God-Talk in America

God-Talk in America

Phyllis A. Tickle

A Crossroad Book
The Crossroad Publishing Company
New York

1997

The Crossroad Publishing Company
370 Lexington Avenue, New York, NY 10017

Printed in the United States of America

Library of Congress Cataloging-in-Publication Data
Tickle, Phyllis.
    God-talk in America / Phyllis Tickle.
        p.   cm.
    Includes bibliographical references.
    ISBN 0-8245-1651-6 (hardcover)
    1. United States – Religion – 20th century. 2. Tickle, Phyllis.
    I. Title.
BL2525.T52 1997
200'.973'09049–dc21   97-3916
                                                                    CIP

For Daisy

הִיא תִתְהַלָּל. תְּנוּ־לָהּ מִפְּרִי
יָדֶיהָ וִיהַלְלוּהָ בַשְּׁעָרִים
מַעֲשֶׂיהָ.

T'nu la mipri yadeha
Vihal'luha vash'arim ma-aseha

Extol her for the fruit of her hand,
and let her works praise her in the gates.

Life is a sacred adventure. Every day we encounter signs that point to the active presence of Spirit in the world around us. . . . For us, the signs have come most often from books and popular culture.

— FREDERIC AND MARY ANN BRUSSAT
from the Introduction to *Spiritual Literacy:
Reading the Sacred in Everyday Life*

Contents

Interlude ... 101

Interlude ... 153

Foreword

⚞ VERY BOOK is a dance of sorts, an engagement of people and ideas that has its own conventions and its own methods of sociability within the rules of a formalized game. The book that follows here is a simple one. Like a Virginia Reel or a Texas schottische, it is a folk dance as unadorned as its title and as unabashedly American as its Norman Rockwell face. Hopefully it is also energetic, like a well-called hoedown.

As was true in the community gatherings out of which our folk dances came, not every reader has to dance to enjoy. There is plenty of room here for those who wish only to observe...and perhaps to clap with the rhythm from time to time. But in every dance, and especially in folk ones, there are always bits of background and circumstance that can make either dancing or toe-tapping a more diverting as well as a more profitable activity.

First of all, my publisher would have me say that this book can be read in three pieces, and he is right. Over a third of its content is contained in the notes, a category that is a bit of a misnomer in this instance. That is, as you will quickly discover, there are some few — three dozen, perhaps — entries in the notes, that, like disciplined children, just offer their bibliographic citations and retire from the conversation. All the rest I have used for expanded citation or — *mea culpa* — for commentary and asides. "God-talk" as a term suggests conversation. It invites and even promises it, to my way of thinking; and the notes are much of the conversation of this book.

My imagistic publisher says — and has asked me to relay for him here — that more than conversation, the notes to this book are the bone to be gnawed on and savored after the pork chop has been eaten. Either way, they can be read in their entirety as a second set in the dance. So also, the body of the main argument can be read straight through without any reference to the notes, except by the curious or the compulsive. As for the third subset of the book, that is a slightly different matter.

I make my living as a journalist. Specifically I make it as an editor in religion for *Publishers Weekly*, the international journal of the book publishing industry. Whatever else that means, it means that every year I see thousands of religion books long before they are published and that I travel the country about two weeks out of every four talking with readers, writers, publishers, librarians, and booksellers — all of them in terms of religion. But I came fairly late in life to this peripatetic and somewhat frenetic way of life.

While religion was always my passion as well as my intellectual hobby, as a writer I was always a storyteller or, probably more accurately, a memoirist. Old habits die hard, especially in the warm diversion of a community dance. As a result, there are stories as well as journalism woven into this one. I have titled the stories as "Interludes." Because they come from a memoirist, the Interludes are all autobiographical. Taken as a whole, however, they are the developing narrative for which the other chapters stand as argued proofs. Lifted out and read in sequence, in other words, the Interludes both predict and exemplify the motifs and patterns of the dance.

Folk dances are not for everyone, but the music that emanates from them is compelling almost beyond anybody's power to resist. The combination of clapping and stomping with instruments played to predictable but not yet fixed rhythms is seductive of that part of us that yearns to be forgetful and free, at least for a little while. This book — this dance — assumes such, anyway.

Certainly this book has been written for those professional religionists — clergy and lay alike — who are themselves callers of the dance elsewhere. Likewise, it was written for those who, like me, are paid to watch from the sidelines, but who have a tapping foot that will not be stilled once the music has begun. But most of all, this book was written for those of my fellow Americans who are dancing in their own spaces on the floor and would like for a few minutes to see the whole pattern of which they are a part.

And so to all of us, call your partners and let's begin.

— One —

From Greece to Berkeley

══ ══

ONCE UPON A TIME.... All postmodern religion books should begin with those words or some variation upon them. The older I grow, in fact, the more convinced I am of the absolute necessity of their introductory presence for readers in our times. In saying this I am being quite sincere and not at all precious, believe me. Believe me also when I say that there are at least two hundred other, perfectly reasonable opening sentences for this book that would be much less compromising. The problem is that those other openers — every single one of them — would violate the underlying thesis of the work itself. But more of that as we go along.

Once upon a time, then, and not too long ago, as I was clicking my way along the Internet, I chanced upon the following entry. The thing itself had been posted by a colleague of mine, John Leech, then of Westminster/John Knox Press, though I did not discover that fact until after I had finished reading his bulletin. I am reprinting John's note here exactly as it first appeared on my computer screen, suggesting to you, as I do so, that in many ways the vignette that follows says it all:

On vacation from seminary (in Berkeley) my then-wife and I drove to Arnold and walked through the groves of Calav-

eras Big Trees State Park. She decided she wanted to go into
town and get a haircut. I tagged along. As I sat reading the
waiting-bench magazines, I heard this conversation.

— So, where are you from?
— Berkeley.
— Oh, I used to live there. Too many people. Why
do you live in Berkeley?
— My husband's in graduate school.
— What's he studying?
— Theology.
— Theology? Huh. Never heard of it.

While I have long since forgotten the point that John Leech
was trying to make in that chat room (assuming I even knew it in
the first place), I have nonetheless kept as a kind of talisman the
printout of his story.

Theology. *Theos,* the old Greek word for god. *Logos* and its
derivatives, the old Greek word for word, study of, conversation
about. "Theology," a Hellenized term and, as Mrs. Leech's hair-
dresser immediately recognized, one far removed from the core
vocabulary of current American experience. Had John Leech been
in Berkeley to study religion, on the other hand, what a difference
that would have made!

Religion is a notion we can all sink our teeth into and do, even
those of us who don't have much truck with it. Despite the fact
that we are the developed world's most theologically illiterate and
morally obsessed society, we are also its most religious one.[1] Additionally, we are fast becoming its most self-consciously spiritual
one...which means that had John Leech's ex-wife laid claim to
the spirituality word, as in "My husband's in graduate school
studying spirituality," it's safe to say that the rest of the conversation would have gone something like this: "Well, he sure picked
the right place for that, but I didn't know you had to study it in

school. Now, I've got this friend, see, and she goes to this meditation thing every Thursday night and you wouldn't believe what
it's done for her. She..."

The truth obscured behind such insouciance, of course, is that
every time we "do" religion as individuals or argue a moral position or attend to our own spirituality, we perform those activities
in relation to theology. It doesn't matter that we have had to
work our theories out pretty much alone and pretty much innocent of any studied context; they are still theology. Likewise, even
though theories of god (or theories of god's absence, which is an
equally valid position in this context) may be what informs religion and morality and spirituality, theology as such cannot exist
in any practical way apart from all those tangible expressions of
its presence.

The resulting symbiosis can be fascinating from a purely
human point of view (though God only knows what anguish it
must cause our observing angels). It is also a conundrum, one that
being greater than any of its parts, requires a name, and that we,
in good yeomanly fashion, have come to speak of as "god-talk."

On those occasions when they do chance to stop and study
us, even heaven's angels must recognize a few exculpatory things
about American god-talk, however. Foremost among them is the
fact that many of the peculiarities of our god-talk, including its
much-touted, aberrant naiveté and egalitarian laxity, arise more
from an acceleration of experience than from any actual spiritual
stupidity on our part as a people.[2] Simply to remember what we
have come from and in how short a period of time is to expose
not only that acceleration but also many of its effects as well. And
since remembering is essentially an autobiographical exercise, a
bit of personal history seems a proper way of pursuing it.

Interlude

FOR MOST CHILDREN, all the spirits that mentor one's growing up — the angels and demons, the ghosts and imagined playmates, the good and bad alike — really do exist and really do occupy given areas. In my own maturing, the place of the spirits and of my associations with them seems most often to have been a closet. My earliest experiencing of spiritual intimacy, in fact, was in the closet that opened off of my first bedroom in the asymmetrical, amorphous way of leftover spaces in old houses.

Huge in its dimensions and cavernous with its ten-foot ceiling, my childhood's closet was sufficiently removed from the household flow as to be only infrequently remembered by anybody but me. It was, in other words, a repository for the curious nonessentials of the adults around me — full of moth balls and almost dispatched toys, the scent of my mother's perfume still caught in out-of-season clothes, of cedar boxes and of my father's collection of newspapers... one for every day of the Second World War from Pearl Harbor to Hiroshima.

Despite its ungainly architecture, everything within the closet was planned and preserved for its utility. Even its shelves were so spaced as to make an uneasy ladder up to the forbidden trap door that opened onto insulation and crawl space. And it was always, from the beginning, in the closet that I arranged and stored myself as well. I was the one who threw out its excess, wrought order upon its collections, sorted its debris for the raw materials of my soul's education. Whatever parent or cousin or time dumped, I sorted by feel in the unelectrified dark or by stealth with a flashlight, spiriting out the useless to the alley trash bins and climbing to the top-shelf repository with the remains. There neither my short-of-stature mother nor my taller but less inquisitive father ever could or would go.

The closet was pantheon for my childhood's gods. It was as full of personalities as was my father's copy of the *Inferno*, illustrated by Doré and secreted years before on the upper shelf, much to my father's recurring puzzlement. The upper shelf's walls sang with awesome pictures of Shiva, Astarte, Hecate, Medusa, all torn from the pages of my grandmother's discarded *Chamber's Illustrated Encyclopedia*. A china Ferdinand-the-Bull (mine were the golden years of Disney) that my uncle had brought me from New York shared the closet's fantasia with crayoned tracings of satyrs much less benign than those Walt Disney would have had me believe in. And the arms of the goddess Kali (brass and beautiful from India, but an adult gift repugnant to my mother who had thrown her away) waxed over the whole of the shelf in constant incantation.

Somewhere just near the attic crawl-through was God the Father. His beard was frequently no more than a cobweb; but still He was there, or passage to Him was. Even as a child I knew that there was no God the Mother and was glad. I did not want one. Gentleness, nurture, support, stroking were sexless in my understanding, belonging to neither gender exclusively and to both identically. It was Kali with her many-handed sexuality whom I wanted as the Queen of Forever. In my imagination she would travel the god's body and mine in sweet sensation while fantasy honed the diffuse appetites of youth into focus.

Kali was, in fact, the only one of the closet's treasures to escape its destruction. She alone still sits on my bedroom dressing table.

All the rest have long since gone as victims to my maturing or the house's new owners. I threw Shiva and Astarte away before I was fully ten years old. In high school I had to study Dante and, for convenience, moved him back to the more accessible bookcase. Doré's ghouls and phantasmagoria by that time were more eternally etched into my faith than they ever could have been into the pages of any book. Ferdinand I had broken one adolescent day by slinging him against a brick wall. In a rush of need to know what it was to kill someone I truly loved, I had hurled him away from me. Even today I can still feel the slick heat of him as he slid from my hand to his multifaceted destruction. Like so many toys for so many children, he served better in death than in life, and I never mourned him. Bit by bit and doll by doll, the other treasures were carried out and dispersed to other children, to nieces, nephews, neighbors, some even to my own children.

During Vietnam and not long before his death, my father burned his World War II collection. He had always believed in fairness, made a kind of goddess out of freedom, referring to both of them as "her." When he burned the newspapers, I suspected that he had at last lifted the skirts of idealism and found to his horror a freemartin, a mandrake without parts. After his funeral and before my mother sold the old house, I sorted out and emptied the closet for the last time, keeping back only the Kali but moving it to a much more public place on my dresser. Now only the outline of the never-tested trap door and the odor of my mother's perfume remain when I push back to remember the closet.

Each time I go back to remember, of course, the perfume grows more faint, more lost in the loss of odor that is memory. Once the perfume has gone, only the trap door and the going where in time I never went will still be left to me. And after that, Kali will bless a bed on which I no longer am, her brass and my self having changed places with each other for the last time.

— *Two* —

In the World of Overload

IN GOD-TALK as in every other form of earnest conversation, the environment in which the talking occurs is as central to the content of the discourse as is its grammar or its vocabulary or the logical flow of its argument. In subtle but potent ways, conversants define, with their circumstantial gifts and limitations, the possibilities within which meaningful discourse can range.[1] An idea or perception cannot be less than the normal fare of their daily talk, or it simply presents itself as no more than chatter or social dalliance. By the same token, a stream of talk that exceeds by too many concepts the basic repertoire of its participants will shortly come to feel to them like gobbledegook or, if impassioned, to be no more than, as Shakespeare said, words "full of sound and fury but signifying nothing."

It is the former rather than the latter principle, I suspect, that will ultimately prove to have been the greater determinant. That is, unless I miss my guess completely, history will show that the inability of intentional conversation to be less than its participants was one of the five or six most influential agents at work in late twentieth-century religion, at least theologically speaking. That one quirk of human discourse, in other words, is the net wherein we shall catch the conscience, if not of the king, then of our subject. It is also at the center of my closet memories.

Adult Americans over sixty years of age but not yet settled into their mid-seventies (my generation, that is — we who are also known as the "Builders" generation) are the oldest or most senior of the active conversers in today's god-talk. Mercifully, or so I am pleased to suppose from my present, more youthful vantage point, the eighth decade of life seems to bring to its constituents surcease from overmuch concern either with theology or perhaps just with its abstract niceties.

For those of us who have not yet gone over that great, delicious divide, however, religion and theology remain at the very least an ever-present scrim through which to mute or enhance or simply view daily life. For many of us religion and theology are the mistresses that govern our conduct and usually inform our evaluation of conduct (particularly of conduct we can't quite seem to manage or control). And for a surprising — almost shocking — number of us, they are part not only of conduct and judgment, but also of self, of identity and allegiance from the time we are adolescents until we pass into that presumed spiritual tranquility of advanced age.

Like every sustained analysis of complex, fluid social issues, the chapters that follow here rest on some assumptions that a reader, of necessity, must accept or, at the very least, indulge me in for the purposes of the argument at hand. The assertion that my generation is the most senior of America's god-talkers presently chattering away on the subject is the first of these assumptions. Along with it is the corollary that ours was also the first American generation to exhibit and employ the traits that now, to a large extent, determine the current conversation. Or to state the matter symbolically, ours was the first generation to have, on any statistically significant level, my closet.

There is, first of all, a certain literalness to my opening remembrance. Closets as closets did not exist in many American homes before this century. For one thing, the affluence that closets enclose did not exist. And while there were thousands of places for a child to retreat and dream before closets came along, there is an effectual difference between afternoon dreams, Tom Sawyer style, on a river bank or in a treetop or under a dense arbor and dreams in a constructed space. But that is of only minor impact here.

What was and is important for all Americans today is the type of relative largesse — intellectual and material — that was contained in both the literal and the metaphorical holding spaces of Builders as a generation. My family's stack of newspapers chronicling every day of a war may have been unusual in its completeness, but the presence of saved clippings, of quickly dispersed and multiperspectived reporting on any part of the world's business, was not, and is not, unusual for my own and subsequent generations. The ability to form emphatic opinions about contemporaneous matters beyond the range of one's own personal experiencing is as old as humankind, but the ability to support those opinions by an authority beyond hearsay and sheer personal opinion is not. Such grandeur of citation is heady stuff. It's downright empowering, in fact. It makes a child, reading and absorbing in a closet what the *Times* says, almost the equal of her parents in validity and — here's the rub — vastly more empowered than her deceased grandparents had ever been with only their static encyclopedias.

The birth of the slick magazine as a serious fixture in the mailbox, in the bathroom, and in an evening's conversation was simultaneous with the Builders' births. Right beside the World War II newspapers in my closet was a stack, almost as complete, of all the *Life*'s that had helped us armchair soldiers fight World War II's battles one by one. More than just the ubiquity of the magazines themselves, however, was the thing they were physically. Filled with color, they were twice as authoritative and five times more accessible than had been their tabloid antecedents. Filled with pictures — with actual photographs we could see and see in detail — they were exponentially more informative and powerful. It was from *Life*'s pictures that I first learned to feel compassion. If the Boomers learned it from the shots of My Lai and of napalmed Vietnamese screaming as they and the death on their backs ran flaming toward nowhere, I learned it from the leaping bodies flinging themselves out of Atlanta's burning Winecoff Hotel, from the bombed-out beauty of Normandy's destroyed children, and from the photographed silence of Nagasaki twenty-four hours after ground zero.

The presence of books — so many books, in fact, that some could even be spirited away to a private hiding spot without a major hue and cry and others could be cannibalized without detection or consequence — became the commonplace with my generation. And it was the books that mattered most in our new feast of information. Whether because they had come first to the party and were for that reason trusted familiars; whether they were (and are) far more permanent; whether their very fixedness precluded easy correction and therefore educed greater editorial respect for an exquisite accuracy; whether their cost and their keeping still were great enough to continue to mark them as a characterizing property of the influential and thus more prestigious; whether their genial size and sustained involvement simply render experiencing them a more substantial event — whether a dozen such possibilities, all of them plausible, intervened or whether only some of them did, the fact still remains that books were our final authority, the gauge against which all other sources were measured. Even the bulbous-tubed radio that sat on a side table next to my father's easy chair and brought us the progress of the world at the flip of its dials had to — and did — do homage from time to time to the authority of books in order to undergird its own broadcast position.

Later, when General MacArthur announced to an astonished America that old soldiers never die, they just fade away, I was sitting on the floor of a classmate's living room with the rest of my high school civics class watching a peculiarly shadowy screen from which Mr. MacArthur's evaporization did indeed seem absolutely imminent. Nevertheless, even after it had lost its snow and managed to get its images outside of a fishbowl confinement, television was to do as radio had done before it. It would continue to cite the book as authority and to become, almost unwittingly, the natural showcase for the men and women who write the books.

The point, then, is that we who were born Builders got our name for good reason; and the reason has to do with the fact that all the building materials had been delivered to the job site just before we got there ourselves. And what a construction site it was!

I don't remember now who first gave me the term "cumulative literacy." Undoubtedly it was some sociologist somewhere to whom I can pay only my anonymous respects, but certainly his or her term is a good one, as slick and facile as it is accurate and insightful. Cumulative literacy denotes a mind-set, a context of circumstances, that both underlies and results from the Information Age and that, while it undoubtedly is as old as human language, entered into its present period of aggressive growth and excitation only in the America of the 1930s. It certainly has run rampant in the sixty-some years since.

As a term, "cumulative literacy" references three phenomena: acceleration, diffusion, and obligation. When speaking of acceleration in relation to cumulative literacy, one means that as information flows in, it empowers, excites, and then invites in ever more and more of itself. But information is a living, dynamic thing that, like all living organisms, struggles not only for its place in the sun but also to broadcast itself as widely and as economically as possible. Historically this has meant that as information has accumulated, no small part of what it has brought with it is greater, more efficient means for its own dissemination. The result is our present, always-quickening maelstrom of data, interpretation, and theoretical projection. To know at all nowadays is almost instantly to know even more.

Secondly, as both information and the means of its ready transfer have accelerated, there has developed a kind of diffusion of our accumulating knowledge that is more nearly a profusion. Knowledge — and especially the kind we refer to as general knowledge — no longer requires us to have specific intellectual skills or tastes in order to access it. Americans who don't read books (and fewer than 10 percent of us will read a book this year) don't have to. What books contain, at least by way of objective fact if not of aesthetic experience, will show up on television or sound out from a radio or flash by on the Internet or saunter in from somebody else's reading group or jump out of a tabloid's factoid or shine forth précised from the pages of a magazine. That is, those of us who scorn television can't avoid newspapers or magazines entirely. Those of us who find radio intolerable probably can't avoid all conversation, certainly not that which is simply overheard publicly, but which is nonetheless created by those who do listen and reference radio. And most certainly those of us who can avoid the "talk" parts of our culture will never manage to escape the music part of it, be that out of a radio or out of a passing boombox or simply out of an offspring's CD player.[2] Etc., etc. *ad infinitum et ad nauseam.* Or if not to the point of nausea than at least to the point of cumulative literacy — a phenomenon which, as I have said, is characterized by yet a third and even more telling, if not outright burdensome, property.

Were cumulative literacy only an acceleration of information and its profusion, we could quite honestly say that, as a term, it is no more than a ten-dollar label for life in the Information Age with a mass-media overlay. But cumulative literacy means to describe more than that. It means to describe as well our uniquely postmodern (once again, we should add "often burdensome") responsibility toward the employment of all that information. Now that we have it, we feel we cannot ignore it, or choose not to employ it, or even defer to the paucity of understanding that has accompanied our acquisition of it.

Areas of choice and decision that the generations before us assigned to tutored professionals with their banks of arcane knowledge millions of us now feel a moral — sometimes even a religious — obligation to enter into for ourselves. And all of this because the arcane knowledge of the professions did not stay dutifully contained within its category cages, that is, it did not remain as it was — professional and arcane.

For example, I know little or nothing about medicine or eastern European political history, at least not as sciences whose disciplines I have formally engaged. I nonetheless must still pay (with attention and intention) the price for all the popularly accessible, media-predigested overviews of them that I have, however unwittingly and involuntarily, received. I (by which pronoun I mean to imply all of us) cannot hand over responsibility for my own health care willy-nilly to some white coat just because it is a white coat; nor can I turn over carte blanche all of my compassion mechanisms to some pin-striped blue suit in Bosnia just because it is a blue pin-stripe and rides in an embassy limousine that sports little American flags on its hood. Such a turning over, in my mind and that of my fellow Americans, would be culpable conduct and, more specifically, an abnegation of my "god-given" responsibilities. The operative words here, of course, are the "god-given" ones, which is precisely why cumulative literacy is one of the three or four most informing factors in American god-talk's conversational environment right now.[3]

In addition to all of this, we must take note of another dynamic that is at work among us: there are so many ways to get at the information upon which cumulative literacy is built that the system has begun to flow in reverse. Life itself has become a veritable thicket of ways for information to get at us, ways that are inescapable for most Americans and that are themselves no longer separate or discrete. Today's information, unlike Marshall McLuhan's, is not medium-specific; and such medium-specificity as information may enjoy becomes daily less and less of our message. The only possible exception to or variation upon this developing circumstance is that books still command center stage in popular respect, and the information contained in books still moves among us as if with a greater validity. To look at books and analyze their content, then, is to study not so much books per se, but ideas. It is to analytically engage ideas and concepts that have been carried into the general conversation through many more vehicles than just the books they began in and that have done so with a unique authority.[4]

All of which is to say that when one sets oneself the task of describing and interpreting something as omnipresent and fluid as god-talk is in America today, one must do so within a context of the new, responsibility-bearing literacy and with studied respect for all the means of its delivery. Books, movies and television,[5] magazines,[6] chat rooms and the World Wide Web, commercial newspapers,[7] talk radio,[8] idle conversations overheard, colloquia deliberately attended, music — they all tell the curious observer something about god-talk by what they include and by what they exclude and by the frequency with which they do both.[9] To look at all of them would be beyond the scope of any single study, yet to look at one vehicle alone seems limiting of, if nothing else, the sheer richness of observable possibilities. For that reason, both because books do indeed command such pride of place as is still present among information vehicles[10] and because they are the part of America's information business that I deal with every day professionally,[11] I have chosen them as my primary, but hardly my only, diagnostic tool.

There is one other reason for my selecting books as the principal proof text for the observations and assessments that follow here. It was books that first signaled in the late 1980s by their shifting patterns in sales and content emphases, the religion and theology ferment that is occurring in this country at this moment. This ability to be prognostic and predictive as well as diagnostic makes books and their sales patterns a kind of litmus test against which to try conclusions suggested by the other forms of communication active in our culture and in our heads.[12]

So the questions then become ones not about god-talk in theory, but about god-talk in the actuality of today's cumulatively literate America: how can it and we as its creators be characterized, what are we saying, and where does it appear our conversation is going? I want to begin the attack on my Gordian knot by being more concrete not about this new kind of literacy per se, but about some of the points of its greatest impact on late twentieth-century theology, spirituality, and religion. That process alone should suggest the answers to many of the questions we began with.

Put more specifically, identifying some of the areas of cumulative literacy's most dramatic impact on god-talk should answer several important questions about that talk, questions like: In what context and out of what frames of reference are we Americans buying all these books about religion and theology? What are we searching for when we are out there on the Internet all hours of the day and night talking about God? What takes us there and what do we come with? Who are the readers whose disposable dollars are encouraging more and more column inches about religion in newspapers and magazines? What is the engine that drives so many callers to engage religion on radio talk shows and why is theology folded into so many casual conversations? Where do the reading groups and the small-group discussions and the parachurch gatherings all come from psychologically? From what part of our national or cultural or statistically average soul do these things arise?

There is one other cluster of concerns implicit here. When we come to the business of doing god-talk these days, we all come as adults fed and nourished from an environmental chalice — or a cauldron, if you will — that is unavoidably communal as no other in history has ever been. What are the theological issues and conclusions and consequences of this ubiquitous cultural soup from which we all feed.... And we all do feed, whether we privately like the mix or not. And as is true with every fine stew, each piece of it has made its own, integral contribution to the pot's bouquet and flavor, if not to the actual comestibles in our individual bowls.

In order to address these questions, beginning with some specific examples of the theological, religious, and spiritual effects of cumulative literacy, I want to detour once again. I want to turn aside this time to a sunnier and infinitely less dangerous spot in my childhood.

Interlude

MY MOTHER was a woman of her times, having not a forward-looking bone in her body nor the least desire to delve into the profound. She was, instead, merely brilliant and eerily content. Her frame of reference was always the day she was in, and her enrichment of its possibilities always drawn from extant literature and premodern history. My mother seemed, in fact, constantly to be looking backward at a stunning view and to understand her role in life as that of an appreciator rather than of a creator. This turn of disposition gave her a kind of urbane, citizen-of-the-world distance from the voguish and a natural affinity for the authentic, traits that made her appear always insightful and not infrequently prophetic.

Mother's penchant for unfettered assessments and her casual courage in living them out loosed me from many of the more transient expectations that beleaguer growing up in any era. At the same time, they also granted me time and opportunity for a kind of unguarded familiarity with her interior life. It was she, for instance, who first taught me that one should pray during the busiest hours of the day by doing so herself—every afternoon of her life, as regularly as clockwork, after she had finished our mending and before she began our supper. I was never once, so far as I can remember, included in this ritual, but I still absorbed its efficacy. And it was my mother who first showed me that words are like closets, deeply private space with inevitable and usually public results.

When I was old enough to sit on a rather rickety wooden stool and listen for any length of time, I loved most the sound of her voice talking in the kitchen — as much to her bowls and dishes as to me — while she did her baking or, after prayers, cooked our dinner. She spoke often in the late afternoons of my grade-school days during World War II about the great authors whom she had read as a girl and whom, I sensed even then, she missed a bit in her crowded, domestic role.

She particularly loved Cicero. She reverenced almost to the point of Calvinistic commitment his notion of *summum bonum,* the highest good. She reveled in his acerbic worldview: "Spartam nactus es, hanc exorna," which loosely translates to "Sparta is your heritage; so make the best of it, Kiddo." But most often she quoted sections of the *De Senectute,* the essay on old age. Looking back now, I realize that her absorption with the piece was as much a poignant awareness of her own approaching age (for I was born late in her life) as it was appreciation for the syntax and style of the famous orator.

I still remember the kitchen in which we worked. It seemed to me that the flour bin was always swung out over the dough counter and that a bowl of oleomargarine was always warming in the window sill. Three afternoons a week it was my chore to beat in the red dye that would turn the distressingly white, lardy mass into a streaked facsimile of the butter we could no longer obtain. While I whipped (precolored margarine was one of the symbolic luxuries of my postwar adolescence), she rolled biscuits or pie crusts or both, and Cicero flowed into the rims of my bowl and over the edges of her bin, filling the white hollows and corners of the shiny room with his sonorous Latin and her impressive translations.

In the years after that, I moved on to high school and my mother moved on to predyed margarine and eventually, as the deprivations of wartime receded, into having real butter once again. My time in her kitchen, like her pleasure in having me there, diminished.

In high school, because it was required for a diploma and because it seemed as natural to me as a first cousin once removed, I had begun to read, in translation but for myself, the substantial Latin of the great Romans. I came also to appreciate both my mother's pleasure in their words and the real consolation that she had undoubtedly derived from essays like Cicero's conversation between ageing friends. High school gave way to college, and my mother's kitchen to a one-eyed hot plate for a stove and a dormitory window sill for a refrigerator.

Cicero was joined, in the original this time, by Livy, Catullus, Horace, and, to my surprise, Homer. Yet even when I elected to major in Latin, I never questioned the origins of my decision. I wanted to be a writer, and intimacy with the vocabulary and structure of Latin and Greek was, to my way of thinking, intimacy with the language of the gods.

It was not until my senior year when a magazine editor, in accepting a story of mine, remarked, "Your style has a kind of classical balance," that I began to understand. She of the apron had been shaping more than pie shells, dyeing more than margarine.

— *Three* —

From "Who Is Man?" to "Who Am I?"

═══ ═══

$\mathcal{T}$ODAY'S GOD-TALKERS in America, from the Builders and
the Boomers right down through the eighteen- to thirty-
something-year-old Busters among us,[1] are unique in history.
They enjoy an untethered absorption with their subject.[2] They
are the recipients of an accumulating literacy; and they can draw
at will from a technologically accelerated bank of general information that is constantly impacting their discussion. This new
kind of information (most of it translated out of theory and into
real-time experience over the last sixty years of my own life),[3] is
multicultural, multinational, multidisciplined, and multifaithed.

Unlike the wisdom that centered earlier times, the information
of postmodernism governs by explicit data rather than symbol or
suggestion and empowers by the expansion of facts rather than
by their distillation.[4] Traveling widely in Walden on a daily basis
may once have been a virtue, especially among those who personally rejected it in favor of the enervating streets of commerce
and personal success; but it is a self-indulgence today. Instead, our
present times demand of the spiritually responsible a dynamic,
factual contact with the whole world of human affairs, and we

value carefully scheduled side trips to Walden primarily because they are good for the individual, rather than the group, soul.

When I left my mother's kitchen with her Cicero tucked comfortably into my mental suitcase, I entered a college where I was to study anthropology with Francesca Boas, daughter of Franz Boas, who had fathered that strange new subject within his own daughter's lifetime and memory. Francesca was to hand me and hundreds of my fellow collegians names like Frazer and Mead certainly. But far more importantly, she was going to accustom us to cadences not Cicero's and to lines of argument and ways of knowing that were not his either. She would first show us all these wonders and then validate them — validate them on the basis of their effectual existence in fully realized human beings whose lives were scattered across thousands of years, diverse cultures, every continent and myriad religions, all of which were different from our own.

I left my mother's kitchen to study the relatively new discipline of psychology with an instructor named John Hornaday. Fresh from doctoral studies at Duke University, he had worked for almost five years under a man named J. B. Rhine in a totally new, totally unheard of, totally suspect field called parapsychology. Hornaday was going to talk to me and my fellow undergraduates about Freud, who we knew for a fact was suspect, but also about Jung and Fromm; and he was going to do so in terms of our own self-perceptions as maturing young adults. He would dare to handle publicly in classroom conversation currently inexplicable but documentable phenomena and experiences that a century before had been the stuff of a holy magic or a suspicious scandal.

I would leave my sheltering closet only to be required, in my majors' seminars, to read James's *The Varieties of Religious Experience* before I ever opened Aeschylus — and this in order that I might better appreciate the latter's genius for my more lavishly furnished world. I would register for (and luxuriate in) one of

the last classes ever offered by my college in pure trigonome-
try. I have remained ever afterward confused about why trig's
somewhat simplistic but comfortably obvious principles had to be
incorporated as a mere footnote into the complexities of emerging, postnuclear general math. But then I was among those who
began basic science in laboratories to whose periodic table wall
charts two or three new elements had been appended by hand
before we graduated....

...The list could go on, though with diminishing drama, for
there is a limit to how much shift and burgeon any one period of
time can experience and still remain stable enough to talk about
itself forty-five years later. The point is, however, that when I
write of my mother's house, I must write more as a memorialist
than as a memoirist, for an age died in that place and in millions
of others like it in the Western world. When my contemporaries
and I closed the doors of our mothers' houses behind us, we
locked ourselves out of five hundred years of human habits and
entered into disjuncture. And the new ways of being and seeing
and — inevitably — of believing that were so abruptly thrust upon
us were only the first inklings of the new[5] formal disciplines — the
mind sciences, the maths, the comparative -ologies, and the theoretical and physical sciences — that were to come to full potency
in the closing years of the millennium.

Not all of these new bodies of information were destined to
affect god-talk directly. Some were, of course; but most were to
erode established theology and religion almost tangentially. By
changing the conceptual world of those who think, talk, and practice God in their everyday lives, the new disciplines would change
both the religion that we who were the newly informed could
accept and the theology we would be driven to create.

•

"What is man?" is about as old a question as there is. It is also a theological one. So also are all its near kin like "What is body?" "What is consciousness?" "What is mind?" "What is intelligence?" "What is soul?" "What is spirit?" "What are emotions?" "What is reality?" "What is society?" etc., etc.

"What is man?" is so profoundly theological, in fact, that for most of human history it could be neither asked nor answered outside of a religio-theological context. The great "religious" insult of the Enlightenment, after all, was its establishment of the notion that asking "What is?" questions was acceptable conduct within nontheological discussions. What neither the Enlightenment nor all the years since have been able to extricate from theology is not the asking, therefore, but the answering of "What is?" questions...that and the application of the answers after they are proffered. Like Siamese twins with a common heart, answers to "What is?" and human god-talk seem inseparable even in the hands of the most skilled practitioners.

In the world at large over the last few decades, there has been at least a baker's dozen of disparate factors that have converged first to form, then to excite, disseminate, and refine the "What is man?" questions. We now lump both the queries and our new understanding about them under the capacious umbrella term of "mind sciences." Psychology itself, which was the progenitor of the contemporary disciplines contained in the mind sciences, came upon us only slightly more than a century ago. Hardly without its own precursors, psychology can trace its lineage from mesmerism straight back to the most ancient of philosophical and religious texts. But the popularity of the earliest pioneers of psychology as we know it, especially of Mesmer, the Freuds, and Jung (of whom more a bit later), demonstrated two things: the ripeness of the times in which they came and, prophetically, the enormity of the impact produced upon the general or popular culture by research scholarship conducted in a literate, mass-media, multiple-outlet context.

Beyond the rather explosive growth of psychology, psychiatry, parapsychology and the clinical research surrounding them in academic and medical contexts, there were concomitant in the everyday world, as well as inside the academy, certain other matters that further stirred the "What is man?" pot: matters like computer science; the analysis and construction of artificial intelligences; vast, painfully intimate, but highly informative experience with psychedelic drugs and — blessedly — expanding familiarity with some therapeutic ones; and ever-more-sophisticated scanning devices of the physiology and machinations of the vertebrate central nervous system, to name but a few marchers in a long parade of the obvious.

As neurobiology, psychobiology, neuropsychiatry, psychosurgery, psychochemistry, and over two dozen other legitimately recognized disciplines arose within the taxonomy of formal study, the very proliferation of their naming testified to the richness of their newly discovered approaches to asking "What is man?" The popular hue and cry that followed behind the professional ones engaged not only the drama of the question but also its particularization. "What is man?" picked up first the fascination and then, almost immediately, the urgency and poignancy of "What am I?"

Popular books became the first effective agents for carrying late-breaking bulletins about new answers to the old mind/brain/intelligence questions out from the laboratory and operating theater into the office coffee break and the family dinner hour. Admittedly, these lay books of scholarship in the mind sciences, when they began to enter the general marketplace some three and four decades ago, traveled rather sedately at first. It was not until the 1980s that they began to leap so inelegantly off their press beds and straight onto the regional and, in some cases, the national bestseller lists. As their commercial success increased, so too did the public broadcasting of the ideas they contained and the fame of their authors.

In 1981, Daniel C. Dennett, Distinguished Professor of Arts and Sciences at Tufts as well as director of the Center for Cognitive Sciences, cowrote with computer scientist Douglas R. Hofstadter, *The Mind's I*.[6] Its publication, a classic in the publishing industry's canon of unanticipated-success stories, is still regarded as the watershed event in the history of popularized mind science, and Dennett himself became probably the most visible of the early movers and shakers in the field. A decade later, this time alone, he published *Consciousness Explained*.[7] *Consciousness* was an even more daring and even more widely circulated analysis of current research on the processes of human perception and mentation; and it questioned, ultimately, the very existence of consciousness as anything other than adaptive biological response.

Following *The Mind's I* other books came in fairly rapid succession. What we must note about these books, aside from the iconclasm of their ideas and the sales figures that establish their commercial success, is that they were written by men and women so distinguished in their fields that their very names militated for a respectful consideration of what the books were saying. Their names commanded as well the kind of ready media attention that immediately furthered the general range and influence of their ideas in ways that would have been unthinkable fifty years earlier.

There was *The Emperor's New Mind: Concerning Computers, Minds and the Laws of Physics*[8] by the distinguished mathematician and theoretical physicist Roger Penrose, who with Stephen Hawking constructed the theoretical confirmation of the Big Bang singularity. *Bright Air, Brilliant Fire*[9] was written by molecular biologist Gerald M. Edelman; and *The Astonishing Hypothesis*[10] by Francis Crick, the distinguished British physicist and biochemist who collaborated with James Watson in the discovery of DNA....

...The list extends by at least several dozen more titles. We were becoming, cumulatively but surely, very literate in the intricacies of our new kind of information. We were opening with fact and reproducible experiment the mind's mysteries, even to the point of annotating some of her dearest myths as well. We were also discovering that nowhere was there any kind of uniformity of interpretation about all that new information and those new data once we got them. Dennett and Frick, for example, were, and have remained, miles apart in their theories of consciousness.[11] What uniformity or consistency there was, in fact, lay instead in our clear grasp of what had been demolished.

René Descartes — he of *cogito, ergo sum* fame — was the seminal philosopher from whose theories of the human mind much of modern psychology was constructed and upon which it and its precursors had depended for well over three hundred years. He also — because of the easiness of his "I-think-therefore-I-am" formula, no doubt — has come to be the reductive symbol for many, many other thinkers from his era. Descartes et al. postulated that what each of us perceives as a "self" is really a kind of homunculus. He and his contemporaries taught, in other words, that somewhere inside the heads of all of us — Descartes claimed the pineal gland was the exact site — there is what Daniel Dennett still refers to as the "Cartesian theatre." There Self sits like a little queen, viewing, as on a many-monitored wall panel, all the various parts of her domain and governing the whole accordingly. Implicit in this Cartesian system is a resultant and absolute separation between mind and brain, just as there was the assumption that intelligence and consciousness are both characterized only by reason.

It is easy to review Descartes's legacy — both his and his era's, in fact — in such a way as to disparage him and to present his principles as quixotic notions.[12] Whatever else the mind sciences have done for us over the past ten to fifteen years, they have surely turned Cartesian debunking into a safe indoor sport. They have also rendered as untenable the old, Cartesian-based positions of the free-standing homunculus called Self; of thought as itself existent, much less as a credible proof of existence;[13] of the Soul as a locatable integer; and of the discrete distinction between mind and body — just to name a few of the more serious of the newly created vacancies.

What the mind sciences have not done, as we have already noted, is to provide us with a validatable commonly agreed-upon new set of workable premises for understanding our selves in relation to all these parts — or nonparts? — of humanity's perceived experience. Where late twentieth-century mind sciences have left us, in a manner of speaking, is post-Cartesian and confused.

Only time and hard scholarship will provide us — if indeed anything ever can and does — integrating answers about the structure, interrelationships, and functions of all the pieces of our existence that we honor as internal to, rather than external of, each individual one of us; but we cannot spend the intervening time in ignoring the presence of the questions just because we're busy waiting for their answers. Nor can we ignore the linchpin nature of our present lack of answers. Whatever we do or think or decide is to some greater or lesser extent shaded by the presence of the new, unresolved questions and the demise of the comfortable old answers.

If the exhilaration of new worlds of understanding to be conquered...If the unsettling vertigo of traveling in foreign heights and depths with no maps...If the experiencing of all the emotions in between those two extremes, even...If any or all these states were limited only to the ranks of professional scientists and the egg-head few who concern themselves with matters too mighty for the rest of us, then none of them would matter at any effecting level. The mind sciences and all their brouhaha would not be a blip on the cultural radar screen. Or at least they wouldn't until they had resolved themselves and their differences into a cohesive whole they were willing to hand down for our pedestrian uses. That, historically, has always been the way of things . . . it has been, but isn't any more.

It is quite possible that as a society we could have dispassionately enjoyed, but remained largely unaffected by, the magazine and tabloid reportage that spun off from and/or referenced the books about the mind sciences and that, in doing so, greatly enlarged our public awareness of both.[14]

It is possible, at least for the sake of argument, that we might as a culture have come through the drug experimentations of the 1960s and since, without extrapolating the interior/internalized experiences of millions of Americans into some kind of public concern with theories and the absence of theories about mind, self-awareness, and perception, about the mind/body juncture, about spirituality or about mentation, intentionality, and emotions. I doubt it, but it is possible.

It is possible that we might have confined to the already persuaded a fascination with the arcane principles of alternative medicine or the ancient ones of Dr. Rhine's parapsychology or the aberrant, unnerving ones of psychosurgery or a dozen's dozen other such results of expanding information in a shrinking-world experience. I doubt it, but it is theoretically possible.

And maybe, just maybe, we might have made it through a level of computerization that imposes something close to absolute machine intimacy on a majority of us without succumbing *en masse* to the obvious questions: Do I think this way? Am I a machine? Am "I" a machine? Am "I" and I real? Are we the same? etc., etc.

All of this is arguably possible. What was not possible, however, was any escape from the ubiquity and cumulativeness of all of them together. From the bag lady to the university president our postmodern confusion about how we operate as creatures was shared knowledge, and the debunking of our former absolutes, a common cynicism. That every Tom, Mary, Dick, and Jane among us knew of such matters and felt free to have opinions about each of them matters almost not at all to pure science. The nearest popular knowledge comes to impacting pure science these days is in the royalty statements of some of its practicing popularizers. What caught and is catching and, from every current indication, is going to continue to catch the ramifications of our informed confusion and cynicism is theology.[15]

The question "What is man?" — once it makes that slippery slide over to the particular of "Who am I?" — is one half of the West's great theological query. For the majority of us who do god-talk in this hemisphere, all other questions depend from the great duality of "Who am I?" and "Who are You/you?"

The masses of non-book-readers among us may go along innocent of the particulars, if not of the generalities. The more intricately informed among us may find themselves rewarded for their heady efforts by having to frantically tread water in a sea of questions. Neither group, however, can escape our present flux in human definition; and neither group is going to grab as a believable life raft a theology, private or public, that does not incorporate into its scheme of things the sea-changes we have experienced.

Specifically this means that while there is no unanimity of data or academic theory about the nature of human interiordom, there is near unanimity within the popular and pervasive perception of it. The operative "folk" principles seem to me to be that the brain is a machine like unto the familiar computer; that that brain, which is probably mind as well, is body; that the body and, therefore, the mind and/or brain, are not "I"; that "I" is greater than all these component parts. And most significant as well as the logical apex to which the other premises lead, "I" is a spirit, a noncorporeal, integrating but knowable mirror and replica in miniature of the Great Spirit.

Today's so-called "seeker" is about the business of connecting with that original and originating Spirit. He or she is also about the business of connecting with others who both search and at the same time image that which they seek. The most remarkable characteristic of all this looking and spiritual striving, at least from a professional religionist's point of view, is not that it is going on, but that it is going on with almost no sectarian or even tradition-oriented guidance. The average seeker in America today is being shepherded to a large extent by commercially published books that owe allegiance to the experientially validatable and to a perceived mystery. It is the mystery, perhaps, more even than the insistence upon experiential validation, that defines our current search—a perceived mystery that by its very *mysterium* overrides and exceeds doctrine; is engaged more as health or well-being; and is approached more as the Worshiped than as an Overlord with expectations, demands, and purposes. Yet the theology that does not engage these shifts and any religion that attempts to operate out from a theology that does not engage them are doomed to failure, at least in the short run.

To put it more humbly, " 'Who' or 'what part of what' prays when 'I' am on my knees and to Who/Whom by what means?" is a commanding question. For the theologically inclined—and that is by recent count about 96 percent of us in America today[16]— it has already proved powerful enough to intrude itself into the evaluation and assessment of religious and sectarian doctrine, of moral codes, of politics, of clergy, and of humanity in general. It will continue to do so, because it is cumulative literacy that has become theologically apparent; and the real message here is that it informs almost every sentence in today's god-talk. But before we leave the matter (a small pun on my part, as will soon be obvious) of cumulative literacy there and lest we underrate its power, I want to consider just one or two more areas of impact in which new information popularly delivered has changed the whole theology of the street.

— *Four* —

Out of the Mouths of Physicists into the Ears of God

≡ ≡

ⓦHAT IS the proper definition of humanity and what the proper interlocking of all our human pieces and parts are questions that may still (though perhaps not for much longer) be fairly described as subjective. But side by side with "What is man?" is another great, equally contextual question, "What is matter?" Currently, it may be characterized as an objective question, even when it occurs in carefully deliberated dialog among the very deeply religious. That is to say, the first question of what is man, even when pushed to the limits of its everyday usages, is still "personned" in most of our parlance; and the questions that devolve from it, including the god ones, seem to be likewise rooted in a "person" (i.e., "subject) perception, by and large. The second question of what is matter seems to be almost universally and uncritically accepted by most of us as a question rooted in a material (i.e., "object). In neither case were matters always thus, and in both cases, as most of us already know from personal experience, public perceptions are in flux.[1] God-talk and god-talkers are just beginning to deal with this set of the shifts that advancing information has thrust upon us.[2]

As we have already seen in our brief look at the mind sciences, the clean divide in popular literature between science and theology — a separation that was always tenuous in the first place — is beginning once more to blur.[3] So likewise is the divide, both professionally and popularly, between the physical and the mind sciences, the findings in any one of them spilling over almost immediately into implications for the others.[4] As both meldings continue,[5] the concept of process as itself being agent (or Agent, if one prefers) will inevitably become more and more central to our popular understanding of them. That shift in perception — a pivotal one in anybody's worldview — has already begun at a popularized-science level and will mature in an America whose general citizenry, until fifty years ago, had no theological jargon with which to conceptualize, much less name, such a possibility.[6]

Even the Native American's Great Spirit, which is as near as this land mass ever came to indigenous nontheistic religious practice, can hardly be said to even approach the unempersonned agency of Confucianism, Taoism, or of much of Buddhism. Yet no exogenous belief system has ever swept so dramatically across the American theological landscape as has Buddhism in the years since World War II, Korea, and Vietnam.[7] The tools for talking about unpersonned or impersonal or less-than-personned god arrived on our shores just in time first to capture the American imagination and then to fill an American need.

Ironically, as process or order begins to function more and more comfortably as agent/Agent or as a defining characteristic of theistic agency in popular acceptance,[8] the Physical Sciences are becoming more and more comfortable with reassuming some of the animation and perceptions of traditional theology and — herein lies the greatest irony — of premodern, lay conversation. Consider, for example, as a case in point, the work of mathematician Frank J. Tipler.

Few recent commercial books in the Physical Sciences have made as much stir as did Tipler's *The Physics of Immortality*, published by Doubleday in 1994.[9] (So great was the public presence of his work at the time, in fact, that *Omni* magazine chose a Tipler interview as one of the major features in its "16th Anniversary Collector's Issue" that year).[10]

Tipler is professor of mathematical physics at Tulane, where his contribution and reputation have become considerable. But what Tipler did with *Immortality* and has continued since to do in popular appearances and interviews was perhaps even more significant in the long run. What Tipler did was to give authoritative academic voice to the shifting relationships, within both vocabulary and conceptualization, between science and theology.

The Physics of Immortality is an extended mathematically argued description of the Omega Point Theory,[11] the author's preface to which concludes with the words: "The time has come to absorb theology into physics, to make Heaven as real as an electron." It is a startling task and one that Tipler proceeds over the next 517 pages[12] to accomplish, at least to his own satisfaction.[13] Later, confessing to *Omni* that his work was "disturbing a political agreement between theologians and scientists to keep their fields separate," Tipler was even more direct about the implications of his work. "My mathematical theory tells us," he said, "that the ultimate theory is 'personal' — so it can be called 'God.' "[14]

For thousands of Americans who have read Tipler's *Immortality* or the interviews and articles that have spun off of it, however, the fact that Professor Tipler is even out there on such a limb is as affecting as are his conclusions, especially since most of us have to take the latter on sheer faith after a few pages of the good man's math-sprinkled text.[15] In other words, at the lay level of our own everyday lives and conversations, the repercussions of Tipler's work, while admittedly delimited by a vague or fuzzy comprehension of the science involved, elicit nonetheless a kind of low-key but pleasant excitement mixed with the sweet incense of verifiable mystery. It is a heady combination at any time; it is especially seductive and embraceable in an age and among a people grown weary beyond all comfort of Enlightenment and its attendant responsibilities.

But is Tipler's an isolated presence, a fluke as it were, or are there others of his colleagues doing the same popularizing thing and having an equal effect? If so, which of their ideas, perhaps obtuse or perhaps just beyond the grasp of most of us, are nonetheless impacting us and our god-talk with hope and an uncanny attraction? It's a deceptively clear question with an encyclopedic set of answers, but let's look at one or two subsets of the answer.

The new disciplines within Professor Tipler's field of physics and mathematics — the astrophysics, the quantum physics, the nuclear physics, the mathematical physics,[16] the complexity physics, the chaos physics, etc., etc. — have in fact had an even easier time than have Dr. Dennett's mind sciences in grabbing an accepting public's attention. Given the "hardness" of their data — i.e., their greater specificity and reproducibility, and the more overt range of experimentation possible in many of them — it seems at first blush almost paradoxical that the theories and principles of contemporary physics should be better known (or at least more casually bandied about) than are those of the mind sciences. Yet the truth is that a reporter would be hard pressed to find an American over ten and under seventy who did not know pretty particularly what space travel and aliens are, and pretty vaguely but confidently what black holes, time warps, and $E=Mc^2$ are.

Most Americans within those generational parameters would also know at some greater or lesser level of clarity what parallel universes are; that time is a dimension and quite possibly that it is the fourth in what may be a ten or twenty-six dimensioned original; that there was a Big Bang, the results of which are still echoing across the cosmos; and that creation *ex nihilo* is probably just as likely as the book of Genesis says it is actual.

If our reporter were to narrow the age window to Americans over ten but under forty-five or fifty, he or she would find, I suspect, that most of those queried had heard and/or at some degree of depth really understood, that something called the far future is out there and that the future is running backward toward us in one sense and has already happened in a noncontradictory other sense; that quantum theory explains three of the four forces of the created order, that Einstein's theories of relativity explain the fourth, and that superstring theory seems capable of uniting them all; and that string theory seems to "prove" that an observer observing affects the outcome of an action. They might even know at some tentative level that there are now respected physicists who contend that superstring theory outright "requires" the presence of an Observer for existence to exist.

The list of the "knowns" and "almost-knowns" of new physics that are abroad in popular conversation and conceptualizations today is astounding; but it also has been so gradual in its accumulating that for years we accepted the incorporation of its information and half-information into our worldview almost unawares. The reason behind such innocence in our handling of portentous change is a construct of several factors, but the two greatest of these are the sophistication of the sciences' popularizers and, of course, cumulative literacy.

We watched the process, all of us, all at once: The sheer horror of nuclear bombings and the constantly reported upon, constantly photographed, constantly politicized programs thereafter in nuclear control.... The doleful face, sad eyes, wild hair, and bizarre lapses of Albert Einstein that domesticated him within his own

lifetime into America's favorite stereotype of genius. . . . The glam-
our of *Star Trek* (the books, the movies, the TV shows, the CDs,
the sound tracks, the fanazines, the features, the whole megillah)
that likewise domesticated outer space and made it more imaginable than Nebraska for a kid living in Baltimore or San Francisco
or anywhere in between. . . . The charm of R2D2 in George Lu-
cas's hands or of HAL in Arthur Clarke's and ET in Steven
Spielberg's. . . . The drama of a NASA, a Cape Canaveral, a Hunts-
ville constantly coming in to supper with us on the kitchen TV
set. . . . The photos of deep space exploration and Hubble teleme-
try coming into the family room via dozens of slick magazines
to chat with us (not to mention, of course, to breakfast with us
via the newspapers with which most of us begin our days). . . . The
poignancy and national engagement of *Challenger* with the shame
of its loss mixed up in the patriotic glory of its crew members'
sacrifices. . . . The poignancy as well of a Stephen Hawking who
combines unspeakable personal bravery with Einstein's penchant
for easy domestication as an icon of genius.[17] . . . The vigor and
media-savvy brilliance of writer/scientists like Carl Sagan and
Isaac Asimov. . . .

This list, too, could go on, but the point would seem already to have been made: the newest branches of physical science
have enjoyed a singular wealth of access not only to the popular
intelligence but also to the popular imagination, an access considerably beyond any available up to now to the other forms of
new information.[18] The result is that their questions as well as
their suggested possibilities and certainly their discoveries, having been broadcast in a kind of surround-sound environment
from multiple points of origin,[19] have fallen upon ever richer and
ever more fallow ground. Their success in taking up residence
in lay minds and sensibilities, in other words, has been a self-
potentiating process, and, ironically enough, its greatest and most
lasting contribution may be not to science at all, but to theology.[20]

"What is time?" for example, may have started out as a question of physics, but it became one of theology almost before it hit the airwaves or the newsstands. What is time, and what does it mean to be lifted out of it? What is "real" when looked at from "outside" of time; and if time can be exited, is what is real inside of it really real at all? How does life arise and what does it mean if — or since — it does exist elsewhere than on our earth? What does that mean about us and, more importantly, about the intentionality of God? What is light after all? What is its role in creating coherent reality, and what is the meaning of its fundamental duality as wave and particle? What is place or locality and why can some photons, like the sparkles of Mr. Scott's transporter, be in two of them simultaneously? What does that mean for us and for our apparently inherent dependence on the notion that we really are somewhere? Is the whole really greater than its parts as quantum theory suggests, and are all the parts really inseparable, really interconnected by fields that are inviolate? Is prayer, given such a system, really only applied physics? And can mountains indeed be moved because they aren't "there" in the first place except as we observe them so to be? ...

These and dozens of teasing, gnawing, barking questions like them are cosmological and scientific in content, but theological in conclusion. And by casting such ultimate questions in the language of established experimental methods and passing them on to interested, but lay, people, popularized science has, however unintentionally, helped to return theology to people, making it an acceptable concern for the informed and restoring intellectual excitement to popular god-talk. It has also gone a long way toward replacing private passion and institutionalized doctrine with questing belief as faith's central authority. In the final analysis, then, god-talk in America and the religion that does or does not attach to it are going to have to engage not only the questions raised by new information, but also a change in both the attitude and the composition of those who are wrestling with it.

This accommodation to new ways has several other pieces to it. I want to introduce at least two of them before we push on to the other theologically active phenomena besides cumulative literacy and expanding information that are at work in our time. I want to look at an example or two of some effecting new theses in, first, the nonlaboratory and, second, the applied sciences. By virtue of their more narrative nature, the findings and conclusions of the nonlaboratory disciplines are frequently more difficult to evaluate and their results for popular theology, far more diffuse and idiosyncratic. For that reason alone, they deserve, at the very least, some deliberate consideration here.

The case for our stopping at the applied sciences is a bit different. On a sliding scale that runs from pure theory down to absolute how-to, the applied sciences obviously are nearer to the how-to end than to the theoretical one. In the same way, on a sliding scale running from pure theology to practical morality, the applied sciences are nearer to the moral end of the stick. Predictably enough, because of the greater immediacy of their presence in everyday life, the applied sciences, then, have given us some of the most theologically volatile intersections between postmodern information and responsibility and our former ways of talking about and understanding God. For that reason, they too seem to me to require a bit more attention than do some other areas.

So now, on to some nonlaboratory sciences, or more accurately and less prejudicially, to some less laboratory-oriented sciences, for this too is a matter of sliding scales.

— Five —

In the Middle

═══ ═══

FOR CONVENIENCE, Michio Kaku, professor of theoretical physics at the Graduate Center of City College of New York and cofounder of string field theory, divides physics into two bundles — the physics "of the very small," by which he means quantum mechanics, and the physics "of the very large," by which he means relativity.[1] Taking license from Kaku and by extrapolating shamelessly, I want to make another useful (but totally unorthodox) distinction. I want to lump together, for the purposes of facilitating our look at cumulative literacy, some fields of study that I shall call "the sciences of the middle."[2]

By sciences of the middle, I mean those that are more perceptually human in their sizing and in what they reference and, as a result, in their natural ability to impact religion, theology, and spiritually.[3] The centrality that allows these disciplines to be lumped together in popular discussion is not so much the nature of their methods and materials, in other words, but the immediacy and intimacy of the impact of their findings upon the perceptions of ordinary people and upon folk thinking. It is through the rubric of that commonality that I mean to juxtapose some of the newer divisions of long-familiar academic fields like archeology, anthropology, sociology, and biology as "middlers."

Archeology and anthropology alone have spawned such new sciences as archaeometry, cultural anthropology, papyrology, paleoethnology, ethnolinguistics, and a whole litany of similar polysyllabicisms, most of which end in "-logy." Nobody ever said, of course, that any of us has to define all these new fields of specialization, or even that anybody outside a university setting has to have ever before heard of them as such. The truth is that most of us can't and haven't; but we have all been influenced by the popularized results of their existence. If those results are something of a mish-mash in our heads, at least in terms of which field of formal study has produced which premise or fact in our accumulating bank of information about ourselves and our imme-diate world, we may be forgiven. If we ignore their consequences upon belief and traditional theology, we won't be.

When in 1990 the students and followers of the late Joseph Campbell sought a means by which to continue and expand his work, they established the Joseph Campbell Foundation as a not-for-profit organization "seeking to formulate a mythopoetic response to contemporary literalism and cultural retrenchment."[4] As a mission statement, it's a bit of a mouthful and far too clunky to be very rousing; yet in everything except its lack of a lively animation, the foundation's statement encapsulates not only Campbell's work but also its living consequences.

More than any other single human being in modern times, I am convinced, Campbell changed forever the syntax and semantics of popular god-talk by changing everything from its vocabulary and frames of reference to its juxtapositions and catenations.[5] The formative element of such massive changes, however, was not so much in Campbell's brilliant passion or inspired scholarship, though those certainly were prerequisite, but in his charismatic ability to communicate and popularize his interpretation of the human condition by using his own and other scholars' work in anthropology. It was also certainly in his being present within that precise moment of history that could hear and incorporate him. And most assuredly it was in the coterie of highly skilled people who were attracted to him and his work, not the least of them another lasting communicator of our culture's religious business, Bill Moyers.

Campbell's ideas are too extensive and probably too subtle to suffer adequate reduction, of course, but it may fairly be said that he denied the primacy of materialism and determinism as the only or even as the most appropriate ways to interpret either individual or communal life.[6] Life and history, he taught, both have a transcendent reality that lies beyond the reaches of material measure or determination; but theirs is a reality that may still be seen and studied, nonetheless, by means of the fingerprints and foot tracks that reality leaves behind as evidence of its having been. This "mythic dimension," to use Campbell's words, is to be found in the literature, the art and architecture, and the religion of every people, but most especially in their mythology. Campbell truly believed — and was the first in epochs to make the rest of us believe — that every book about religion should begin with "Once upon a time." Those words, he would have said, are the door beyond which truth waits.

Myth, in Campbell's scheme, was body to the Mystery, its corporeal and observable expression. Universal in their basic plot lines and central characters, myths capture and record in terms of superhuman beings the fundamental life cycles of each of us and of our species in general. Like religion, which it so often serves, myth to be myth must impose system and pattern upon life and grant safe passage through its crises and transitions, problems that, as Campbell saw, are beyond enculturation at their core.

Why must we all have stories of a beginning to explain us, and why, having them, do we record in almost all our stories that the first act of divinity was the imposition, either by creation or pro-creation, of order upon a watery pre-Chaos? Why should we need the questing hero and the always symbolic talisman for which he searches? For that matter, why must the hero always endure the terrible journey that will involve almost all of his vigorous life in transit? And why the forest/desert isolation that commences his search and steels him for it? Why must there be another world or worlds into which the hero looks and/or travels and into which the dead move without hope of return? Why, indeed, to these and several dozen more commonalities to human myth?

Because, Campbell would have said, myths detail through metaphor a needed structure for all the relationships and connections that are the nexus undergirding us and the reality relieving us. The ideas conveyed in myth are elementary ones in the most robust sense of "elementary"; and beneath their cultural contours and ethnic elaborations, they constitute one describable set of stories pointing to one set of truths.

Prior to Campbell's work as a public scholar, the perception of similarity of story among peoples of common origin was fairly well-known. That is, average citizens found it in no way disturbing that Greece had Zeus and Rome had Jupiter. The fact that they were both storm gods and so was Judeo-Christian Yahweh was a little more privileged as information. As a divine similarity, moreover, it could easily be regarded as accidental or possibly curious because it was a fact in isolation. It was in isolation, that is, until Campbell began publicly to retell the tales of many very dissonant cultures and then to explore not only the global similarities of their myths but also the significance of those similarities even being there. It was Campbell, in other words, who first suggested to millions of Americans that "since all humankind participates in these universal ideas, the myths and art of other cultures are the moral equals of Greco-Judeo-Christian culture."[7] And as if to make matters worse, Campbell was credible!

Joseph Campbell, in fact, was a very careful scholar. He may have painted with a broad brush, but he did so with lovingly mixed colors on a professionally primed canvas. He both knew whereof he spoke and had the text proofs to defend his positions once he assumed them. His passion, however, drove him to a wider audience than that sitting in his lecture hall at Sarah Lawrence College. At first books were his megaphone out to the waiting hordes that were to be his converts.[8] It was not the books, however, that were destined to solidify Campbell's penetration of the public consciousness and win for his ideas the centrality they now can claim in American god-talk. It was his old admirer and able-in-his-own-right friend Bill Moyers and the powerful new medium of television.

The Power of Myth, a kind of summary on wheels of all of Campbell's ideas, was taped shortly before his death in 1987, but aired posthumously. As a six-part, one-hour-to-an-evening viewing on PBS, the interviews between Campbell and Moyers were "unprecedented" in the numbers of people who watched and "they were rated higher than any public television show had ever been rated before,"[9] just as the videos that came from them are still among the genre's top sellers consistently.[10]

What Campbell had finally done was expose to a massive audience by means of image as well as words the fundamental similarities across cultural and temporal lines of the group-specific stories and symbols that integrate and inspire group behavior.[11] He had exposed us to ourselves as well, demonstrating quite nicely that the representations of those stories that are our own we call religion and that the representations belonging to another culture or era we call myth. The consequences of this truism are so obvious and so much with us that only a few words of commentary are really needed.

Thus, since Nordic mythology had Yggdrasill, the Tree of Life that pierced the cosmic layers and bound them all together; since the Babylonians had the sacred *kiskana* tree in the Grove of Eridhu where Anu the sky god first made human beings out of mud; since the ancient Aztecs, remembering in myth a holy and perfect tree, told stories of Tamoanchan, the paradise where both the gods and human beings were created to live in harmony under its shade until some of the lesser gods broke the taboo of reverence for the untouchable tree and plucked its flowers, thereby destroying paradise; since the Hindus speak of *Idavarsha,* or the Garden of Ida, where the sacred *Kalpadruma,* Tree of the Ages, and *Parajita,* Tree of Every Perfect Gift, grew; since all of these identities and near identities exist, are there not questions that thinking people must ask themselves? Are we not almost required by this information to ask ourselves what we are to make of the singularity of Hebrew story now? What exactly is the sacredness now of Genesis? Where on the scale of myth to text is its proper definition?

Not only, in other words, does proof of such ubiquitous similarities raise the defining question of why one system of belief is "better" or "truer" or "more effective" than any other; it also raises questions about whether any of them is. In time it almost assumes the hidden presence of a universal truth that can be entered into, like a grand ballroom, through many doors. More important, it presumes that all those welcoming doors that open onto the ballroom differ from one another only in the exterior decors with which their outer surfaces must blend when the doors themselves are tightly closed.

What must be commented upon specifically here as being equally influential but less obvious, however, is a kind of corollary truism to Campbell's observations about myths. We — most of us anyway — now concede that the operative distinction between myth and sacred texts may be related to one's point of view, to whose stories are being talked about by whom and when. The corollary is that this popular truism can quickly turn upon itself and reduce all holy stories to myth instead of elevating any of them to sacred texts — which is exactly what has happened, however subliminally, for many post–Joseph Campbell Americans.

Moreover, and just as provocatively, Campbell's position, logically extended, suggests that the poetry and metaphors of myth, rather than its historicist or literal details, are the truth. Indeed, the history and details of myth, under such an assessment, can become suspect as being no more than enculturated servants to the intention of the story. This last possibility has meant for hundreds of thousands of thinking and seeking Christian and Jewish Americans[12] a near obligation consciously to reexplore their sacred texts in pursuit of a greater truth than that which they had in youth been taught to see.

As important to popular theology as Campbell's suggestion of universal efficacy in all established faith systems was, the reexamination of texts by eager laity proved to be a body blow to religion and institutionalism as well. It implied from the very start that the institutionalized church or synagogue, the invested pastor or rabbi, had deliberately cordoned off the "real" truth over the centuries for reasons of professional self-interest. The Christian teaching that "there is but one true way to God and that is through the man Christ Jesus," and the Jewish concept of chosenness and *Halakah* as requisite became theological hostages to this almost universal suspicion or cynicism.[13]

The failure of formal theology and institutionalized religion in this country to find unified resolution to the questions and charges raised by Campbell's work and that of those who preceded and have followed him has done nothing to improve the public image of either.[14] Rather, it has empowered the questions and charges, in a sense allowing them to simmer like some informing spice in the general melange of America's popular godtalk for the last forty years. Just as significantly and probably consequentially, any talker who wants to influence or shape the business of God today is going to have to engage these fundamentally challenging questions, like them or not, in some cohesive, coalescing way.

Much of Campbell's work in similarity and analogy had to do with, and was dependent upon, the work of Carl Jung. Jung, who had worked in his younger years with Freud and later clashed with him, was himself a dynamic scholar and an enormously effective popularizer, having been one of the first of the moderns to play to and gain a huge following. Coming upon the scene literally just a few years before television and video were ready tools for learned dissemination, Jung had to depend primarily upon books and lectures to achieve public stature, but he did it well; and his has proved to be an enormously stable popularity. There are, for example, several hundred books *about* him presently on the market.[15]

His now-famous separation from Freud freed Jung to pursue psychoanalytic experimentation in far broader terms than had Freud. That is, where Freud had taken the single patient and presumed a pathology, Jung took many particulars and presumed a neutral pattern. It was, of course, this part of Jung's work, i.e., that with the mythic implications and structures of archetypes, that was to become most widely associated with his name. But Jung's wide-ranging exploration of the geography of human subjectivity; his reverential drawings of the interior architecture we build for ourselves with memories, dreams, and reflections;[16] and particularly his forceful promotion of the model of our unconscious as imagistic and universal — these ideas were to change humanity's understanding of itself. They were also, just as fundamentally and no doubt consequentially, to change theology. Indeed the walls of separation between Jung's work in subjectivity and a mythopoetic, symbolistic paradigm for the study of religion and religious experience are, at their very least, semi-permeable; for Jung they became almost nonexistent.[17]

Jung's conclusions about the uses of religion; his magisterial dicta about the universality of experience from which religion arises and about which memories of the universal unconscious religion must evoke or play to if it is to be apprehensible; his almost poetic exposure of the necessary role played by symbols in the soul's communication with, and integration into, the other parts of experience — these were to find and retain their own audience. They were also to find their expansion in the work of others who, like Joseph Campbell, followed Jung and employed well the seminal fruits of his lifetime of study.

Emphasizing only two giants of formative change, in other words, in no way implies the absence of many others.[18] Our mid-century was abundantly peopled with able minds dedicated to the formal study of mythopoetic theological issues. I would be disloyal to my own spiritual autobiography if I did not mention specifically men like Alan Watts, who opened the harmonies of East with West to me,[19] or Mircea Eliade, who made comparative religion a salvific experience for me and whose *The Sacred and the Profane* gave popular god-talk a whole new (and still employed) modern vocabulary.[20]

The audience for the work of men like Campbell, Jung, Eliade, and Watts and public receptivity to their ideas of the similarity and universalism in religions have been sustained and expanded, of course, by the work of others who have followed them.[21] Much of this growing recognition — even general incorporation as bedrock premise — of equality among religions (that is, of one-god-sought-through-many-means-but-one-and-the-same-once-found) and of the universality of human need for the divine has found its reinforcement in other of the middle sciences. Some of the newer branches of archeology that I jested about earlier, for instance, have fired the popular religious imagination as much as the professional academy's intellectual one. The media coverage of dig after dig and of find after find

from Donald Johanson's Lucy[22] to the frozen hunter of the Alps
has reinforced our general readiness to assume evolutionary process as a given and our basic brotherhood as a species-specific
fact.[23]

Familiarity with and the discovery of pleasurable excitement
in reading about such discoveries have undoubtedly increased the
general readership for scholar-popularizers like Hershel Shanks[24]
or Charles Pellegrino,[25] whose work in biblical archeology has
done so much to confirm a more judicious rejection of literalism
in textual readings while affirming as even more spectacular the
suggestive wonders of a mythopoetic approach.

Lest even so cursory an overview as this one become tedious
with detailing the names and ideas of the well-known, however,
suffice it here to make only one last observation. In an odd,
almost paradoxical way, much of the formative material that
modern, "middle-science" scholarship gave to theology as it has
evolved in the mind and thoughts of average citizens was not facts
and theories, but the ability to abstract the thing itself. Watching
scholars pull religion/theology out, set it down in front of them as
if it were indeed an object upon a laboratory table, walk around
it in study with impunity, and then dissect it/them in plainly accurate or plausible ways taught everyday people a lesson, or at least
a new method of approach. We learned the illuminating benefits
of observing and assessing our theology, and we learned that one
can do that observing and assessing without guilt or irreverence
or personal vulnerability. In many ways, in other words, popularized scholarship's greatest contribution has been that it has
empowered as much as it has informed god-talk in the streets, offices, and living rooms of this country. I want to develop this idea
in considerable detail a bit later. Right now, I want only to record
its presence and to mention that it has been yet another middle science, sociology, that has contributed substantially to this
distancing or abstracting ability.

Sociometry, demographics, the sociology of religion — they have enabled and given us the informed insights of several of the country's best known and most quoted scholars. Sydney Ahlstrom's *A Religious History of the American People* is something of a classic, having stayed in print since 1972 and having served as a prototype for several dozen subsequent popular or near popular similar studies.[26] Among the scholars producing these studies, none is more believed, more respected by his peers, or more frequently cited by the popular press than Martin Marty. With his pastoral but incisive assessments of many characteristic forms of religious behavior, Marty has produced dozens of books. In doing so, he has also over the years gradually provided us with the tools, standards, and vocabulary for objective, dispassionate, nonpejorative analysis of theology as it is applied by people, especially by Americans, in their religious observance.[27] These same concerns have also found powerful but almost poetic expression in the hands of the literary critic Harold Bloom, who in writing his bestseller *The American Religion*[28] in 1992 said that he saw himself as inventing yet another middle science, the science or art of religious criticism.

Likewise, George Gallup, Jr., has provided for millions of Americans the comfort of broad statistical studies that, by quantifying almost every conceivable presentation of theological concepts and religious activity, have allowed Everyman (or woman) to locate his or her own spot upon America's religious landscape. Like George Barna,[29] who functions as a cautionary agent primarily to millions of America's Evangelical or conservative Christians, Gallup prognosticates as well as describes, and almost always to the benefit of the devout as well as of the desirous. In books like *The People's Religion*,[30] which he wrote in 1989 with Jim Castelli, Gallup has managed to expose through a seemingly inspired use of statistical studies the cultural and social ramifications of religion in this country.

These scholars, with their popularizing, have facilitated the gradual transformation of god-talk from an exclusively learned and professional activity to a general one in one other way as well. Their work has furnished the kind of frames of reference that have empowered the media — and most especially the periodical, print media — to cover with impunity more and more areas of religion and theology. Whereas print media were once susceptible to charges of prejudice and to vilification from the religious and religions, they now can cover religion and theology with the cutting objectivity of reportage, because they can both fortify and protect themselves with reams of statistical validation and comparative data. Wire services like Religion News Service, which supplies over two hundred of the country's newspapers with religion copy; professional organizations like Religion Newswriters Association that provide guidelines as well as an energizing network; highly visible and enormously skilled reporters like Terry Mattingly at Scripps-Howard, Gus Neibuhr and Peter Steinfels at the *New York Times,* Ken Woodward at *Newsweek,* and Richard Ostling at *Time,* to name only a few — all of these, too, have been of inestimable influence in the shaping of America's god-talk and in our choices of the places in which and among whom it transpires.

But enough of the middle sciences that deal with the world at large. I want to make one more stop in the universe of cumulative literacy before we move on, this time in the world of the applied sciences. So, as the song says, let's get physical.

Six

Of Micro and Macro

≡   ≡

EDICINE is one of humankind's oldest absorptions, predating almost every other science by eras if not eons. Yet medicine's progeny as much as, if not more than, those of any other science, new or old, have richly impacted theology in the decades of our cumulative literacy.

Medicine is, of course, a middle science, even by my own definition of that somewhat ill-defined category. That is, it certainly takes its measure from the measure of humanity itself. But it differs from the other middlers we have looked at in that, at its core, medicine is an applied science. It is evaluated on the basis of its totally human results; and those results are almost always instantly discernible, constantly reported upon, and chronically on the edge. Medicine, in other words and as we all know, is the media's darling. It needs no more exposure than that which human vulnerability already assigns it in order to command our earnest attention.

To the extent that medicine and all of its highly sophisticated, contemporary offspring — cardiovascular surgery, gerontology, radiology, oncology, neurosurgery, and dozens more like them — are applied to our vulnerabilities, to just that same extent are the questions raised by them theological, ethical, or "spiritual" ones for us. The lines that separate those three categories seem, in general, to be a matter of simple immediacy. To take them in reverse order, it is a fair generalization to say that for the desperately ill undergoing treatment, the issues and decisions raised by contemporary medicine's advances are spiritual. For the near circle of their families, friends, and associates, the issues are more frequently moral or ethical. For the rest of us, more distant but observing, either of those positions inevitably will become theological, given sufficient time and conversation.

What the new, more technologically sophisticated branches and subbranches of today's medicine have done, in other words, is present us as individuals, as families, and as a society with near miracles of therapeutic technology and a whole panoply of attendant questions. What we as a culture have done about those questions is to demand that people — just plain ordinary people — answer them while standing in the midst of circumstances that are almost always emotionally overcharged. The ironic new twist to all of this is that the resulting highly individual case-by-case answers thus evolved have begun accumulating into a kind of folk or popular wisdom that has shaped not only the studied, professional field of bioethics but also the more fluid and politicized ones of theology and popular god-talk.

The questions generated by postmodern medicine are, in the main, mechanistic in tone.[1] That is, they are in the main tied to an image of human beings as machines or constructs whose pieces and parts (along with the final disposition of all of them) are to be evaluated and then dealt with in terms of some externally defined efficiency factor. Euphemistically, such considerations are known as "quality of life" issues. Politically, they mean "Can Dr. Jack really go around assisting folks who want out to get out?" and "Can the nearest women's clinic really abort everything that just walks in the door?" Practically, they usually mean what do we do about Grandma now that she's ninety-two, blind, in a nursing home, semi-comatose with her third bout of pneumonia and the to-resuscitate/not-to-resuscitate decision is up for grabs again.[2]

Somewhere in between the euphemisms, the politics, and the practicalities is a broad and pain-filled plateau where the mechanical analogies all translate into the biggies: What is life? Where and by what means may it be defined? When may it be said to have ended? What are the levels of its value and of its value relative to other life, and can that question even be asked with impunity? What right does one human being have to take other life and/or what *obligation* does one human being have to take other life and when? For whom or with reference to whom is that obligation operative? Why and because of whose/Whose agency is such a question even necessary or possible?[3] What, if any, are the proper uses of disease and pain, suffering and deterioration? What their origin and what their justifications?

This list, like all our other previous ones, can go on for quite some time before it is in any danger of repeating itself, but the point is made. As with Pandora's box, the ethical/theological questions that once were the province of professional philosophers have now been released into the public domain by the public dissemination of medical advances, and they are all too well known to want extension here. They are, when everything else is said and done, deeply frightening, deeply threatening questions about whether personned intention or impersonal process or — worst of all — some vaguely understood variation of possibility between the two, has been and remains at work with us. They are also questions, inevitably, about how and how much we can, should, and must enter into the processes we are now possessed of before we run some risk of offending the intention we pray is there. Our opinionated answers as a people — perhaps made so strident and obsessive by our fear — continue most of the time to be couched as action and/or rhetoric rather than as the reasoned distillate of systematic thought. Abortion and euthanasia are, of course, the angriest manifestations both of the questions and of our approach as a society to dealing with them.

There have been, for example, no great, centralizing, or synthesizing books on the subject of either abortion or euthanasia, though heaven knows there has been a veritable flood of minor and under-read ones. Whole pine forests have died over just abortion alone.[4] Nor has there been any lack of electronic media coverage of both issues. Certainly there has been no shortage, either, of soap-box orators vociferously willing to attach their own futures to one posture or another.

Looking at us from outside, in fact, an observer might legitimately conclude that on issues of life-definition and intentionality at least, we are a society composed entirely of either the radicalized or the expediently reticent. That is, a few of us scream while most of us either know what we think and don't care to share, or else have made up our minds to risk making our decisions on an each-case-as-it-comes basis without having any kind of overarching theory to position and secure us.[5] The central problem with such a situation as that, especially in a media age of mass literacy, is distortion of the public consensus and an expanding confusion. The radicalized make good copy and the reticent almost never do.

To be fair to ourselves, we should admit that it is hard to be either passionate or ebullient about one's defense of the middle of the road since, as the old joke says, almost nothing ever happens there except accidents and steady progress. Nonetheless, neither popular nor formal theology has articulated either a convincingly attractive or a divinely compelling set of answers to the questions about when life is life and about what that definition (assuming we ever arrive at it) should mean in public policy as well as in private faith and action.[6] That lack of ethical commonality, that kind of fundamental rudderlessness, is a harsh circumstance even in the best of times. It is made bitter and divisive twice over when ecclesial and theological authorities choose to expend themselves in defending historic positions, as often as not against one another, instead of engaging in the *aggiornamento* of evolving doctrine.

It was not too many decades ago, we must remember, that modernity had its own major confrontation between theology and a middle science over the tension between seeing humanity as a created order and viewing it as an order in creation that is best treated as such. That ruckus was and still is Darwinism,[7] and its absolute refusal to suffer resolution is one of the most frightening things about our very similar postmodern confrontations with abortion and euthanasia.[8] (It is also, for concerned religionists of almost every theistic tradition, the most potentially destabilizing consequence of NASA's announcement in mid-1996 of the discovery of archebacterial life on Mars, and for the same reasons.) When theology arrives too late to enlighten and sacramentalize change, it ceases to do the work of heaven and takes on the chores of hell.[9]

Technologically enabled, postmodern medicine's operational premise of body as machine has graphically informed more than our beginnings and endings, however. It has affected just as mawkishly our most pleasurable moments in between: our sexuality. The unrelieved bonding between identity and sexuality is the stuff of high religion and deep myth, a matter too ancient and too fixed to even be protested. When, therefore, my sex is not what my gender seems and certainly not what I feel that I was wired for, who am I? When a skilled surgeon can reassemble what I am to agree with how I feel, who am I after — and what was I before — that surgery?

Hard questions that fascinate not just the afflicted but many other people as well, yet they pale as questions in the face of the real, heavy-duty ones of homosexuality. The transvestite and the transsexual historically were anomalies and sometimes even interesting anomalies like dwarves and hunchbacks, but they were not theological cyphers except, perhaps, to themselves. Certainly they were not walking violations of divine law. Then DNA comes along and genetics comes along and biochemistry comes along and somebody starts suggesting that sexual preference may be like one's hair color or body size — a given. Suddenly the established order is threatened and the fiery questions whose torment we all know so well by now really begin.[10]

How much choice do I and/or does a homosexual have? Can I/he/she really treat sexuality like natural hair color and by sheer will choose to dye mine differently for public presentation? Or perhaps sexuality is like body size and each of us can be held accountable, at least within certain parameters, for how we expand or contract it by our activities and choices? Can the clay really say to the potter, "Why madest thou me thus?" and get away with it? Or is there any potter even to ask? And if so, what kind of cruel joke am I and/or is my friend? Or is the divine law something for another time and place? And if so...?

Ahhhh...now there's a slippery slope to warm the cockles of any canon lawyer's heart, for if one part of the Law can be cast aside, then what of all the rest? What, Dear Lord, of the social contract? What of the attitudes and subtleties of submission and dominance, of seduction and aggression? What of "natural" hierarchy in society's most basic unit and social paradigm, the family? And the minute we begin to ask these questions, we have slipped on our holdless slope down from theology to religion and then it is that the devils begin to laugh in earnest. And all of this happens to us simply because we postmoderns received, not an apple, but a microscope and then after that a better one and after that an even better one and then...*ad infinitum.*

God-talk...how the heart feels it must speak of compassion and how the mind resists that disarray of vital emotions. How difficult to turn *imago dei* around upon itself and say but if humanity is the image of god, then as with images so with the original that is being imaged...and the heart trembles, knowing its pains and losses and circumvented dreams.

Another and far less wrenching way that increased public literacy about medicine has directly impacted popular theology is almost a result of indirection. By its very stringent (and very necessary, I must say it again) insistence upon a machine-like interpretation of the human body, postmodern medicine has tripped a resounding protest — one that asserts loudly, even militantly at times, a "No, by God, I am *not* a machine!" reaction. In this particular insurrection of the spirit against the system, moreover, books and seminars seem to have assumed even more than their customary place of prominence. They have become the most efficacious vehicles of challenge. Many, if not the bulk, of them also have been produced by physicians. M.D.'s like Deepak Chopra and Wayne W. Dwyer, Andrew Weil and Larry Dossey and dozens of others have gone on to become bestselling authors with quite literally millions of devoted reader/followers.[11]

Call them New Agers — and one in every five Americans today is[12] — or call them gullible or call them the historically orthodox laying their claim to ancient efficacies...call them what we will, the fact still remains that millions of us[13] have begun once more to believe unabashedly in the power of prayer to heal, in the potency of the laying on of hands to correct and alleviate, in the life-affirming ability of the spirit to tend and keep the body.[14] And while such postmodern notions of alternative medicine may have begun as a generalized but loose reaction to too much depersonalization of illness and age, they have grown to fill (or, some would say, to fill once again) a proactive and very theological space.

The interchange between body and soul and spirit and the ready acknowledgement of their necessary and inviolate interconnectedness are part and parcel today of most Americans' sense of who they are individually — of their personness, if you will. The result of that significant shift in viewpoint has been a kind of elevation of the body and its necessities into a spiritual realm and a concomitant, acted-upon introduction of the spirit and its needs into the everyday physical. The emphasis on "wholeness" is everywhere operative and honored, and all space is potentially holy or sacred by virtue simply of its capacity to know and hold human beings. It is an interesting progression that, ironically, is almost historically circular; but it has also taken on the absolutely new strength of a highly informed and acquired naiveté that is not unlike the grace-filled naiveté of the elderly who, knowing and having known it all, choose to believe as a result rather than as a denial.

The men and women who have led the seminars, written the books, popularized the ideas that have culminated in this new harmony and system of active belief may not be as pure as their words would have us think. They may, as some critics contend, indeed be placebo practitioners or merely comforters of the otherwise comfortless and even healers of the only suggestively ill. Their efficacy is of no moment here. What matters, at least right now, is not even so much whether or not they are believed or by how many millions of us. What does matter is that as a result of them and their work, a new relationship has been presumed between body and soul and a "new" integrity of all our parts has been reestablished. Who goes now to his or her prayers goes conscious of and responsible for and equally concerned with all the parts that we are. Who goes to his or her prayers expects as well that the Recipient of those prayers will be just as conscious, responsible, and concerned — which makes us much closer in expectation to Father Abraham than to either Martin Luther or Cotton Mather.

But given all of our popular fascination with medicine and especially given all of the current emphasis on self-help and alternative healing methods, why has even this brief overview of some of postmodern medicine's contribution to cumulative literacy not included psychiatry as well? Surely the medicine of the interior life is of as much theological import as the medicine of the more tangible body? Why relegate all our recent, exponential growth of understanding in this area, as I seem to have done so far, to the tentative theories and laboratory data of the mind sciences? Well, to tell the truth, I have not so much relegated as delayed until now. The sciences of the mind, once they cease to be theoretical and become applied, differ from their fellow middlers in several, and for popular theology, some rather disturbing, ways.

To the extent that scientific investigations of the mind are concerned with human disease process, they are obviously "middlers." And to the extent that treatment of diseases of the mind can be distinguished from studies of the functions and structure of the brain and nervous systems, we can separate psychiatric medicine out from laboratory experimentation. But we also have to recognize even as we do so, that any such segmentation is at best tenuous and that its particulars are often of mixed content.

All the mind sciences, whether pure or applied, "feel" as if they deal with something noncorporeal and therefore as if with something "spiritual" or "other." Mind itself is in many ways the place where God and Man separate — or more accurately, where the business of each meets that of the other. Mind belongs to neither Heaven nor Earth, but is their common appointment.[15] For this reason, the questions raised by the postmodern experimentation and studies of the mind sciences seem to take their measure more from God, the Tao, and the universal than from humanity. It is only in their applied form as psychiatry that the mind sciences lose much of their "removed," philosophical quality. When they deal in the treatment of disease, they cut much closer to home. And cut they do. More than any other branch of contemporary medicine, they demand new definitions of who and what we are as thinking beings and, most disturbingly, of personal culpability, responsibility, and accountability. The result

of each significant, clinical advance in psychiatry is, for this reason, almost always translated publicly into something more, and
sometimes quite violently so.

The most recent example of such a conflation is, to my mind,
that which attended and still attends Prozac. Introduced in the
late 1980s as a psychotherapeutic drug solely and with a very
quickly established record of clinical success, Prozac became almost as quickly a theological hot potato. That is, it became a
source of spiritual shame for some of its beneficiaries and a cause
for a great deal of popular theorizing about the role of will in
the soul's life. Few single books alone have ever had the impact or evoked the storm of reaction, for instance, that Peter
Kramer's *Listening to Prozac: A Psychiatrist Explores Mood-
Altering Drugs and the New Meaning of the Self* did, and it has
since been followed by dozens more books and popular articles
on the same subject.[16]

Additionally, like all the advances made by other sciences
whose findings militate for new definitions of life and its component functions, whether interior or exterior, the advances of
psychiatric medicine have not yet evoked any cohesive or popularly significant, integrating response from established religion
or theology.[17] As with euthanasia and abortion, formal theology
may ultimately fail to map out any position of consensus or general unity of answers to the questions raised by psychiatry and
especially by psychiatric drug therapy. That remains to be seen.
What is clear now, however, is twofold: Most of us have decided
what we think about the nature of psychiatric illness and the
role that psychotherapeutic drugs play in it and/or about what
we would choose as a course of action for ourselves if we ever
had to. And secondly, more and more of us are managing to separate our private decisions from any "official" religious doctrine
we may otherwise claim. We are instead assuming our stances on
the basis of our individualized understandings of God or of God's

will. Any consensus that cannot be articulated is dangerous not only to its opponents, but also to itself, primarily because it can never exercise in the broad light of day and grow. Yet it just may be that god-talk in America has already become or is becoming addicted to the unspokenness of a number of articles of faith. If so, then ours is a most inhospitable place in history.

One may justifiably contend, of course, that established religion's failure to successfully wrestle the issues raised by medical advances has been a result of the deep infiltration of those issues into almost every part of human spirituality. In a more politic way, one might even suggest that religion's whimpering silence is a result of a time lag and of rapidly changing subdisciplines that are in such a state of flux as to almost defy ordered response just yet. Both would undoubtedly be true. But I think we must acknowledge as well that the delay has been, at least in part, a consequence of a kind of institutional cowardice obscured from itself by an energetic and almost all-consuming fixation by formal religion and theology upon two or three other of the middle sciences. Because they deal with more overt and less intimate territory than, say, pharmopsychology or gender medicine, these other areas of advance have been easier to comprehend and less dangerous to address. Consider ecology as a case in point.

Ecology, bless it, deals with us and our right-here-right-now world. It is neither up there nor down there, but here where I have been or, theoretically anyway, where I can go. And of the many legitimately distinct new fields and subfields of human study, none has bonded any more dramatically with and adhered any more immutably to god-talk than has ecology. So tight is that union that it has itself spawned subdisciplines and its own subset of labels.

Where once we spoke of conservation or environmentalism, we now hear all around us news of more specific and far more distinctly religious areas of formalized concern like eco-spirituality, eco-theology, eco-therapy, and eco-feminism. Prominent among these is "earthkeeping," a label that is enjoying wider and wider currency among religious organizations — Christian, Jewish, Islamic, and Buddhist alike — in this country.[18] As a rubric, earthkeeping presumes an active recognition of the spiritual and physical interdependence of the earth and humanity in terms not only of the environment as such and the conservation of its bounty, but also of more sociological and economic issues like poverty, hunger, population, employment, etc.

The sensibilities that have led to this pitch of concern found their earliest popularized expression in the work of Rachel Carson and most particularly in her now classic *Silent Spring,* originally published in 1962 by Houghton Mifflin.[19] What Carson caught in *Silent Spring* and gave first voice to was human yearning, the keening cry of the severed longing for home.

Because all yearning is at its core religious or a celebration of the same unity that is religion, ecology as Carson articulated it was a natural companion to god-talk and became an equally natural and easily affiliated concern of America's god-talkers. This, not surprisingly, was a public passion that was expanded and instructed by books.[20] Carson, who is still revered by younger writers in the field, was followed by others: by Thomas Berry, himself a religious;[21] by Matthew Fox, the Roman Catholic priest who for his troubles was excommunicated by Rome and welcomed into a new priesthood by Canterbury, primarily on the basis of his commitment to contemporary god-talk;[22] and even by devout politicians like Vice-President Al Gore, whose *Earth in the Balance*[23] drew empowered attention to the problem. In fact, publishing books about the religious and/or spiritual ramifications of the earth herself and a proper reverence for her became a lucrative as well as a culturally laudable business in the America of the mid-1990s.[24]

Nor was the evoked reverence all couched in the traditional perceptions of Judaism, Christianity, or Islam. As one of America's fastest-growing faiths, Buddhism also, with its deep, philosophical involvement with physical space and intentional living, excited much of our early public awareness of ecology. As the number of practicing Buddhists has grown in America, the very presence of their ideas has likewise increased greatly the freedom many Americans feel in talking about such things as the spiritual implications of earthkeeping for individual lives. Especially has this new freedom to think and react "spiritually" to environmental issues empowered those who previously were religiously unaffiliated. In combining the teachings of Buddhism and the disciplines of ecology, many of them have chanced upon a resting place for their intentions and a comfort for their longings.[25] For others within our so-called "dominant culture," however, the most vital or vitalizing experience with the soul of ecology has come from sources even nearer to hand.

While the methods may have been inept at times, while motivations were sometimes less than noble, and while the results are even now far from sufficient, the fact still is that we as a culture began almost forty years ago the process of achieving unified and equal enfranchisement for all citizens in this country. We will eventually accomplish that goal. In the meanwhile, it is obvious that the process itself has been of benefit in many, many ways. Incorporating African Americanism culturally, socially, and politically into the mainstream has obviously enriched the whole country in general and its music and religion in particular during the last few years. The African American community's charismatic heritage and spiritual candor seem, quite literally, to have rejuvenated, just in the nick of time, old rituals and forms that were threatening to fade away as modernity itself faded.

The Native American, whom white colonialism and white supremacy had afflicted with a ferocity equal to (or, some would

say, in excess of) that directed at the African American, likewise
had a characterizing religious tradition and praxis. It was, however, worlds — pun intended — away from that of either black or
white heritage and destined to be integrated by way of ecology
rather than by music or the ecstatic. Native American religion
was firmly anchored in the natural cycles and sacred places of
this land mass long before a dichotomous Christianity arrived to
"save" it. As a result, it did not suffer so readily as did black religion the disruption or subversion of its animism and shamanism.
The Native American, moreover, was routinely removed from any
proximity to or familiarity with the dominant culture, a political
circumstance of cruelty that had at least two redeeming virtues: it
further insulated our one indigenous religious system from much
enculturation or erosion;[26] and it lent to Native American ways
the jesuitical cachet of the exotic.

When the time came, then, for the reshaping of America's national attitude from exclusion to inclusion, there was a confluence
of several things that reinforced each other and by extension
the connection between ecology and god-talk. First, there was
a popularization under way, effected out of both political and
humanitarian necessities, of Native American ways of being.
There was the burden within white America of intellectually
perceived concern for the environment and its potential exhaustion, of emotionally perceived disgust with rampant consumerism
and its disappointments, and of spiritually perceived severance
from a rural and/or agricultural history. There was also in religious America, both observant and lapsed, a vague, unarticulated
restiveness of soul, a rejection of old and basically European for-
malisms in worship and praxis, an uneasy sense of life's having
grown too cerebral. There was a pervasive mourning, as it were,
for the body misplaced, for the physical and routine and daily in
all of life's peregrinations and for the benediction of union once
more among all the parts of our experience. The newly discovered

and newly voguish Native American spirituality not only spoke to these needs; it was a lived and living answer to them that had an immediately at-hand, observable praxis.

The suddenly attractive sensibilities and precepts of Native American spirituality became a paradigm for merging the facts of environmental biology with the emotions of postindustrial existence and endowing the result with the imprimatur of religious value. Ecology enhanced the politics of incorporation, the ways of the incorporated subculture eased the pangs of the larger one, and both found a common vocabulary in the lexicon of the spirit's ways. They became, as one Native American friend said to me, prayer beyond the pale of language. Ecology and all her children had settled in at last, and they obviously intended to stay a while.

The theological questions that have resulted from ecology's dramatic advent and our even more dramatic public embracing of it are both substantive and multitudinous, many of them swinging over very quickly into ethics as well as pure theology. What is responsible stewardship of resources and who should pay the private cost for each moral judgment that comes from each particularized answer to that question? Are we indeed only visitors on a lent space and, if so, who is the landlord and what the nature of accountability due him or her? At what point may the events of natural law and cause and effect be interrupted with both benefit and impunity? Why, if they can be so correctively addressed, were they so imperfectly provided in the first place? Etc., etc.

This list, too, goes on and on; yet no overview of god-talk as it presently is and as it is presently becoming in America can ignore or even sidestep the theological questions raised by ecology. One of the major differences, however, between this and most of our earlier sets of questions is the fact, as we noted originally, that for whatever reasons, established religion has indeed begun to produce substantial quantities of curricular, lay, and professional literature on every possible permutation of ecology.[27] In many ways, the religious tradition or establishment that delivers the best set of applications (or the most comfortable set of standards to apply to the answers, inasmuch as answers are suspect in a postmodern world) of ecology to god-talk and god-living may just well be the tradition or establishment whose other precepts will prove most attractive by proximity. It is a fact of ecclesial life that every communion in this country is seemingly aware of and struggling with.

But as must already be obvious, when we talk about the attractive power of ecology for popular theology, we are introducing into our overview something more than just the driving forces of cumulative literacy or the impact of a new kind of information. We are introducing an emotional context, one that informs all of our present god-talk in America and that lies at the very center of much of its vitality. Before we take on the emotions that are animating god-talk today, however, I want to visit another closet — one, this time, that belonged fiercely and incontestably to my mother and that belongs still to my understanding of her.

Interlude

WHO CAN FIND a virtuous woman? for her price is far above rubies...

She seeketh wool, and flax, and worketh willingly with her hands...

She is like the merchants' ships; she bringeth her food from afar.

She riseth while it is yet night, and giveth meat to her household, and a portion to her maidens,

She considereth a field and buyeth it; with the fruit of her hands she planteth a vineyard.

She perceiveth that her merchandise is good; her candle goeth not out by night.

She layeth her hand to the spindle, and her hands hold the distaff...

She is not afraid of the snow for her household; for all her household are clothed with scarlet.

She maketh herself coverings of tapestry; her clothing is silk and purple...

She maketh fine linen and selleth it; and delivereth girdles unto the merchant.

Strength and honour are her clothing; and she shall rejoice in time to come...

Favour is deceitful, and beauty is vain: but a woman that
feareth the Lord, she shall be praised.
Give her of the fruit of her hand; and let her own works
praise her in the gates.

—Proverbs 33:10 *et passim*

They are ancient words, these thirteen sentences of King Solomon's. They constitute one of the oldest pictures still available
to us of idealized femininity as earlier societies defined it. And
despite the fact that they are royal and scriptural and therefore
removed from any part of my own background by history, class,
and privilege, they still exercise an unavoidable control over me.
The moment I read them, I react autobiographically, not to the
words themselves but to my own experience of the combination
that they mean to describe; for what they describe is the ancient profession of housewifery and the combination they name
is that of woman and place. Or perhaps of woman preceded and
ordained by place.

The place of my experiencing the combination — the house I
grew up in — was as solidly middle-class as any college professor's house ever was, and as blessed with singularities as it was
devoid of pretensions. It had an entrance way and living room
that ran the entire length of its front and a kitchen and bath that
did the same to its back. The west ends of the kitchen and living room were connected, as one moved from back to front, by
a huge pantry/breakfast room and a dining room that opened out
through doubled french doors into the living room.

On the east side of the house, unfortunately, things were not so
direct. There there was a long, thin hallway whose chief purpose
appeared to be that of congesting all of our domiciliary arrange-
ments. Its second and more amiable purpose was to connect the
adult first floor to the raised landing and spartan stairwell that
gave access to the nonadult world of the second floor bedrooms
and my attic playroom. Those chores having been satisfied, the

hall's last duty was to connect the east end of the living room to a line of doors...doors to my father's study, the linen closet, my parents' bedroom, and finally to the back bath and kitchen, in that order.

The very listing gives one some suggestion of the size of the linen closet in question and of its importance in the scheme of things. What it does not do — nor will anything ever — is explain why a ten-foot-high space that was some four or five feet in width and some six or seven feet in depth had solid shelves from its back wall to its door jambs. I owed one of the most specifically physical delights of my growing up years, however — one of the few, genuine sensualities of my early to mid-adolescence right up until I got too curvaceous to enjoy it any longer — to that particular, architectural oddity.

Every year there came that glorious day of spring when we "did" the linen closet. On that day, once the household linens had been withdrawn to the safety of freshly draped beds that she had readied to receive them, my short-of-stature mother was faced with a tier of five painted surfaces she could no more have accessed than she could have flown to the moon. Instead, for a number of years, it was my job at that point to climb onto each shelf, Spic n' Span bucket in one hand and drying cloth in the other, and wash it down. Even in early adolescence and with a rapidly lengthening body, this operation involved my lying as flat on my belly as possible and stretching as far as possible, if I were to have any hope at all of even so much as kissing the back corners of each shelf with my sponge.

The all-over damp of the pine-scrubbed and freshly toweled shelf boards, the half-confinement of the shelf just above me, and the opened hall door behind me, the distortion of all sound into soft and meaningless mumble, the odor of moist plaster where the sponge had stayed too long against the shelf's edge — together these were the wine of summer and the clarity of winter in a seasonless space. I would stay there as long as I could, stay, that is, until a smart rap on my instep reminded me that cleaning, not sensating, was what I was supposed to be about.

But the luxuriant privilege of annually entering the closet head-first and literally took most of its richness not from the physical sensations involved — they were too few and transitory — but from the enormous centrality of that space in my mother's daily habits and from the exacting projection of herself that she had made of it over the years.

We did not have a washing machine. That we did not was purely a matter of economy. Whatever else she was, my mother was frugal — not mean, never mean, but frugal; and the truth was that washing machines cost more than people did in those days. As a result, while our neighbors began, house by house, to buy machines, Mother looked longingly but declined stoutly. We instead continued to sort our soft goods just as we had for as long as I could remember.

The "delicates" — meaning her lingerie and my underwear, the dresser scarves she had embroidered and the doilies she had laced and the flour-sack kitchen linens she had hemmed — these she washed herself by hand. The "flatwear" — meaning our sheets and towels that were too heavy for washtub laundering, together with my father's shirts that "had to look professional" — were sent out twice a week to the commercial laundry and were sent back to us twice a week on the laundry's delivery truck. The "wash" (I never could ascertain what Mother thought her other categories were) my dresses and hers, my father's underwear and hosiery — these we took once a week across town to the washer-woman who had a washing machine, two daughters-in-law, and a thriving family business.

The treasure of the heart buried in all these hours of occupation, in all this routing and sorting, fretting and maintaining, is that for my mother and for thousands of householders like her as far back in time even as Solomon's virtuous woman, the possession of cloth and cloth goods was freedom. Of all the domestic wares, including food itself, cloth was the least susceptible to easy or quick replacement. Yet without it, a family could have no public life. Without cloth and clothes, a family would have to cower inside its own doors, confined by either its poverty or its sloth; there could be no social intercourse between the members of one family and those of another without cloth. In a way that is hard for us to recall now but by whose value systems I still innately make my judgments, how well my mother made, decorated, and maintained the fabrics committed to her keeping was an irrefutable index of her commitment to our comfort, our self-esteem, and our easiness as a family in the world around us. Like the Fiddler's Goldie, washing our socks was an act of the purest and most lucid love, an easy translation in her mind of abstraction to evidence — or if one wants to put it biblically, and Mother would have, of belief into works.

Remembering is a dangerous sport and one which we employ so sentimentally at family reunions and around our supper tables that we sometimes domesticate demons to our own detriment. Such is not my intention here, but neither can I so easily leave the linen closet just yet. I am deterred certainly by the fact that the reverence which Mother exercised there was indeed biblical and that the love which she served through it was so traditional. But I am deterred also by the still riveting memory of what that closet and my mother daily made of one another.

Each weekday morning, after she had handwashed the delicates and hung them, Mother would gather up the rest of the dirtied clothes from the bathroom bins and carry them to the long hall. There — always in childhood with me sitting on the landing of the upstairs staircase across from the linen closet door and watching — there she would take from her pocket the linen closet key and unlock its darkly panelled door.

I was grown and gone from home before I ever stumbled in a book across the word "chatelaine." I wished then and still wish that it might have been otherwise with me — that I might have had that lovely and euphonious word within my tongue's reach during all those young hours of watching her, that I might have known how long and honored a tradition among women was hers, and how elegant in its heritage. Instead I thought of her as "sacristan," for it was a word I did know, and it fit in every way the demeanor with which she conducted her duties. And even though I think now that there is little substantive difference between the two words, I still sometimes long for the lost generosity that it would have been from me had I been able to say to her, "Chatelaine."

And chatelaine she was, though she went to less extreme lengths of self-consciousness than did the originals perhaps. She wore no snips or scissors dangling mid-thigh from her belt, no needlecases of cork and silver, no wallets of wax and signet. Instead, she simply carried the linens' key in her dress pocket; but once she had used it, once the closet's doors had been unlocked for the day, both she and it emanated historic precision.

The uppermost shelf, blessedly, was beyond Mother's low stature and therefore never employed. (I used to wonder how I should ever squeeze myself between its front edge and the closet door's upper jamb were she ever to change her mind and decide to occupy it.) The second, third, and fourth shelves down from the top were taken up respectively with our blankets, coverlets, and throws; with sheets, pillowcases, and mattress covers; and with wash rags, bath towels, bath sheets, face towels, and finger or guest towels.

It was the fifth and bottom shelf, however, the one which served as a ceiling for all the washing paraphernalia and laundry baskets stored on the floor underneath it, that was Mother's true adytum. Here she stored the patent medicines, folk remedies, and palatable chemicals by which she managed our physical lives. Cellophane packets of both smelling salts and sweet-clove buds ready for crushing; vials of witch hazel and tins of camphor; tightly secured bottles of collodion and peroxide; blue ones of milk of magnesia and clear ones of mineral oil and boric acid, glycerine, and Listerine; sticks of silver nitrate and caustic; boxes of Epsom salts and plaster of paris, their moldering label indecipherable in the closet's half-light...they were all there.

They were hers to catalog and inventory, to add to and subtract from, to sort and arrange and then rearrange again by some secret system lost to me in chemical mystery. And they were also hers to administer or to withhold according to the witchery or benignity of some wisdom that she and she alone held and that all of us — even my father — bowed to.

Even as a very young child still too immature to serve yet as scrub lady to her needs, I loved the sheets shelf; and every chance I got, I shinnied up the shelves to run my bare arms back and forth across the voluptuous tufts of the towels, much to the chatelaine's annoyance. But the lowest and last shelf...the lowest and last shelf was different. I was, from my earliest memory, enjoined from ever touching the last shelf or its contents. It was a proscription accompanied as no other in my small life by threats not only of parental reprisals but also of dire, irreversible consequences. This last was more than reasonable, given the very real danger of what was stored there. Its effect, however, was not so much that I fanatically adhered to the law of avoidance — though goodness only knows I did — as it was that I fanatically adhered to Mother.

Her ability to manipulate and employ such powerful potions with impunity lent her their authority and efficacy in my mind. By knowing them she somehow became allied with them, and I as much feared her as loved her. This ambivalence was no doubt excited in me, as in all children, by my own impotence in the face of her mastery and by the attractiveness of the very things in which she had chosen to house the forbidden. Here was the only collection of bottles and jars in the house, and I loved bottles and jars — the way they cupped in the hand, the way they contained with margins I could grasp and carry, the way they could open and still close back without scar or leak. These were diversion and pleasure for me and I begrudged her her control over them.

And then of course, there is that other thing, that third and final fascination. Because Mother was short of reach as well as height and because common sense said that one could not keep daily goods beyond arm's reach with any hope of efficiency, the banks of stacked linens and the rows of herbal and chemical containers were always kept stacked neatly to the front of their respective shelves. It was, in fact, part of each day's early morning routine that the stacks and rows were checked for precision of arrangement and for the exactitude of their alignment. To do otherwise was to invite disaster, for behind those banks and rows of household appointments and just at the right place for me to see it easily from my seat on the floor of the hall landing was infinite, dark space, the chaos of no-thing.

Impenetrable and neutral dusk whose near borders were kept by care and prohibition and into whose maw the necessities of our familiar life threatened daily to tumble — I early assigned to that space beyond my mother's careful domain the bottomlessness of spiraling dreams and the smokiness of imagined caverns, making of it my first preserve for darkness and out of Mother my first, approachable protector against its terrible possibilities. Thus always and in all places has it been between humanity and its mothers, or so we are taught. It is only a caprice of fortune that my own formation was so absolutely literal as well as so physical. Or perhaps the caprice is simply that in choosing the writing life,

I chose the one adult profession whose first obligation is remembering what we all have known, and whose second is to name, as particularly as human pain will permit, that which has been remembered.

— Seven —

About the Many Uses of "Once Upon a Time"

=== ===

ᏫᏒOSTALGIA! Despite all the damning words that have been spoken about it, it is an intricately woven thing and compelling — this last in part, no doubt, because it is both contradictory and unavoidable. To live at all is to suffer its outrageous agonies, and not infrequently to enjoy them.

Nostalgia is condemned out of hand, in fact, only by those brief ages in which social and political stability are in such vigorous good health as to stave it off, and/or by individual writers who are temporarily in a similar, if idiosyncratic state. Times like ours are more appreciative; times of such uproar and instability as ours, much more respectful of nostalgia's powerful role in human affairs. And a role it certainly has.

If cumulative literacy and new knowledge have become the principal context in which god-talk is happening in America these days, unquestionably nostalgia is the principal emotion coloring it. That is, a whole complex of emotions that are nostalgic in origin and energy are doing the coloring, and Once Upon A Time is everywhere.[1]

While no one is isolated enough to think that Americans are the only ones who are psychologically seasick in an ocean of postmodern sociopolitical, technological, and economic changes,[2] it is still true that we are suffering as violent a case of motion sickness as anybody at the moment and that it has made us yearn for land with a fair degree of desperation. The difference between Americans and peoples of other geopolitical units — at least with regard to nostalgia — is that among us cultural nostalgia more readily becomes religious nostalgia.[3]

Like it or not, this land mass was settled out of religious motivation by people who very early in the process saw the society and the government they were creating as a substantivization of a religious vision. Our political, cultural, and literal ancestors were not theocrats exactly, but they were so close to it that one would have considerable pains to discover a better word for exactly what it was that they were. This land was the new promised land of Christian Old Testament prophecy, the kingdom on earth of the Christian god as understood primarily by Evangelical Protestant Christians with some spicing and piquancy added to the original mix by liturgical Christian sensibilities.[4]

This near unanimity of opinion about how the world was to morally operate in its most distant outposts far removed from the corruption of established interests or old prejudices was the most congenial of attitudes for the new notion of democracy. It was also very susceptible to becoming so intertwined with the democracy it was nurturing as to be inextricably joined at the head, the fortunes and health of either being felt and experienced by both.[5] America's religious disposition was its political and social disposition. When something went amiss in American society or when society itself simply suffered the inevitable processes of change, the effects were evident in American democracy and in American religion. They still are, just more so at this particular moment in our national time.

The reasons for our current nostalgia are too numerous and multiform to be treated either adequately or appropriately here;[6] but a brief summary of the religious elements and implications woven into its general character certainly is not. Such an analysis should provide us not just a picture of our nostalgia per se but, far more usefully, a presumably prophetic description of where institutional religion is going to have to go if it is to satisfy our new perceptions of the old impulses that traditionally have sustained it.

Nostalgia by its very nature is quasireligious anyway, wherever and whenever it occurs. It is a longing of the heart and sometimes of the remembering mind for a place of the heart, for the fixed center, for that imagined and usually romanticized state of prior equilibrium in which current tensions were incapable of existing because current circumstances as yet did not. For Americans ending the second millennium of the common era and stepping over into the eschatology of a new thousand years,[7] the descriptions of the desired center are almost exquisitely religious.[8] Perhaps nothing attests to the truth of this statement more dramatically than does the abrupt and widespread adoption by thousands of Americans over the last ten years of the "centering" rhetoric and practices of Buddhism. Books and manuals and tapes about centering altars, centering tools, centering prayers inundated the marketplace and were bought up almost as quickly as retailers could unpack and shelve them.[9] What had begun almost as a cult phenomenon quickly became a national and truly religious one.[10]

The private homes of those who were less than affiliated with an established monotheistic faith (and of a sizeable number also of those who were firmly attached) developed centering spaces or meditation areas, and their owners built into their domestic schedules set times for the practice of centering disciplines. By 1994, even the ancient Christian rubrics and prayers of centering were being revived and openly employed by the orthodox and the simply needful alike.[11]

Yet overt and obvious as such an employment of centering as centering is, it is still available only to the spiritually adept or inclined or able or whatever other word one may choose to describe those of us blessed with the gift of spiritual self-knowledge. But because centering per se is an option only for a limited, if significant, number of the predisposed, it will never be one of the major means by which our national nostalgia can give either religious vent to itself or be assuaged. That nostalgia lies too ubiquitously upon the land and affects far too many types and conditions of humankind to be so narrowly relieved.

The longer I consider the breadth in America's current nostalgia, the more it seems to me to be composed of three almost indivisible areas of intense yearning: the yearning for home, the yearning for "American" values, and the yearning for spiritual connection — though not necessarily in that order. The American longing for home is, I would suggest, the greatest of these; or certainly it is the part so intensely and viscerally felt as to have completely pervaded, infused, and shaped the other two.[12] It is also, so far as I know, unique to our time in history. I certainly can find no other period or people who have experienced such a wrenching sense of domestic dislocation as we.

I would suggest, even further, that what we really want when we long toward "home" is more than a physical place and the safe-haven of warranteed intimacy, or even the emotional stability of a center, though there is every evidence that we do want these things as well. But what we want first is far more earthy and much less locative. We want Woman. We want that ur-combination of skilled protectress and terrible priestess that was my mother's kitchen and her linen closet with her in them. We want the drier of herbs and mixer of potions, the mistress of the linens, the chartress of all our courses, the chatelaine. We want her back as she used to be as well as where, the "as" and the "where" being covalent in the formula.

"I was young and now am old," the psalmist once wrote, just as he got ready to commence a long, poetic discourse on what he had learned in all the intervening time between his two estates. I always thought his words were one of literature's more graceful introductions to what basically is a tiresome genre ... so I shall employ them here. I was young and now am old; and from that stance, I want to say with all sincerity, that longing for traditional woman is not, in and of itself, either anti-feminist or necessarily politically incorrect. Part of it, however, may be historically so.

There is a sharp, critical difference between the chatelaine and June Cleaver, a difference that separates not only those two definitions of woman's gender role, but also the public expression of how they are celebrated, remembered, and longed for. The chatelaine of King Solomon's paean and my youthful memories is as old as civilized time itself, if not older. June Cleaver is a brief anomaly who came and left with America's golden mid-century and functioned only in the relatively confined strata of society that could afford her.[13]

Being no more and no less than a shadow of the original, June's ancient physical powers and governances had been untimely ripped from her by machines and affluence. The fact that both June and Betty Boop (her sister in parody) produced daughters and granddaughters who managed to break out and once more assert their primal power, albeit in ways far less magical than those of former times, speaks to the irrepressible vigor of femininity.[14] It does not, however, mean that June and Betty should be canonized except — very, very pivotal word "except," and especially so here — except by that Boomer generation whom June reared and for whom she became the appropriate definition of mother and/or grandmother, as the case may be.

The loss of the June and Ward Cleaver understanding of home and gender is as legitimately a loss as is any other deeply felt one; and it must be allowed its mourning time. But as an experience in our history, it is better dealt with as a shift in "American" values and institutional hierarchy than as a spiritual disjuncture. Nor must we forget in all of this that fully half of the yearning for what used to be before the Cleavers is being done by women themselves — women who feel diminished in power and sphere of influence, in spiritual vigor and acumen, in sexual subtlety and primacy, in maternal depth and focus, in familial position, and in intuitive experience. And if those painful losses are not driving American women to the faiths of their great-grandmothers (and it is doing exactly that to many of them),[15] it is certainly driving them to produce and consume a veritable glut of religion/spirituality/inspiration books about every one of them.[16]

The women who read and write these books, who belong to the small-group clusters that engender and incorporate these books, who conduct the seminars and maintain the networks that empower and are empowered by these books — those women are all, because of the very nature of their tasks, doing god-talk. Theirs is a conversation more consequential for American religion and probably for American theology and certainly for American spirituality than any other going on in the country today.[17] Its conclusions and resolutions will filter through and march into every room in America's theological house and houses before it is done. And if the sale of books is any indication, the gender and semantic devices of American god-talk will be firmly established as feminine before they are done.

This kind of mass movement back toward some of the authority of my mother and of all our mothers before her has to do also with a longing, by both sexes, back toward a place and a way of life that made the old ways possible. The consequences for any group of people of shifting from an agricultural and rural to an industrial and urban lifestyle hardly need elaboration here. Since history's first naming of the Industrial Revolution, we have been aware intellectually of what that disjuncture meant to western European culture; but intellectual perception is very different from personal experience. While the former may offer some sustaining perspective on the latter, it can never obliterate its pain.

In just the same way, all the sociological sophistication in the world could not save us Americans from the grief processes of this century: grief over our lost frontier; grief over the demise of the sustainable, small family farm as a lifetime's total industry and experience; grief over the loss of earth rhythms as being also occupation's rhythms; grief, certainly, over the loss of the natal community as a lifetime's context....

... The list is long and poignantly familiar, but always it speaks to that move from field to pavement and, in transient America's case, always it speaks as well to the demise of the woman-blessed, rhythm-hallowed life that the land supported and job markets cannot.

Our doleful mourning for this loss is no different from that of any other part of bereft humanity. Sociologists might say that its expression runs the gamut, surfacing as the violence of escalating abuse against the redefined wife, daughter, sister, or mother and as the Humpty-Dumpty approach of the men's movement in attempting to put it all together again;[18] that it also gives expression to itself in the fury of feminism and more quietly in the rise of Marianism;[19] that confusion over our loss drives the abortion issue sotto voce beneath the raucousness of its street life and finds sweetest expression in how we love children. They would probably be right; but whether they are or not, certainly we do know, in all of this unease, that we have lost more than ur-woman, more than the hands that shaped and secured lives while they kneaded our bread and mixed our potions. We have lost the place in which she who is lost could do and be these things. When we lost the farm, we lost her. When later we lost the village street with its backyard gardens and its artisans' shops attached, we lost her daughter. We lost Papa as well.

Then World War II came, and Mama left too ... not to join Papa — he was at war — but to build his airplanes and guns and bombs so he would come home again. But except for that brief golden postwar time of the Cleavers, Mama would never be Mama again. Like Papa's, her work would lie now beyond the front door. Even more subtly but importantly, home would cease to be the thing being created and built by Papa and Mama and become instead the base from which each of them had to draw the strength to create and build outside of it. Once that happened, we had lost completely the physical centering that had been their center and that fixed them forever in one spot to serve as ours. We had also lost the intimacy of work and the immediacy of its rewards.[20]

What we think we know about those pre-1940s earlier homes of farm and hamlet and the earlier roles played out within them, we memorialize now with symbols. The "handmade" quilts of craft fairs and mail-order catalogs, the kitchen kitsch of Pennsylvania Dutch and charming geese, the garden ware of painted saw blades and kissing sunbonnet children, the pine Americana of Wal-Mart and the muted blooms in Victorian nosegays — they are talismans to our loss. They are our proofs of what we tease ourselves to remember. But as they fade in efficacy, they assume increased significance as icons of what must be replaced.[21] So too do the humbler old crafts that at one time truly did employ them.

While I have no direct count of how many more gardening books, quilting books, cabinetry books, breadmaking books, herbs and herbalist books are published and sold in this country now as opposed to ten years ago, I suspect that the increase in their numbers has been appreciable. I *know,* however, that the number of them produced by religion publishers has increased dramatically. Positioning these domestic crafts as the meaningful works of the hands that free the spirit to be and to know itself is not only psychologically accurate, but commercially shrewd and religiously responsible as well.[22] It also veils, though it cannot hide, the nostalgia that seeks to find some former ease in those half-remembered ways of arriving. I know additionally that the number of commercially published books that add or even emphasize the spiritual benefits of the crafts they teach has likewise jumped over the past six or seven years.[23]

The home as altar, as the place of spiritual centering and the soul's exercise, and as the substance of connectedness replaces the religious institution in those roles by just a little bit more every time one of those books is sold, read, discussed, applied. What has for centuries been true in Jewish and Buddhist practice daily becomes more so in Christian, if not yet in Islamic, practice among us.

And the Christian church, both Protestant and Roman Catholic,[24] like it or not, is being shaped almost as perceptually and certainly far more doctrinally by yet another part of our yearning for home and for mother. Mother Church...an antique phrase if ever there were one, and an appellation for Roman Catholic Christianity that had not been heard in our land for years but must now be ubiquitous, for I hear it everywhere I go these days.

Much of what we conceptualize the hamlet as having been and much of the cohesiveness of the stable nuclear family as we celebrate it in actuality was not those things at all, but the village church. All the pivotal gestures and events of individual lives were lifted out of their obscurity and memorialized there. The continuity of human generations was blessed as well as recorded there; and a township discovered and sanctioned its social and ideational consistencies there. And almost without exception the worship conducted in the American village church and the theology cited there were Christian and Protestant.

As a fact of history, that means that a majority of us presently doing the yearning today never saw a priest in any pulpit we ever sat in front of as children; never saw a rabat or clerical collar on any man whose pulpit we did sit in front of, much less a black, buttonless shirt; rarely looked through ornately elaborate stained glass; were never choir boys (or girls) and never carried a cross in procession, with or without a corpus; never saw a monk and only occasionally a nun; never said "Father" to anyone except "Papa," and not very often even to him; and never — absolutely never! — smelled incense or watched a thurifer swing a thurible to dispense it. Yet two other things are very true today as well.

First, when most Americans — Christian or otherwise — think in terms of "church," they image that construct in these essentially Roman or historic images. The religious objects and site shots of television and the movies, the book jacket illustrations striving to suggest benign or helpful content, the canned "religious" shots in newspapers and at least two-thirds of those in slick magazines, the wraps and labels on the CD and audio albums of chant and a lot of Bach and Handel...these things all are built upon priests and incense, crucifixes and altars, candle-lit naves and vibrantly stained glass. God/Inspiration/Religion, in other words, rises in most of our minds as "church"; and "church" rises not out of the puritanical simplicity of American Protestant worship, but out of the rich fecundity of Mother Church. We think, we yearn, we reach out....

...Which is the second great consequence for American Christianity — and, by proximity, for American religion — of our homesickness. The reaching out has created at a popular level a kind of emotional familiarity and a set of positive Pavlovian associations for millions of American, Protestant and Catholic, with the rubrics, images, and accoutrements of historic[25] and Roman Christianity.[26] While this is primarily an emotional reaction or conditioning rather than a theologically argued ecumenism, it has nonetheless become a major — and, in my judgment, uniquely American — factor contributing to a rapprochement between Protestant and Roman Catholic Christianity that would have been unimaginable half a century ago.[27]

Although I doubt that any demographer or sociologist in the world could ever separate the persuasive power of nostalgia from the persuasive power of practicality[28] or of genuine theological shifts, I do think that at a commonsense level we can draw some defensible conclusions. The movement toward greater unity within Christendom in both doctrine and practice is informing all of Christendom right now, especially within Europe and America, just as syncretism among all the world's major faiths, especially its monotheistic ones, is informing all of religion at the moment. There are at least a dozen good reasons for this coming together, not the least of which is Pope John Paul II himself. Enormously pastoral and exuding the benignity of a visceral compassion, John Paul has made it clear at almost every possible opportunity[29] that his is a papacy dedicated by policy and papal personality to the model of a complementary confederation, if not a unity, of Christianity's great divisions.

Scholars and observers, including the German theologian Wolfhart Pannenberg, have contended for some time now that within the next century Christianity worldwide will have only three such divisions — Catholicism, Orthodoxy, and Evangelicalism.[30] That may well be true. It is equally true, however, that within the American context those divisions have already begun, in a singular way, not only to accommodate to that shift, but also to ease the lines of tensions that might threaten a beneficial and beneficent cohabitation.

It was in America, for instance, and not elsewhere that the remarkable "Evangelicals and Catholics Together: The Christian Mission in the Third Millennium" was drawn up.[31] The work of fifteen leaders and elected heads of religious bodies, the document was the result of a year of intense consultation and, when it was released in the spring of 1994, the recipient of intense attention.[32] Leaders from both the Roman and the Protestant communions in North America rushed to add their signatures (although two of the original fifteen who came from the Southern Baptist tradition — SBC Home Mission Board president Larry Lewis and SBC Christian Life Commission executive director Richard Land — felt forced to withdraw their names "due to 'continuing misperception' that they spoke for the SCB in signing it").[33]

It was in America also that a year later a group of equally prominent and legitimately empowered leaders and scholars from all three Christian traditions — Orthodox, Roman Catholic, and Protestant — met in what *Christianity Today* called "perhaps the most significant moment of rapprochement since the April 1994 'Evangelicals and Catholics Together' statement" in order "to pursue further the so-called "New Ecumenism," *which has been expanded to include participation by Eastern Orthodox Christians*" (emphasis mine).[34]

It was also in America that the new *Catechism of the Catholic Church*,[35] when it was released in 1994, became an instant bestseller, riding all the lists in a sweep unprecedented at that time by a religion, much less a theological, title. From my perspective as a professional bookwatcher, one of the most satisfactory components of the *Catechism*'s success was the fact that booksellers began early to report that they were relatively sure that it was selling to Protestants as well as to Roman Catholics, and in percentages that some suspected were as high as one in three copies sold.[36] This kind of integrated embracing, unique to American religion, must arguably arise from something likewise unique to our American present. That something, I believe, is the emotional preconditioning of popular nostalgia and of its first cousin, hungry curiosity. Its effects upon American religion, I believe also, are so far-ranging as to be inestimable at this point in time.

A third consequence worth mentioning here may be more of an aside than a fully formed consequence. It is, nonetheless, true that nostalgia has contributed to, if not driven, the inordinate and absolutely generalized popularity of John Paul II among Americans. One has only to look at the phenomenal sales figures for the pope's books — in the millions for his 1994 *Crossing the Threshold of Hope*,[37] for example — as well as for books that are simply about the pope, to find irrefutable testament to the breadth, depth, and singularity of His Holiness's popularity. Nor do I think it stretches things to suggest that Mother Church and homesickness for Mama have merged as well into a fascination with the second most adored religious figure in the Western world — Mother Teresa — and with female, especially medieval female, saints in general. Mother Teresa's *Simple Path,* for instance, stayed on national bestseller lists for months;[38] and books by or about Julian of Norwich, Teresa of Avila, and Hildegard of Bingen have proliferated over the last five years.

Just as the lines of demarcation between a deep longing for the primal feminine and a nostalgic yearning for home are very blurred ones, so too are the lines that separate our sense of home from our sense of values. And it is not even of values as such that we speak these days; it is "American values" we talk about, always with the quotation marks in our voices.

As a phrase on its way to becoming a cliché, "American values" enjoys all the shorthand economy of the cliché, while also suffering all the intellectual messiness of its imprecisions. But American values — and/or "family values," which is another cliché for naming a subset of roughly the same thing — do exist, if for no other reason than that we employ them as a reality in our national conversation. While most of us may not go around talking at public gatherings or in formal meetings about our yearning for the force of the wise woman or even for home, it is virtually impossible in this country right now to speak in either of those venues about any form of political, social, cultural, economic, or religious policy without speaking immediately of traditional values, whether "family" or "American."[39]

The distinguishing element that separates — at least to the extent that they can be separated — the "family" from the "American" within the rubric of traditional values is little more than the size of the arena being referenced. Family values are those that deal with human responsibility at an intramural level — gender roles, child rearing, marital and sexual ethics, disciplined choices and attitudes, loyalties and priorities and all the modes of conduct that lead to them — and at an individual level when and as each family member interacts with society beyond the home itself.[40] American values, by contrast, address the larger arenas of human responsibility — politics, law enforcement and law-making, civil institutions and their governance, public charity, foreign policy, economic policies, individual freedom and diversity, etc. They affect the individual only as they impact the conduct of his or her possible life and as they inform any citizen's personal dedication to the establishment and perpetuation of compatible values in the public square. In theory, family values accumulated would be American values and become its proofs. By contrast, American values, if I understand them correctly, serve primarily to empower and enable and secure family values both here and, the geopolitical weather permitting, elsewhere as well.

The most telling commonalities that family and American values share are point of origin and time. Both claim the Judeo-Christian principles of the Ten Commandments as the source of their beginning and their authority. Proponents of "American" values tend to update that citation by frequent, selective references to the Founding Fathers; but then, the Fathers themselves used to cite Sinai, so any argument is at best circuitous if not outright redundant[41] ... which bit of history, of course, is why yearning for former sureties — typical of all societies in stress — is so inextricably tied in the American experience to religion and so easily appropriated as a proper subject of god-talk.[42]

By the commonality of time, I mean something different from the Sinaic moment of shared origin. I also mean not so much a year or decade in our history as a stage in it, a period in which our movement in cultural attitude, if not in actual polity, was from semi-rural and agricultural to urban and consumerist. I mean, as I have already suggested, our mid-century. How one delimits that vague period is fairly arbitrary. I choose to regard it usually as stretching from the Great Depression to Vietnam. Others commence a bit later with World War II and America's so-called "Golden Age." Sadly, however, none of us seems inclined to argue about Vietnam's place as the terminus.

In other words, it seems to me, as I listen to us talking and as I read the books and articles we are writing and selling,[43] that the family and American values being talked about are those that were active in and characterized by the small-town ethos of less-rural, less-agricultural but not-yet-urban America. This does not mean that the principles operative in that small-town Golden Age were not those of the Founding Fathers. It means that the principles we yearn toward restoring now are those foundational principles as they were construed by mid-twentieth-century, rather than by any originating eighteenth-century Americans.

While it may be, as some cynics claim, impossible to codify American values, we can at least name some of them;[44] and in my opinion, the most efficient way to do that is to think "Midwestern," "mid-century," "small-town," and go from there.[45] Far removed from the conflicting cultural ways of the immigrant-populated coastal cities, from the poverty and depersonalizing noise of the tenement, from the impotence of a cash-based existence and the constant proximity of inescapable greed, from incipient despair and all the lack of mores that permits it ... far removed from all these enervating things and dozens more like them, was Norman Rockwell's small-town America. And what many of us really want to do, if only we could, is live inside a Norman Rockwell. (I suspect as well that a lot of Americans regret only the fact that there is no picture of God by Norman Rockwell; it would have saved us a great deal of effort in trying to describe One now.)

We remember or choose to think we remember a time when "community" — one of the key values in our list of American ones — meant a moral unanimity. As a people and to our great credit, we have been singularly tolerant of doctrinal differences extant among us (and even of some doctrinal peculiarities) so long as moral and cultural ones weren't hiding beneath them. One of the abiding legacies of our Evangelical Protestant Christian beginnings is a strong memory of religious persecution at the hands of the State and a strong insistence on absolute freedom of the individual and of individual belief. The potential anarchy inherent in such a posture lay essentially unnoticed and unaroused for two centuries. A common moral history born religiously of the Mosaic code and the Golden Rule, a common theocentric allegiance to God as supreme ruler of human affairs, a common sociopolitical heritage of Eurocentrism, a common legal history evolving out from *lex romana,* a common economic theory of capitalism and *laissez faire*[46] — these things never existed everywhere and completely, but they did exist almost everywhere and almost completely. They certainly were true of enough of our citizenry to blanket and persuade the rest of it into conformity. They constituted what Stephen Carter and legions of other observers so constantly refer to as "the religion of the public square."

The sustained use of the *religion* part is absolutely accurate.[47] Another of the abiding legacies of our Evangelical Protestant Christian beginnings is a strong emphasis upon "works" (as they are called doctrinally) as opposed to words. That deep-seated belief that overt action is more religiously diagnostic and significant than are the words a man or woman speaks has left us with a very low tolerance for moral diversity but, ironically, with an almost passive attitude toward the invisible or intangible varieties of spirituality.

At the same time, there was — and is — in Protestant Christianity a complementary belief in the formative effects of outer or extrapersonal experiences upon the individual soul. The conduct permitted in the public square was — and is — religiously significant; and defining that permitted conduct properly was a religious imperative because everything the person may experience sculpts in some way the soul's future.

As a result of both these tenets, the "religion" undergirding American public life seems — and actually is, but not for capricious, sectarianly perverse reasons — much, much nearer to morality and overt acts than to worship and spiritual striving. It is this dichotomy that makes theological issues out of events and policies that in some other time and place would simply be political ones.[48] It has allowed, has even compelled, today's observant Evangelical Protestant Americans, in other words, to emphasize codes of conduct as a litmus test of human worth in ways that both confuse many of their non-Evangelical fellow citizens and that have had as well the divisive result of making the Evangelical appear to be both unattractive and stridently radical.[49] Evangelicals[50] mean it when they say they are fighting pornography or legalized gambling or NORML or gay rights for the sake of their children's souls. They are; and they are entitled to be respected for all the history and dignity of that positioning, whether one agrees or not with its present-day ramifications.

The morals and values of the America that we and Norman Rockwell remember also meant working together for the accomplishment of easily agreed-upon group goals. In addition to being

the result of a shared cultural and religious heritage, these principles, held in consensus, were also quite clearly of political and
social benefit — public safety, an educated electorate,[51] orderly
personal deportment at home and away, absolute integrity of conduct and honesty in public office, a free-market economy, equality
of legal justice in theory and in actuality except for the exceptions,
freedom of the individual within Judeo-Christian parameters and
freedom of political society from responsibility for the individual,
etc., etc.

As we know when we really force ourselves to think about
it, the world created and run by these values is not necessarily
good for everybody; nor are these values — many of them mutually exclusive or contradictory in the best of times — possible
in a pluralistic, urbanized polity. But it's nice sometimes to think
that they might be or to delude ourselves into thinking that they
ever were. It's particularly consoling (and inflaming) to think that
way when one is surrounded by furious debates about school curriculums, ongoing social programs, equal opportunity and OSHA
stipulations, NAFTA and foreign trade, freedom of speech on the
Internet and in the local public library's shelves, etc., etc.

Ahhh, those lovely times when we all knew and agreed on what
was right and good — all of us outside those crowded cities, of
course. And ahhh, how lovely also when we all knew each other
and cared for each other and left the front door open and the
car in the driveway unlocked, etc., etc., etc. Ahhh, once upon a
time....

Once upon a time, but no longer... and subtly the loss of these
romanticized blessings slips into a perception that somehow we
have failed, that we have slipped from what we were (blessed of
God) to what we are (obviously damned to some kind of immediate, if not eternal, torment) through some fault in us, that we have
sinned — and religion along with theology is once more in the

mix, brought there by a nostalgia as unrealistic and as powerful as any nostalgia ever was.

Much that went on in that small-town era was good and real, of course. No one denies that. But when the bulk of us swapped the homeplace for an apartment in the city, we inadvertently and unintentionally put ourselves into a place and a circumstance more conducive to crime and gangs and violence, more susceptible to drugs and their cancerous destruction, to isolation and moral dereliction, to.... We all know this list as well, and to extend it further seems unnecessary. What does need to be plainly said, however obvious it may be, is that what all these listed evils consume, among other things, is our sense of safety and well-being, our sense of purpose and significance, our sense of control and of goals greater than self.[52] What they consume is the human spirit; and that is a moral concern that for us, given the nature of our society, must become a cornucopia of religious, spiritual, and theological questions.

The ways in which we Americans have tried to reverse our contemporary evils or limit their consequences since Vietnam have become exercises, in almost every instance, of social engineering administered in religious rhetoric or of religious zeal embodied in political programs — which intertwining, for all the reasons we have discussed, is about as American as one can get. Whether initiating those policies and programs that allow the apartment dwelling family to mimic the habits of the homeplace family and its values and lifestyle — whether restoring America's "values" — is productive or simply anachronistic is a question that has no answer as yet. It is being asked, however, certainly with persistence and, more and more frequently nowadays, in the context of American god-talk.

However we may come in due time to assuage our longing for former moral habits, we can be sure of two things. First, for us as citizens, the old ways of approaching such issues and of integrating public or communal values with private ones or at least of ignoring the conflicts between them will not die quickly.[53] Secondly, among us as private individuals, our penchant for comfortably separating overt religious profession and allegiance from covert spirituality will not soon disappear.

From time to time, I will chance upon a paper or essay that refers to these two idiosyncrasies of ours as being complementary evidences of a common characteristic — our ability to separate established or institutional religion from personal religion. That is absolutely true; we do. But we do something else as well, and for the same reason. The longer I have lived with that wording about what we do, in other words, the more persuaded I have become that its phrasing is subtly erroneous. At the very least it is misleading in that it jumps a step in the actual progression of things. What it fails to acknowledge is the fact that most Americans assume that all spiritual activity is at its core religious and theological, and that's just not true for everyone, only for the religious and the theistic.

One of the unique components of today's god-talk is that, in this country at least, it is happening in the midst of an enormous, an unprecedented, ferment of spiritual concern, a good deal of it among the areligious, nontheists, and/or the only vaguely theistic.[54] For the first time in our history, it would seem, the religious in America are having their theology influenced by proximity to the passion and anima of many who are not formally religious or necessarily theistic and never wish to be. Understanding and accepting that phenomenon is, it seems to me, fundamental to actually hearing the god-talk going on around us just now.[55] It is most assuredly a prerequisite to accurately analyzing the third and last major part of our current nostalgia — that for spiritual connection.

Interlude

――― ―――

$\mathcal{J}$WAS sixty-two years old the spring I went to Rome for the first time. How I had managed to delay so long is beyond me now, but the omission had never seemed strange to me. To be honest, it had never even struck me as an omission. Then came the inevitable religion publishing meeting that had to be covered and ten hours later I was in Rome, notebook in hand, ready to do my journalistic duty as a paid observer. The problem was there wasn't much to observe after about one o'clock in the afternoon.

It was June, and the heat was already oppressive beyond that of late August in my part of the world. Even the Italians kept remarking upon its severity, assuring those of us in the press that Rome was almost never so sultry so early. They gained considerable credibility, with me at least, when I noticed that most of the exhibitors, speakers, and attendees who had come into Rome from northern Italy were almost as desiccated as we were.

Whether the weather really was so unseasonably difficult or whether there was a large holiday intention covertly built into the conference by its planners right from the start (which I also suspected), I could never determine. It probably would have made no difference anyway, even if I could have. The truth was that the traditional Mediterranean mid-day break for rest and a leisurely lunch marked the absolute end of any reportable activities at the conference and, so far as I could see, of any activities at all beyond the perfunctory ones required by the people who validate expense accounts. The result, hardly an undesirable one from my point of view, was that by the second day of a week-long conference, I had turned my after-lunch attention away from business and out toward Rome with its very adequate subway system and its eternal treasures. For the remaining five days, I turned into a tourist at the stroke of noon about as readily as Cinderella metamorphosed at midnight into a disheveled and dusty serving girl.

With a colleague or two, I wandered the Forum, climbed the Coliseum, cooled off in more churches than I ever really looked at, and enriched several dozen street vendors, the majority of them from Tunis and Algiers, by buying some of the most charming memorabilia that I have ever seen. Since I'm not a buyer of souvenirs — not ever, as a matter of fact — I concluded that the heat must indeed be singularly dangerous. It was with no small relief then that I discovered, once I was home and cool, that I still was pleasured by the trinkets I had brought back with me. But delight in small tokens was only a minor departure from my normal reactions and habits.

So likewise, as a departure from usual subjective patterns, was my sense of surprised awe in looking up at the arches of the Forum and understanding for myself the massiveness of their authority and the security of their presence.... So likewise my sense of unwanted and unrealized connection to bleeding story and anonymous death as I rested under the tiers of the Coliseum, and my sense — somehow most distorting of all — of the flooding of that place in the name of sport and of what such a thing must have smelled like for those waiting beneath the walls.... So also my sense of quiet homecoming when, on the train toward Ostia and the Tyrrhenian Sea, I saw the pillars and sea walls of the old Roman port and understood for an exhilarating moment or two that this really had been; that Rome had been; that there once had been all of this and it was mine by extension of the commerce and power and political genius that had flowed out from those towers and broken pilasters to me and mine. . . .

So all these emotions that were powerful for me in the heat and that have remained powerful in the lesser heat and greater cold of the intervening seasons since I first felt and absorbed them. Like my pleasure in my trinkets, they have grown and settled and seasoned, becoming an emotional reality for me in my interior life. But they too were almost as nothing compared, both in memory and in the moment itself, to my coming into the Pantheon.

I had not come to Rome as a naif. Not only was I physically well into late middle-age, I was, by profession, an experienced traveler — an experienced experiencer, in fact — trained to look with a calculating eye and think with a suspicious head. All of them are qualities that, having been fiscally reinforced over the years of my working life, tend toward a kind of blaséness and sometimes even to a truly dangerous objectivity that threatens to strip the significance from reality. But beyond those learned and acquired ways of engaging the world I am paid to watch, I was not a naif in matters of the spirit either.

Religion is my beat only because religion is and always has been my passion. From my earliest memories in my mother's house, religion, mystery, a sure intimacy with an actuality beyond, a third eye or the flick of the vision seen out of the corner of a physical eye — these things have always been there for me. I have served them as a Christian and believed, as I still do, that it is in Christianity only that I can approach and serve them.

That does not mean that I have not recognized intellectually and emotionally the similarities of religious experience among all peoples nor that I have not been schooled in the varying organized religious expressions of millions of other people. Obviously I have, just as I have read literally hundreds — and, I hope, read with empathy and most assuredly with personal benefit — of the spiritual journals, diaries, and manuals of many, many who, like me, have seen and felt and served, though invoking by other names, that which all my life has called to me.

No, it was not a naif who, surrounded by a noisy group of fellow travelers, stood at the base of the steps leading up into the Pantheon and gawked. As an adolescent taking my first formal classes in the Latin my mother had so surreptitiously siphoned into my soul, I had early learned to appreciate the relief of opening the next lesson in our textbook and discovering a big, full-page or at least half-page illustration. Not only did that *desideratum* mean that the exercises were to be shorter within the lesson itself, but it also meant that we were to be instructed in Roman customs and history, an infinitely more pleasant prospect than parsing, memorizing, and declining ever were destined to be.

The only picture of the Pantheon (outside of those in some art history texts) that I can remember ever studying intently was the one in that first-year Latin book. I can remember, oddly enough, flipping the first page of our next lesson, seeing the photo illustration, thinking, "Oh, good, there is one!," followed instantly by, "Lord, that's the ugliest building I ever saw!" ... which was what I, for my part, was gawking at that afternoon in Rome. The damned thing really *was* the ugliest building I had ever seen.

My husband and I live in the country now, on a farm that is slowly threatening to reengulf and repossess us as we grow older and less able or less inclined to fight back. One of nature's more effective means of repossession, aside from our southern Kudzu, is wasps. Wasps manage to bore into, ingest, and process every fence post, every barn piling, every outhouse on a half-tended farm. The end result is that anything wooden begins in time to sag and anything protected from the wind begins to grow gray, bulbous pedunculae. That's of course why we call them paper wasps: they take our wood and produce their paper, making of it nests for the thousands of their own kind who will exponentially increase within a single season the speed at which our destruction can be moved along toward its predestined end.

It was of those oddly unfenestrated, oddly foreboding, oddly controlled but amorphous, mud-gray nests that I thought, as I stood looking at the building above me, of the nests and, immediately thereafter, of my son's attempt, one summer day when he was four, to scoop the gummy, gray silt/mud/clay from the edge of our cattle pond and cover, as one covers a cake in icing, the heaps of dung that so fascinated him. The Pantheon was, in its reality, as ugly as it had been in my first-year text and as near as anyone will ever get to a combination of clay-iced cow patties and impenetrably gray wasp nests. Gawking was the only reasonable response to such a solid, controlled, windowless fixedness as the thing sitting impervious in front of us. It was, and I had not realized this before from either my old Ullman and Henry or my art history texts, nothing more than a man-made cave sitting above-ground.

Someone had told me once, when I was a child and still charmed by such things, that caves are the earth's closets, and just for a moment the analogy rose out of those lost years, flitted into my awareness, and then was gone again...which should have, but didn't, prepare me.

I went up the steps with a close friend and business associate and with some thirty or forty other tourists who, having recovered from their initial surprise, had given up staring in favor of getting out of the heat. In their jostling, chattering, camera-winding company, I pushed through the huge, stolid doors and was alone, abruptly alone on the dark marble floor, alone in the cool, faintly moist air, alone in the unarticulated hum of no-voices wafting around and down from that incredible dome, alone in that light — that strange, inscrutable light — that was the hole in the humming dome. There was no "other" that was not understood and subsumed in that complete light, and I knew in my moment, as I had known in my closet, that God the Father was there above where I looked and that there was no God the Mother.[1]

As I moved to stand at the border of the light — I was afraid to enter it out of anxiety that I might distort it — I saw beyond its diffusing the arching stones of the dome itself as they rose in celebration of their own perfection. And caught for all time around the rotunda of their circumference I saw again Kali and Shiva and Astarte, though they had different names and wore the different garb of togas and sandals.

It is impossible to convey to another what the intense moments in one's life really are. Always such brief openings are too interior to be plumbed, too much the constructs of all the experiences of the private life to be generally referenced. But even if that were not true, the complete telling of this one would lie too close to sacrilege for me to try here. It must be enough, instead, to say that in those few minutes I experienced something as profoundly ecstatic as I ever have. I was physically as well as psychically within the mystery, and it is.

— Eight —

Up from the Belly of Time

≡≡   ≡≡

OSEPH CAMPBELL, like so many of the thinkers who have followed him, was fond of observing that "feeling" life is more
important to the individual than finding meaning in it.[1] Placed
within its proper context, Campbell's observation is probably one
of the most prophetic of a long and very fertile career. The human
truth implicit in it is that until we have experienced or "felt" some
mystery beyond the reach of rationality, most human beings are
incapable of assigning either meaning or spiritual dimensions to
life, much less of participating in more than a perfunctory way in
any religion that may depend from them.

There is a second truism involved here, a kind of negative
corollary. And that is that as a species, people do not have to
perceive extrapersonal or supernal meaning in order to live, or
even to live creatively. The drive to discover and accommodate to
transcendent meaning is not universally present in our order of
creation, in other words, because the prior gift or experience of
having discovered the transcendent to be sometimes transparent
(to paraphrase Campbell again) seems not to be a universal one.[2]

What is odd or tragic[3] or poignant or just plain pertinent to
our moment in history is that in America there is a third category
within this set. There are those who believe the transcendent to be

there and to be the meaning as well as the source of life *only* because they have been told so. In polling the millions of Americans (and our number constitutes about 90 percent of America's adult population) who so believe,[4] no demographer or theorist to my knowledge has ever separated the "I know!" believers from the "I have heard" believers. My strong suspicion, however, is that at some point after World War II and before Vietnam, the percentages tilted, and the latter group began rather rapidly to exceed the former.

Whenever and whyever the exact turning point was, the fact remains that Americans, once we had begun the shift into the last half of the twentieth century, began to lose from our list of direct experiences some things that had been important to us both as individuals and as groups, things that in their commonality had woven us and secured us into communities, things that became increasingly attractive in their increasing absence. We became a society permeated with private and public nostalgia. And that nostalgia, as we have said, entered into our religion and our religious awareness just as surely as it entered into our kitchen kitsch and made Hallmark greeting cards a growth industry.

But religion is not an integer. Rather it is a construct of parts, the most familiar and presumably nonthreatening of which is, indeed, the gentle appeal of place, trappings, heritage, and rituals, and of all the spiritual nurture that they imply. Nurture, even in the most urbanized and postmodern of lifestyles, can still be felt . . . known . . . perceived . . . experienced. It is, quite predictably then, the nurture of religion, not the rigor of its various doctrines that has become its greater attraction for millions of Americans.[5] When we are being fed and comforted, the argument goes, we *know* it! When we are being instructed, we know that too, and the italics and punctuation say it all.

That kind of reaction is not the product of situation-specific thinking so much as it is just basic human nature; but in the case of American god-talk it has had unparalleled repercussions. Buttressed with our cumulative literacy and popularly available information about human psychology and comparative religion, rich with access to the practices and customs of many faith traditions, accustomed to accept individualism and self-governance as virtues, freed by circumstance from proscriptions against experimentation, millions of us — Jews, Christians, Muslims, agnostics, atheists, all — for the first time at a generalized level of popular acceptance began about a dozen years ago[6] to divide religion down the middle. That is, we began to separate religious exercise into two piles: that which nurtures and is spiritual from that which is everything else and official. The former has proved to be the more popular, naturally; but the very process of separation has been the instructive part.

Several "truths" have, in fact, emerged as conversational givens in the process. Not the least of them is that there really is such a thing as sacred space — a building or grove or cave or structure that for some reason fills the emotions and lifts the spirit to ecstasy. Ancillary to that is the truth that plopping cinderblock oblongs down on the cheapest piece of land accessible to the greatest number of the interested and saying a few prayers over the result does not necessarily create sacred space.[7] It may not even always sacramentalize whatever it is it does create.[8] But as surely as there is a Pantheon or a Newgrange, a Western Wall or a Kaaba, there are sacred places and holy sites. We know this, if for no other reason than that we or someone we know or someone whose accounts we have read has been to such a place, experienced it, and told us so.

Beyond what they do to us, we know of sacred places that they are almost never new and/or that they have moved thousands and thousands of people who have somehow further imbued and enhanced them with a cumulative reverence. We know also that such places are the property and purview of no one religion, but work equally as dramatically and effectively for all. We are even persuaded, despite a few caveats, that some places, while not primally sacred, can nonetheless be sanctified by the prayers and adoration and rituals of many human beings over many years (though never to as great a level of subjective impact as that extended to places of spontaneous theophany).

And most certainly we know as an experienced fact that individual lives and individual spaces can have sacred points made holy by the same process and that those individual bits of the sacred are efficacious images of the greater to which they refer and from which they are defined. Just the boom in popular books on creating one's own sacred space would be sufficient to establish it as a potent phenomenon in contemporary spirituality before one even begins to tally up the incredible burgeoning of seminars and retreats and workshops that have been built around the subject over the last ten years.[9]

We understand something far subtler, far more effecting, even, than all of this, however. We understand, by both experience and study that there is more than one way of knowing. The modern or post-Enlightenment way is factual, logical, objectively applicable, but the other way, the old way....

Ah, the other, the old, way is the wellspring and natal earth of what we seek. The other is the soul's chamber, the numinous cavern where knowing and feeling are one as once we were one — body, soul, and mind — and one as we yearn to be again. And what American god-talkers seem to understand about that is threefold: until human beings today can be that at-oneness, we will continue to be eternally restive and searching; That which comes closest to inviting the unity of all our parts is that which honors the senses as the bridges of connection between body, mind, and heart; and that which lies beyond and surrounds and sustains the numinous cavern is the mystery, and those who would engage it are those of us who would do religion as well as spirituality.

What all of this rather amazing lurch forward in generalized religio/spiritual sophistication means at a theoretical level is, obviously, part of the exploration being chronicled here. Probably the first indication of what it was going to mean for institutional religion at a practical level had to do with the matter of physical space and appointments.

Whether used in nontheistic spiritual exercise or in theistic worship or in something in between, the nearer an objective space comes to simulating the subjective cavern and its ambience — the more closet-like it becomes, if you will — the greater the comforting nurture. For our time, that fact has become an invitation to the arts that is without modern parallel because it is fundamentally an invitation to private space or the creation within public space of private cloisters of space. It is medieval, not modern;[10] it is chant, not oratorio; it is poetry and narrative, not homily or discourse. It is, in other words, a recognition that music and sound, repetition and ritual, simplicity and beauty of decoration and exquisiteness of care endow a space as much by freeing us as individual, sensate beings from the disjunctures of time as by invoking spirit into it.[11]

It is on and around these "discoveries" that contemporary American spirituality has already settled its foundations as well as its practices. The irony, of course, is that not one of those well-thought-out practices would have been anything other than apparent to the ancients nor, within formal religion, to saints and monks and holy women. In this we postmoderns have, like reminiscing elders, gone full-circle. We have come back again upon that which once we without knowing were and now in greater richness can be because of knowing.

But because we have relearned how to create, discern, employ the things of the spirit for ourselves and our communities outside of the structure of formal religion, formal religion cannot so readily as in the past use the comfortable offices of space and ritual and art and trapping as substitutes for doctrine or as carrots to persuade the disaffected toward ecclesial affection. These latter things, too, must learn to engage the mystery, and that engagement is the very burden of much of our current god-talk.

Once one approaches the Gordian knot of doctrine or even the lesser one of its successful delivery in America, one hits another part of Campbell's need to feel, an almost paradoxical part. In a country like ours with its long tradition of individualism, one can without difficulty understand why there is an intensification, an almost pathologic exaggeration, of the need to experience for oneself in religion as in everything else. What is at first blush less easy to understand, but is one of nostalgia's greatest gifts to contemporary religion, is the American need to know/feel — to "connect with," to use popular parlance — both the experience of religion itself and, of equal importance, the company of one's fellow experiencers.

It is not enough to know, America's god-talkers seem to be saying, especially not to know only in one's head. Doctrine is not enough, will never be enough, not, that is, until the fire has fallen on us and those in community with us, not until we have seen and known with our whole awareness the subsuming of all life — our own and that of our fellow worshipers — into the Life, not until we with and like them have been pierced with that ecstasy, not until we can say, "We *know* You! Each of us *knows* You!" and *know* beyond mere belief that both are true, not until we and our spiritual community are connected by that one moment or many such moments and have it or them to hold on to forever after in memory and worship...not enough, not ever enough, not until then.

The results of this yearning back toward experiential religion within and/or with affirming community have sometimes appeared as a kind of generalized rebellion against the system. No matter that there is not now, and never has been, any universal religious system in this country to rebel against. Rebellion in place, so to speak, becomes a kind of spiritual good for many in such circumstances — each man and each woman in their own way in their own time in their own groups.

At times, the rebellion has seemed simply to be a matter of pure, unbridled emotiveness. If a proposed practice or event looked as if it might excite reaction from any established religious body while at the same time being religiously scandalous enough to exhilarate its participants, it was worthy of trying. At least a group feels something that way. At other times, the kicking over of the theological traces has been directed inward to the enhancing of group and experience rather than outward in defiance. Far more frequently, the act of protest has been no protest at all, but simply an almost naive indifference to traditional (i.e., "sterile") religion altogether and an equally naive syncretism of those elements which an individual or community of like-minded individuals has found to be both spiritually and religiously invigorating.

Regardless of how one comes down personally on the subject of religious and/or doctrinal iconoclasm, however, it does have its consequences. And regardless of how one values or disparages those consequences, they still, in an era of massive information flow, seep into and become part of the cultural mix; and they still, in this case anyway, influence god-talk across all the old divides, meaning among the staid as well as among the daring, the ordained as well as the unallied, the confessional as well as the agnostic. At a macro-level these consequences can be things as disparate and varied as the steady growth of Yoruba and Santeria[12] or the dramatic increase in organized goddess worship and the spread of Wicca,[13] or the shifts toward lay involvement and ecstatic worship within the more established religions.

Because it began as an underclass phenomenon on the West Coast in 1906 and was hidden by place and status from public attention until our nostalgia caught up with its message, the significance of Pentecostalism upon Christianity, upon religion, and upon god-talk in general was masked for several decades. Now, it no longer can be.[14] Pentecostalism and the charismatic and ecstatic practices derived from, or similar to, it are the fastest growing segments of American religion today.[15] They have been, in fact, for several years now.

Because, contrarily, it was safely hidden within the ranks of institutionalized Christianity for so long, the rhetoric of gender-feminist theology's re-imagining also grew for years relatively unnoticed by its own establishments. It grew until, almost unbeknownst to itself, talk became a groundswell that became a liturgy that became an event that became a near disaster for some organized Christian bodies and an immolation for many of their professional staff members. When over two thousand Christians of both sexes from thirty-two mainline Christian denominations met in Minneapolis in November 1993 under the auspices of the World Council of Churches "in an exercise of re-imagining God, Jesus, creation, the church and everything related,"[16] the liturgy invoked Sophia as Goddess and as Divine Wisdom and incorporated into the Eucharist or Mass symbols and appointments that suggested menstrual blood and fertility rites. The results were, as they say, all over the map.[17]

Yet the brouhaha, for all of its unfortunate sound and fury, was hardly unpredictable or inexplicable. It was, in almost every sense, a confluence of the very factors that religion observers have been noting for several years and that we have already listed here as well. As a people, we know that we Americans are searching for wisdom to counterbalance the sharp sterility of our raw new information. Much of what the hamlet with its communal church did was distance ordinary folk from the shock of immature discoveries and unseasoned ability until such time as both the new skill and the wisdom with which to use it were available simultaneously. So likewise, much of what intuitive, earth-referencing woman did was bring second sight and deep skepticism to new messages. With those traditional safeguards now lost, it is no wonder that the religious patterns in which and around which they once orbited should be the place where many of us would begin to look for them again, and with remarkably little concern for doctrinal niceties.

One of the most sensible things I ever heard "said" on the Internet, a system not necessarily noted as yet for its general profundity, was said in regard to this very issue. The religiously oriented search for personally experienced wisdom, whether it is personified as Sophia or not, is almost always now couched — and historically always has been couched in Western tradition — in female terms. Thus for Americans, both inside and outside the framework of Judeo-Christian theology, the search for wisdom does indeed seem to have found its most cordial expression, as we said earlier, along a sliding scale that goes from ecology to eco-theology, eco-feminism, and eco-spirituality to Wicca and a concern with Gaia, or the ur-Goddess to Sophia and/or the Goddess.

In a substantial way, part of the surprise — even of the insult, if you will — of such movements, once they come within Judaism and Christianity[18] and are presented as issues like female ordination and inclusive language texts or at events like the Minneapolis liturgy is that, for the aware traditionalist, they represent the infiltration into orthodoxy of pagan practices and dangers. Chaos with her ungoverned, watery abysses was in the beginning until God moved, creating order by His word.... It is the beginning story of our three main religions. It is the horror from which we arose....

...Which horror was, I am quite sure, the impetus behind my bit of Internet profundity. A group of people, presumably traditional Christians in the main, opened a chat room called "Gaia

Rising" on the Ecunet system in 1995. Although I "lurked" in "Gaia" for six or seven months, I never recorded the names of the participants, and few ever gave any credentials. As a group, they were trying to make sense of the shifts (which most of the group praised as being "rather like those of the tectonic plates") within America's monotheistic and previously hierarchal faiths. As the meetings extended from weeks into months of animated and at times truly insightful dialog, an active participant named David began to insist so frequently upon one point that eventually he started posting it beneath his name in every sign-off. What he wrote each time was: "Perhaps we should understand religion before we pontificate on Christianity."

Whoever the unknown David may have been, he had the political and religious acumen of the original one, in my opinion. This is one area of the doctrinal discussion where we certainly do need to understand the concept before we deal with anybody's particulars.

The truth is that whether or not and how either spirituality or religion picks up the refinements and disciplines and encumbrances of orthodox theology (i.e., formalized and/or with institutionalized practices in place) are two entirely different questions.[19] Nor do the answers to them change the fact that, like it or not, a very great deal of contemporary religion, both inside and outside of established traditions and driven by an almost overweening nostalgia, has already begun to coalesce around theology that may be less than orthodox, but is hardly without traditions. Re-Imaging's Sophia, for instance, is clearly this phenomenon within the Christian system; most of what we mean by the loose use of "New Age" as a religious descriptive is just as clearly an example of the same phenomenon outside of, or tangential to, any of the three monotheistic ones. There is, in the combination of those two examples, interestingly enough, an example of yet a third possibility.

Sophia is a one-word reduction of a tension that is primal within Christianity and fundamental to all three of the monotheistic faiths. "She" is not the *logos* or "word" of St. John's Christ, but wisdom — wisdom in the way, for instance, that the book of Proverbs speaks of Wisdom as handmaiden to God and coexistent with Him. As we all know, however, her name denoted in its original Greek form the concepts of skill or cleverness or philo*sophic* astuteness, giving us such opprobriums as "sophist," "sophistry," and that fool or moron who suffers from much self-inflation, the "sophomore." Her name, in other words, suggests the contradiction — or her definition in apposition to *logos* does — that is also the tension.

Sophia has been so elevated from time to time within Judaism and Christianity as to be as near a goddess as the Judeo-Christian tradition has. Because she has, from the first, been one of Christianity's most natural icons or means for the move from orthodox salvific Christianity into experiential, salvific knowing, she now becomes the natural vehicle for conveying doctrinally the resurgent feminism of today's religious nostalgia, that is, Sophia and the worldview we call Gnosticism are, like the Virgin and Roman Catholic Christianity, inextricably intertwined in a defining and sacramentalizing union.[20]

What Gnosticism actually is is a very good question, one that has shipwrecked far more informed commentators than I shall ever be. For practical purposes, however, I think we can treat it as a Christian heresy that may have predated Christianity, but that found its fullest exercise in the mix of Near Eastern and Greek faith systems with nascent Christianity; that offered the early centuries of the common era a religious accommodation that, in our New Age, has grown very close to being a freestanding religion in its own right; and that has, within the last thirty years, powerfully affected all three of the major monotheistic faiths in this country.[21] Additionally, while I suspect that the vast majority of

Americans today never heard of Gnosticism as such or gave it two minutes' worth of thought, the truth is that almost all of America's contemporary god-talkers — Jews, Christians, and Muslims, Buddhist, Hindus, and Baha'is alike — have some fairly basic gnostic sympathies and even some outright beliefs. In particular, we are fond of those that feed or promise to satisfy, as Gnosticism does, our current need "to experience God directly and personally without intermediaries"[22] through wisdom or the "knowing/feeling" of religious connectedness.

The quotation marks around "knowing/feeling," like the slash connecting them, are there for good reason, for it is the nature of Gnosticism's wisdom/knowledge that is both its power and its weakness. Gnosticism's is a knowing that falls easily within Jesus' "Ye shall know the truth and the truth shall set you free" prophecy (John 8:32). It is certainly a Campbellian "felt" knowing of the arcane truth encoded into myth and poetry and ritual. It is most certainly experiential.[23] But like any experiential system, Gnosticism is fundamentally idiosyncratic and ineffable with little or no central and transmittable core of precepts, making of its adherents a confederacy of small confederacies of the like-minded at best and random groups of the communally disaffected at worst.[24]

Despite the limitations of relative formlessness within the gnostic perspective, the need to know gnostically — or the compulsive belief that if one could just "know," all would be well — is a compelling one. It is so compelling, in fact, that were I permitted to pick only one topic from within American god-talk today as potentially the most influential, the most consequential, the most reformative for American religion, I would have to pick contemporary American gnosticism, with all due credit as well to the nostalgia engine that is driving it.

The hope of intimate connection with what is and of intimately knowing it is doubly powerful among us because its expression among us is, indeed, essentially unfettered by formal religion and ubiquitous. For example, gnostic hope or yearning is a major impetus to extratradition commercial bestsellers like James Redfield's *The Celestine Prophecy*[25] and channeled texts like *The Book of Urantia* or *A Course in Miracles;* but so is it also to our present popular absorption with the Dead Sea Scrolls, with esoteric and/or extracanonical texts,[26] and even, within Christianity, with the search for the historical Jesus.[27]

There is, in fact, a veritable confluence of gnostic and near gnostic elements gathered together in all these areas as well as in the vast areas in between them. There is additionally, this being America, a cult-of-personality idolization of the scholars working within and around gnostic themes that further excites the issues. This particular part of the equation is probably most evident or popularly visible in the case of the so-called "Jesus scholars" whose books almost without exception become immediate bestsellers and whose names, faces, and excerpted words appear routinely in popular magazines, TV screens, chat rooms, and conference brochures.[28] Yet — and it is a very important *yet* — as most ordinary god-talkers know, popularization must never be equated with vulgarization.

For example, the search for the historical Jesus and for the original scriptures, practices and contexts that surrounded Him matters intensely at a popular level, but that does not mean that it exists for less than devout reasons.[29] Much of the energy of that search — the lion's share of it actually, in my opinion — rests on a pervasive belief that "the church" has come between the believer and the belief, between the Christian and Christ, by inserting all the institutional impedimenta of doctrine, structure, and vested interest. The theory is that "if we can just get at who He really was, we will feel safe in our own hearts that we know what He really wants and promises."

Those enquoted words are doctrinal in the fullest, most dynamic sense of doctrine. They are also the most serious words that

I as a secular Christian routinely articulate to ordained and/or tenured Christians; for they contain or suggest about two-thirds of the present disjuncture between the church and the nominally churched, the under-churched, or the would-be churched. Were I Jewish, I suspect that I might have and feel compelled to express some analogous concerns about the current resurgence of popular interest in the Kabbalah, Life-Cycles research, and the wisdom traditions. Certainly were I Muslim, I would watch with more than idle curiosity the phenomenal growth, relatively speaking, of Sufism in this country and most particularly the amazing sales for translations of the Sufi poet/seer Rumi or the continuing tension between traditional and modern cosmologies within Islamic politics as well as theology.

But beyond the sense of rebellion against outmoded forms and beyond the longing to feel and know and beyond even the desire for community within our individuality lies that most amazingly medieval of all our contemporary fascinations: our yearning toward the Mystery.

It is our spiritual love affair with "once upon a time" that in many ways sums up all the other emotions and intellectual absorptions that are the nostalgia in our god-talk. Somewhere back there in that beginning time... Somewhere back where Chaos was the watery abyss and was... Somewhere back where Gaia birthed Uranus and then was tamed by him or Tiamat did to Marduk and was done to in return... Somewhere back there where it all began... Somewhere back there for most of us in America is Genesis.

Thousands of us over the last three or four years[30] have spent and are increasingly spending dozens and dozens of our leisure hours with, of all unlikely things, the first book of Torah. Not only are we reading commercially published, highly successful books about Genesis,[31] but through the fall and winter of 1996–97 thousands of us were glued to television sets for weeks while Bill Moyers led us, in the company of two dozen scholars, through a *Talking about Genesis* series that for substance and audience has become the capstone of his already illustrious camera career.

Not satisfied with that, we have continued since to replay *Talking* through the wonders of VCRs and tape for thousands and thousands of additional hours. We have also participated for many more hours in several hundred small-group Genesis discussions across the country. It is a startling level of popular involvement with what is patently god-talk of the first water.[32] As a phenomenon, it also cries out for some kind of explanation, especially among those who wish to describe the present state of theology in America.

Certainly the move back toward the earliest scriptures known to us as "People of the Book" is consonant with the kind of diffuse religious nostalgia that is abroad in America today. Yes, there is among us an understandable desire from time to time to see our world of exponentially expanding information through the eyes and innocence of those who walked in wonder rather than fact. Yes, the urge toward finding our scriptural "originals" is evidencing itself as a studying back toward earlier or "purer" sources in many areas besides Genesis, as witness the current interest in early church liturgies or the Kabbalah renaissance. Yes, there is, demographically speaking, a strong push among almost all religiously oriented Americans toward investigating the ground held in common by Judaism, Christianity, and Islam, just as there is an obvious desire to accommodate to our differences by emphasizing the commonalities. And yes, nostalgia and the love of wisdom are admittedly powerful forces in life, the Genesis phenomenon unquestionably satisfying its fair share of both. But our particular Genesis flood,[33] I suspect, is driven by more than just yearning for unencultured doctrine or a more companionable peace. Ours seems to swell up from far deeper caverns even than those.

From our earliest known beginnings as a species, the power of the mythopoetic — its grand benediction — has been that by suggestion to abiding memory and physical experience it can speak a truth too vast and fiery for knowing. For a society not yet living off the earth but living with it, the Beyond is what surrounds the earth which they are, and is divine as well as awesome. For a later society living off the earth and severed from it as user is from the used, the Beyond is what will not succumb to user control. But for an even later society that in using has uncovered more dynamic complexity than human capacity can encode, Beyond is once again that which surrounds and is Mystery. Small wonder, then, that what for four or five centuries seemed to many to be little more than primitive mythmaking should increasingly appear to postliterate Americans as a divine script choreographed by the ancients and edited by truth's beauty. Seen as through the teasing scrim of a shadowshow, all the shapes and forms of being dance there in divine caricature, and the power of their performance is in their immortal candor and the random steadiness of their deceptively flat outlines.[34]

For such postliterate believers and seekers, behind the scrim and behind Genesis's puppet actors is El-Eloyim. Is the tetragrammaton. Is What Was before Moses or Jesus of Nazareth or Mohammed of Mecca and was with Abraham and was the Adonai of Melchizedek. And we *want* as a lover wants the beloved and wants to be wanted. And with Genesis as with the search for the historical Jesus or the intention of the Prophet, we are consumed with the thought that if only we could get through the veil of differing substances and the scrim of accretion and time, we could commune again and please again and conform again. We could be at peace again.

It is, in short, the Mystery we seek and Torah, not Revelation or even some wise *surrahs,* is where we suspect that last we saw it, once upon a time.

Nine

For the Love of Theology

≡≡   ≡≡

WE BEGAN this discussion with the premise that human conversation not only occurs within an environment, but also
receives the lion's share of its methods, emphases, and effectiveness as well as much of its referencing and content from that
environment. So long as ordinary human beings are doing the
talking, every part of that thesis certainly seems to hold true for
god-talk in America today.

The immediate effect of cumulative literacy upon American
god-talk has already been inestimable; it will be at least another
two decades before we can fully and accurately gauge the total,
reformative impact cumulative literacy has had upon American
beliefs, upon spirituality, upon theology, and, ultimately, upon
religion as well. Across all the old barriers of class and circumstance, cumulative literacy has provided readily accessible,
expertly annotated facts and probable facts about both the objective and subjective world, facts that by their very nature impact
constantly on the "big questions" that are god-talk in any era or
culture.

Beyond the sheer, insistent flow of information that demands to
be noticed, cumulative literacy has created its own kind of morality, or perhaps just its own kind of mass consumerist psychology.

It has empowered ordinary people with unprecedented banks of information from which to draw down reasoned conclusions and with which to buttress decisions. But as we have already noted, by providing those tools cumulative literacy has also become a kind of imperative toward personal responsibility that has changed the roles of credentialed professionals and a popularly informed laity in almost every domain of life.

Once was the time when trained and usually certified professionals were responsible for the whole conduct of those facets of life that were thought to require art as well as craft — everything from law and medicine to religion, that is — but no longer. With such a wealth of new, newer, newest information, the lay man or woman feels compelled to recredential every professional whom he or she meets or whose services must be engaged. The professional becomes, in this strange new paradigm, almost an artisan bidding for customers; the lay person becomes subtly but effectively a consumer "shopping," in our case here, for the best theology or soundest religion; the professional and the lay become codeterminers of conduct, credos, and decisions, with the lay person making the final choices and the professional, to a large extent, now becoming the worker bee who effects them.

The influence upon conversational content of a bidding-war mentality, the disjunctures of more fact than can be processed and evaluated, much less incorporated, the consequences in a mass-media milieu of bias or distortion in information delivery: they are but three of the more obvious parts of cumulative literacy that are both furnishing the content of our god-talk while, at the same time, sculpting the discourse.

As we have seen, that content and conversation are being shaped as well by a pervasive nostalgia that has, in essence, become the lens through which we see our theological and spiritual desires. It has almost set, in fact, the parameters within which inspiration can be received or belief exercised. Certainly, nostalgia more than anything else has determined the emphases of our god-talk, while at the same time furnishing the bulk of the energy that has driven it to its present proportion of national absorption. There is, however, a third, powerful factor coming in to play here for the first time in our history as Americans, a process that, while it is to some extent the result of both cumulative literacy and nostalgia, promises to be as great as they — and many would say greater — in its ultimate effect upon American god-talk. I refer to the democratization of theology.

To speak of the democratization of theology is almost to imply that it is one thing, whereas in reality it is, like so much else in a mass-communications age, a construct, an effecting agent composed of several processes. The most pervasive subprocess is the mass dissemination of generic god-talk. Ironically, such standardization is the most visible component in our new mix, even to the most casual observer, while appearing to be the one most underappreciated by invested professionals. In fact, many, many teaching theologs and practicing clergy seem quite pleased to disparage and then summarily dismiss the standardization of the tenets of popular god-talk without serious regard for its implications.[1] Few things, I suspect, could be more foolhardy, just as few could be more self-indulgent.

For example, it does not take a demographer to persuade us that the vast majority of the folk watching CBS's *Touched by an Angel* series have tuned in for the sake of entertainment. Admittedly, a large part of that entertainment experience, according to viewers who have been polled, is the show's so-called "inspirational message," that is, its presentation of ultimate, loving goodness as being the eternal in creation. Even being aware of that predisposition on the audience's part, I would still be willing to wager that not one American viewer in ten thousand sits down on Sunday nights for the purpose or partial purpose of thinking about theology. I am even more positive that not one of them looks up from the show an hour later and says, "Wow, that was really some strong theology tonight!" There is, in other words, no theological intentionality (for lack of a better term) on the part of those gathered millions.

What most of the viewing millions do, however, engage is Della Reese's sense of God and her intimate, authoritative (she is an angel, after all) talk about Him. And if by *theology* we mean definitions of God and of His relationship to Creation, then the cold, hard fact of the matter is that more theology is conveyed in, and probably retained from, one hour of popular television than from all of the sermons that are also delivered on any given weekend in America's synagogues, churches, and mosques.

The differences between it and them — between show and collective sermons — are several. Obviously the two differ sharply in their originating source and tradition and in their medium.[2] Beyond that there is a worlds-apart difference between the two in the relative overtness or didacticism of the theological presentation and, as we have said, in the nature of their respective receivers' intention toward the content. (Significantly enough, the content itself really may not have been all that different, depending on the sermon, a circumstance that makes content a shaky candidate for inclusion in this list of distinguishing variances.) But there is another difference, one that is much less dramatic and, in its total impact, far more substantive.

Della Reese's rendition of God is the same one regardless of the homes and heads it goes into. All viewers are equal and equally receive. And that integrating rendition is going, not only without variations but also without proselytizing vigor or sectarian specifics, into millions of evening homes and relaxing minds on a routine basis. It is traveling in, in fact, on the very same routine basis that organized, Western religion has held from its earliest beginning as the most efficacious spiritually and epistemologically — once every seven days and on the "day-off" hallowed one, to boot!

Now while almost every sermon or sermonizer may claim the same seven-day regimen, few can claim to employ it for addressing millions routinely and simultaneously and with any uniformity of message or worldview. That is, even the Billy Grahams of this world do not crusade weekly on commercial television. Those, like the Pat Robertsons of this world, who can claim routinized, visual presentation to mass audiences, cannot command the size or cross-section of audience that commercial television offers certainly. More significantly, however, they cannot claim the subtle power of addressing a relaxing audience — that potency of opportunity that comes when private defenses are down simply because no agenda beyond entertainment is present or at least obvious.

With no wish to belabor the point, I still must note that *Touched* as entertainment transcends as well not only the doctrinal and religious lines that restrict even the best telepreacher, but also the social, educational, class, economic, and geographic barriers that likewise confine the sectarian in any guise. To assume, moreover, as have so many sectarian efforts lately, that the freedom of movement enjoyed by *Touched* or *Promised Land* or by other books and shows like them is attributable purely to their "guise" as entertainment is equally to misread the phenomenon in the opposite direction.

A piece of storytelling in whatever medium is successful in proportion to its ability to elicit points of similarity and therefore of connection between its characters and its audience. Sectarian presentation presumes its truth and seeks to move its audience toward it; nonsectarian presentation seeks to reflect in its characters where and who its audience is and unite them with it in the narrated experience. When the latter happens on a mass-medium stage across all barriers among millions of people, the result is one part of the democratization of theology. Specifically, it is the homogenization of theology or, put more cautiously, the creation of a foundational theology that is homogenized and/or standardized.

The homogenization of theology happens, then, not so much because a particular entertainment experience caused it. Rather, it happens because a particular entertainment experience accurately captured, processed, and then gave back, reenforced and in coherent form, a theological *zeitgeist* consistent with the lived and perceived values and needs of an audience. With few exceptions and none that I can think of as possible presently, Della Reese's theology is going to win out every time over that of any sermon that runs counter to it, not because hers is more accurate or wiser or divine, but because it is more immediately contextual and more easily employed.

What is different now, what separates us from all the centuries since the golden ones of ancient Greece and its theaters where the same phenomenon occurred, is that because it is mass and informs the whole, a standardized theology is — has become, must be — the substratum of all god-talk today, the fixed rhetoric and the established vocabulary with which it must be spoken. This does not mean the end of doctrinally specific and defined faiths. It simply means that those faiths which would take part in Americans' god-talk are going to have to accommodate themselves and their expression to the presence of a theological *lingua franca* that we just didn't have fifty years ago — either that, or degenerate into self-referencing communities of speakers isolated from each other and the larger conversation by doctrinal idiolect and holy patois.

And those who see the discovery of a base common to all our multiplicities as a "washing down to the least common denominator" or, to speak academically, as the vulgarization of theology are absolutely correct in their assessment, but not in their evaluation. It is the *vulgus* that has always heralded religious change, and that record had best be respected for what it is — impeccable and unimpeachable.

The recognition and employment of common totally theological givens that are the new syntax in American god-talk constitute the first, opening, conversational wedge leading toward full democratization. Right behind it is another battering ram of even greater bluntness. By virtue of its more studied intentionality, this one both reveals and reenforces the attitudes of democratization. As an example and, in the name of consistency drawn from the same medium, let us consider this:

When a televised series, right from its opening introductions to its final credits, is concerned exclusively with the book of Genesis and involves twenty-five or thirty professional theologians in conversation on camera only about Genesis, that is intentional theology. Nothing, in fact, could be more intentional, either on the part of the producers or of the audience who choose out of their own private interests to watch it. And such an extensive and expensive programming effort as the 1996 *Genesis: A Living Conversation* series by Bill Moyers that we have already discussed can happen only because people — just plain people — want to watch dueling theologs and dueling traditions have at each other and at a sacred text in public.

What this means, beyond the obvious presence of the raisons d'être that we noted earlier, is some marked changes in attitude. The first is in attitude about self. Moyers's watchers, being cumulatively literate, assumed their own competence — and, for many, their moral obligation — to listen with employable comprehension to differing and often blatantly conflicting interpretations of the one sacred text that is most central to the monotheism of Della Reese theology.

The exercise of lining expert opinions up and evaluating them like a jury member attending to attorneys for the purposes of deciding what to think is very different from the business of listening to an authority who, judge-like, conveys how matters are. The difference, in other words, is one of empowerment; and individual empowerment — gift of cumulative literacy, in no small part — is an important subprocess in democratization, especially of god-talk.

Second, the success of such popular, intentionally theological events as the Moyers series rests on a radical shift in popular belief about the authorship of the text under debate and in the resulting attitude about how and by whom the text may be safely and effectively used.

No one, least of all me as must by now be obvious, is denying the attraction of the mythopoetic nor the power of nostalgia to draw people back to their early texts. Those things are irrefutably operative and constitute the major impetus behind the Genesis flood. But below these and the other social and psychological motivations we have named is another tectonic shift that is perhaps even more fundamental in its theological ramifications. Until we accepted (without necessarily acknowledging to ourselves that we had done so in many cases) the fact that Genesis was of human, rather than divine authorship, there could have been no Moyers-type free-fall about it.

It is a belief in human composition that allows Genesis to become mythopoetic theology, not literal doctrine. It is belief in its human composition that permits human dissection as much to discover the humanity as the divinity recorded there. It is even (most telling of all) belief in its human composition that allows us to employ Genesis as a series of stories in which questions — sometimes impious and dangerous questions — can be raised about the nature of deity and then tested for accuracy and present appropriateness. It is belief in Genesis's human composition, in other words, that makes it safe for us as ordinary individuals to do theology with it, to do popular midrash upon it — and that's about as democratized as one can get in license and in attitude.

Third, like a musky perfume scenting the presence of a seductive other, the unstated notion of religious and theological commonality among all the traditions pervades PBS's *Genesis*. So too does the corollary that that commonality is holier and far more desirable than are the specifics of the divisions that have evolved out it. The faith of Abraham is greater, in these terms, than the faith of Moses — an important shift in god-talk as well as in attitude.

And for the sake of any skeptics who may still be lingering in the wings, let me say, before we leave this part of our discussion, that the fact I have chosen to cite television does not mean that democratization is either a boob-tube or a dilettante's phenomenon. It is neither. It appertains across media and across the whole spectrum of socialization and intentionality.[3]

In the movies, it is *Babette's Feast* or *Field of Dreams* or *Shadowlands;* and it is as much the later conversational referencing[4] or the small-group discussions that meet to parse the films, as it is individual lives that are won to the films' theology and then cumulatively become the prevailing culture's. In audio it is the nation's librarians reporting in a 1995 survey by the American Library Association that the most frequently requested book-on-tape is the Bible, just as it is the release of commercial tape after commercial tape *about* the Bible.[5]

In books one might say that the theology and the intentionality in texts like *Chicken Soup for the Soul* and all its myriad spin-offs are kissing kin with Della Reese's angels (One would also have to say as well that, like those angels, *Soup* et al. have taken up permanent residence in the lives of millions of us.[6]) But when Jack Miles's *God: A Biography*[7] won the Pulitzer Prize in Biography in 1996, a book of the most intentional theology imaginable won our most prestigious literary award in a creative, not a religion, category; and it won in recognition of its ability, among other things, to successfully penetrate our culture and affect it.

Miles's *God* is not what the tame sit down to cuddle up with on a rainy afternoon. It is what the empowered, with absolute confidence in both their right and their ability, chose to devote their energies to considering. And, at the risk of repetitiousness, it is almost as often as not nowadays not a sitting down alone that happens.[8] George Gallup recently published surveys showing that nearly four out of every ten Americans are currently meeting on a regular basis in small groups for purposes of religious study and experience.[9] In effect, the small-group discussion meeting has become the new seminary — or one of its most active departments, perhaps — and a totally democratized one, at that.

Yet, even given all of these things, it is still not in real time and space that theology's democratization is discovering its most potent instruments of change. Those tools are in virtual time and cyberspace. Like all brand new devices, these too are still largely unmastered; and while they constitute the technology of our inevitable future as god-talkers, they also contain all the possibilities of any untried implements for self-inflicted maiming and danger. For that reason we need to look now, with absolute respect and no small amount of reverence, at a place that my mother would never have been able to comprehend, but one which ur-Woman — or ur-Man, for that matter — would have naively accepted as familiar and innately assumed to be one with hers. This latter truth is much of the force we are about to touch.

Ten

In the Palaces
of Cyberspace

$\equiv\equiv \quad \equiv\equiv$

ℳOST RELIGION SCHOLARS will say that democratization has happened in god-talk many times before we came along and in many other places, yet there can be considerable disagreement among them about just which events in history qualify for the core list. No one, however, questions the fact that the Protestant Reformation was the West's quintessential example of theological and religious democratization or that, more than anything else, it resulted from unprecedented technological advances in mass communication and their consequences — advances that in range and depth blanch in comparison to those of our own last half-century. What we must now consider, however, is more than just the fact that the potential for theological fall-out has been exponentially enlarged this time around by the greater scope of our information revolution. We must consider as well the likelihood that we are in the process of completing a democratization of god-talk that the Reformation in some ways really only began.

It is customary in discussions like this one to speak of levels of theology. As with lists of pivotal events, there usually are as many strata of theological sophistication (Hello, Sophia. Welcome back.) as there are schools of religionists who are drawing up the lists. For practical purposes, however, we may assume that modern, i.e., post-Reformation, lists as a rule begin with a folk faith system at the bottom of things and move upward to a popularly literate, consciously engaged system to a sanctioned and ordained one to, at the apex, the intricacies of professional academics' (i.e., *theologi gratia theologorum*) theology, and include dozens of possible stops in between.[1]

Traditionally, the ideas on the lowest ends of the scale have been thought to have the smallest amount of permanent influence upon the culture and likewise upon the theological *zeitgeist,* because they were, one, uninformed and, two, confined by situation. As we saw in the last chapter, neither of those conditions still accrues. The latter is blatantly untrue, and the former has undergone a radical redefinition. Folk theology can be, and is, massively informed and informing via an almost limitless number of sources, which means that "uninformed" is more a prejudice than an assessment and often references in terms of received traditions and interpretations rather than a body of information per se.

The ideas on the upper end of the theological scale, by contrast, have traditionally been thought to have the greatest permanent influence upon god-talk because, while they too were confined by circumstance and position, they were also: one, informed; two, the intentional result of a lifetime's focus; and three, positioned on the top wrung of a hierarchial delivery system that guaranteed their dissemination and ultimate acceptance. Of these conditions, only number two has remained unchanged (although it has ceased to be confined to the professional, as we have seen). The others, and especially the delivery system, are in total disarray.

While the Reformation established the principle in Christianity (and, by association in Judaism and western Islam, to a less formal but still significant extent) of the priesthood of every single believer and while the technology surrounding the Reformation empowered that citizen priesthood with revolutionary access to holy writ and to some textual commentary, neither the Reformation nor its technology disestablished the ordained pastoral orders or the common perception of information as hierarchial. The truth flowed down; it didn't seep and ooze, and leak. We, on the other hand, are into seep, ooze and leak, only with more rapidity and impact of flow than those verbs imply.

Theoretical theology, up until this century, began with the academically trained and/or the ordained who, when they spoke their ideas, spoke them to small audiences of their peers or of their students. When they wrote them, they wrote in books accessible and affordable only to that same group and a few of the privileged outside of it.[2] Over time, the theories, like receding water, found a new level, not among the folk, the *vulgus,* or even among the influential bourgeoisie, but among the pastoring clergy.

One of the ameliorating functions justifying the ordained working clergy traditionally was, in fact, their role in the truth hierarchy. They served as the narrowed portion of the funnel through which information was slowed, processed, and eventually gentled down into the vessel below. The result of that slowing was, of course, as its rebellious critics are pleased to say so frequently, that much right god-talk and much pure information related to god-talk never got through the funnel and, secondly, that much which did had all too often been changed by its stay in the narrows.

Those charges are undoubtedly true, but they fail to acknowledge some other, kinder results of the process. First, much of the theory and interpretation and postulation that never saw full life shouldn't have. The death by stagnation it suffered was of incalculable benefit to all concerned. Second, much of the theology and many of the related data that did get through were seasoned and detoxified on their long passage out to water the masses, becoming thereby a source of nourishment rather than of spiritual and religious morbidity.[3]

As Americans have increasingly absented themselves from formal religious services and/or instruction,[4] however, they have also absented themselves from those working ordained who, traditionally, knew equally well both the theological innovations immediately above them and the folk realities below them, and were the beneficent connection between the two. Unfortunately, as we are discovering, no connection, no matter how historically rooted, works when only one end of it is in contact with anything.

Beyond the physical removal of many Americans from theological mentoring is the business of all the other factors — cumulative literacy empowering seekers, mass communication of theological concepts, nostalgic yearning for unity and simplicity and spiritual meaning, etc., etc. — that we have discussed. Each of these has done its own part toward driving the folks at the bottom of the old-form theological hierarchy to ask questions for themselves and to want to see for themselves the sources behind any proffered answers. At the same time, each has helped drive the folk at the top to want to become missionaries for information and, like popular heroes, charge into the waiting hordes with all those answers. What the last fifty years have given both groups is the way to get at each other and at many of the relevant texts in some very effective ways, but....

...But those ways are as nothing when compared to what the technology of the last ten years have given every level of America's god-talkers, not only in terms of access to each other and supporting texts, but also in terms of access to both traditional and extratraditional theological theories, interpretations, and applications.[5]

As recently as five years ago even and certainly in the late 1980s, seekers and believers alike were largely dependent upon

the good intentions, energy, and ambition of credentialed popularizers for their extracurricular, quasicurricular, and avant
garde theological supplies; nonacademically affiliated clergy were
largely dependent for theirs on personal libraries, all too frequently acquired in seminary and dated even then, and upon the
materials provided or recommended by other clergy or clerical superiors; even academic theologians, blessed with physical access
to relatively adequate libraries, were still dependent upon learned
papers and conferences for any real access to emerging thought
and data. No more. Like a lock in a canal, the personal computer has raised the water level to a powerful and unmediated
equality.[6] It has begun as well an engagement of such proportions that, once done, it may make Gutenberg look like scarcely
more than an irascible old salt sitting on a pier, watching the real
world go by.[7]

Much of the excitement of theology today and about theology
is a direct result of the fact that there is so much of it. The dams
restraining it have burst, and we are awash in a fecund deluge
of possibility and fact. Congregational clergy that could not afford adequate libraries — who frequently did not even know what
such a library would contain, in fact — can now acquire on CD-
ROM almost every significant theological document in the world.
They can then read all those tomes on the relatively inexpensive
computer that almost every parish or congregation or administrative unit or local public library in this country either owns or is
about to own.[8] The result is that for a pittance, anyone — clergy
or lay — can acquire and repeatedly access at will the most honored, core treatises and commentaries and sacred texts from every
faith represented in America's theological mix.[9] Within each tradition — and this has been of especial importance to those in the
Christian[10] tradition — there is unprecedented access as well to
the documents and history behind contemporary doctrinal and
ecclesial differences.[11]

The proliferation of materials that has been the computer's gift to god-talk has, interestingly enough, not remained limited in its impact or audience to the computer environment, however. At least it has not remained so limited as far as sacred texts are concerned. One of the incontestable hallmarks of a democratizing of theology in progress is always a proliferation of scriptures — not the generation of new or aberrant ones, but the creation of versions, translations, and editions of the established ones, of *textus receptus*. The computer with its Herculean referencing and research strengths has facilitated the work of textual reissuing to a pitch that would have been unimaginable even to our grandparents. And the bulk of that flow has reached its market most directly as books.[12]

The presence of so many apparently equally legitimated and endorsed presentations of the same core text among so many people has introduced into our god-talk as never before questions about the absolute interpretation of any of them, including the original. At the same time it has excited among both seekers and believers greater and greater interest in investigating as many variations as possible before arriving at a personal or personalized amalgam. It is at this point that hypertext, with its militantly informing nature, seems most frequently to come into the picture. For far less than the cost of a new pair of shoes, anyone can buy a CD-based set of scriptures in an almost limitless number of languages and versions and, at the click of a mouse, view a half dozen or more of them simultaneously.

Nor is the successful manipulation and critical comprehension of any of these resources denied to the laity by any lack of the learned research skills that are so much a part of the professional education of clergy or the academically trained. To the contrary, most of these computer-read materials are now so cross-referenced, elucidated, paralleled, and annotated as to require little beyond average intelligence and personal persistence to give up their treasures. The hypertext capability of the CD-ROM environment is particularly cordial to theological study — perhaps more cordial to it, in fact, than to any other popular science. Hypertext's facility for infinite cross-references all before the reader's eyes on a Windows screen is, in other words, almost a mandate for interpretation-within-context as well as for enforced exposure to the universe of possibilities and viewpoints.[13]

Beyond the directly theological, however, and of much greater, ultimate import, I suspect, is access to the data and texts and even the theology that lie outside the channels of received tradition, texts, and fact. Most obviously, for example, the discoveries at Qumran, like those at Ugarit and Nag Hammadi, have for decades been of huge — in some cases divisive — proportions to academic god-talk and god-talk theory. All of that furor and exhilaration seems but a distant rumble when compared with the thunderous impact of their release and the release of materials related to them in CD-ROM format.[14]

The very nature of the CD-ROM impacts here in another particularly significant way. The CD moves in a technology that is far more familiar to most under-thirty rather than over-thirty adults and one that is especially comfortable for youngsters. Additionally, the CD combines audio and video with fixed text in an interactive way that allows the user to control to a large extent the order of information received and the interconnections made among all the pieces of it, a capability that is likewise especially attractive to youngsters and younger adults. As a result of this generational affinity for the medium, much theology that might never have attracted younger users had it stayed text-bound is now getting out to them just because of its delivery system and with almost no prior intent on their part as users.[15] As a variation within the business of electronic god-talk, this proclivity among the young for the electronic and imagistic is central to understanding America's future god-talkers as well as to understanding the power of new media to further excite their theological conversation in multitudinous directions.

The results of enabled access for so many ages and conditions of humanity to so much textual, historical, and applicable scholarship and theory in theology have been manifold. Two of them are of particular relevance right now — the greater realization of the Reformation's intention toward the priesthood of all believers and the creation of a constituency of the equally informed, at least among those who wish so to be. In such a milieu, factual information can become proportionately less prestigious as it becomes increasingly the property of all equally. In information's place of primacy, inspiration, mysticism, and theophany can become, if not the new hierarchy, then the new informants to be cultivated and enticed. In such a milieu, too, there can be the rejection (and even the isolation by the majority) of those men and women who are too bound by tradition or prior allegiance to candidly engage the new information and the actualities it has invited in. In such a milieu of so much and such variety, there can be, as in the physical sciences, the pervasive feeling that somewhere, somehow a theological Universal Theory of Everything is lurking in the shadows, waiting for us to stumble into its loving arms. These potential shifts, as we know from just plain observation, have indeed occurred in this country. They are all very much a part of who we are as a people right now and very much a part of all the conversations that compose, in aggregate, our current, American god-talk.

And when we speak of that conversation and of all the conversations that compose it, we may be very sure that for the first time within the centuries of the common era, it really is god-talk that we are discussing.[16] At an effective level, the difference between theology and god-talk is not merely just that of some clever bit of word-play or of some cutesy attempt to be egalitarian. The difference fundamentally is that god-talk both implies and is oral or conversational communication. It is people talking openly and directly to each other about god and everything related to god over a sustained period of time — and nothing had ever given humanity that opportunity[17] until the computer first enabled the CD-ROM and later spawned the Internet, for it is on the Internet where god-talk is purest conversation.[18] In fact, the Internet is, in many ways, the interactivity of the CD-ROM exaggerated into a communal affair with much of the *bonhomie* that that term implies.

No one knows exactly how many of us are using the Internet, much less exactly how many of us are using it to engage in or further our god-talk. But we are beginning to amass some facts that relate to both those questions. The first of these is the obvious one that there has been an exponential growth since early 1995 in use data themselves and presumably, therefore, in the Internet/ theology activity that renders them remarkable.

In August 1996 Nielsen Media Research reported that 25 percent of North Americans over sixteen years of age had Internet access. That translates to more than forty-eight million adults, with youngsters (assumed to be a proportionately higher number) uncounted.[19] It translates as well to a near doubling of users within less than twenty-four months. How many of those users came on-line in part so they could do god-talk we will never know. What we do know is that by late 1995 religion was one of the top three interest areas among American net users.[20]

In addition to surveying for users, we also can count with some accuracy the "hits" at selected religion sites as a way of suggesting, if not absolutely measuring, theology-on-the-net activity. For example, *Christianity Today*, both as a principal organization and as a journal of conservative Evangelical Protestant Christianity, has maintained a section on America Online (AOL) since 1994. In April 1996 alone, that site received over three-quarters of a million visitors, readers, and chat room conversers. Gospel

Communications Network, another Evangelical Protestant group, which operates several home pages directly on the World Wide Web for itself, logged 4.7 million visitors to its sites for the same four-week period.[21]

We can also count, as George Gallup did in May 1996, the number of religion/theology sites and references available on the Internet. Believing site/reference counts to be a more accurate gauge than user hit counts, Gallup's Princeton Religion Research Center staff further delimited their survey to the use of one and only one search engine, Lycos. The Gallup study found a veritable cornucopia of theological opportunities. The hit sites available within Lycos's reach alone range from "56,000 electronic places with the word 'god' in their descriptions" to the number of additional ones that are specific to the deities of particular world traditions (i.e., 5,700 to Vishnu and Shiva, 4,500 to Allah, 30,000 to Jesus, 8,900 to Moses, 5,000 to Buddha, etc.) to the number of sites specific to religious practice (i.e., 16,700 electronic places where prayer is discussed and 15,000 where worship is) and everything in between.[22] The effect of reading, let alone of trying to comprehend, a report like Gallup's Lycos tabulations is just short of intellectual exhaustion and emotional paralysis.

Lest someone — cowardly soul that he or she may be — take that exhaustion as an excuse and say, "Ah, ha! That is the point! There's too much ... so much that it won't matter ...," lest that relief be seized too quickly by the faint of heart, let me add one more figure, one that has to do as much with Gallup's findings about those religious praxis sites as about the theological ones.

The Barna Research Group, another of the country's most respected and most quoted demographic firms, is dedicated almost exclusively to tracking religion and god-talk in America. In July 1996 Barna released some "shocking" figures. Based on recently completed surveys, the firm predicted that "by 2010 C.E. somewhere between ten and twenty percent of all adult Americans will be having their *total* [emphasis Barna's] spiritual experience on the Internet," including not only their worship but their spiritual instruction.[23]

Why this is so becomes the immediate question. What is there about the Internet that attracts folk in the first place and, in the second place, what that attracts so many of us to it as the site of choice for god-talk? Oddly enough, there seem to be several apparent answers that, because of their very obviousness, obscure some other, and I think, more seductive ones. At the risk of being dismissed as a benighted romantic, I want to talk first about the poetry of the Internet, about that experience which ur-Woman and ur-Man would, I think, have declined to regard as being at all unusual.

We all — computer buffs and phobes alike — refer to the Internet geographically. We conceptualize it as "place," not as "thing." From the first this peculiarity has fascinated me. It has become ever more fascinating as I have listened to or read more and more television and print interviews with communications experts. Time after time, the experts will try initially to explain the Internet as a system. It is almost as if they have taken some kind of before-the-fact, professional vow that, by durn, they will do it right this time! But within one or two sentences, every one of them will relax back (with this enormous look of relief for those on camera) to surfing, lurking, hitting, chat-rooming, siting, highwaying, etc., etc., all of them about as locative and physical as any lexicon of terms ever gets.

Like it or not, the Internet is a place, and we all know it. We know as well, even those of us who aren't rocket scientists, that it is just as "experienceable" as the three-dimensional places our bodies travel in. Yet the two equally valid and perceivable places are different from one another; so we invent the rhetoric that recognizes their distinctiveness and call one "real" and the other "virtual." Of late, we have even expanded the former to "real-time" space as opposed to "virtual," an elaboration that I find to be even more confirming of my suspect romanticism.

"Real-time" exists on both sides of a computer screen. Just ask anybody who pays the provider charges on one each month or just look at the relentlessly present little clock in the lower margin of most screens. Time is there, but it doesn't "feel" like it's over there on that other side! In many ways, it's through-the-looking-glass time, and we all are Alice. Not only is the "time" in virtual space a big part of why the space is "virtual," but also it is very much like the time that existed in three-dimensional space before we became dissociated from that space and the earth-time it keeps.

Beyond the time (or, more correctly now that I've argued my case, the kind and perception of time) factor(s) lies the non-corporeal nature of virtual space's citizenry. Millions and millions of people are out there! More people than I ever, ever would have any hope of engaging otherwise. More people than I would ever, ever have any hope of picking and choosing friends from otherwise. More people than I would ever, ever have any hope of watching — "staring at," so to speak — or any hope of daring to be candid with otherwise. They're like angels or spirits or devils, all these ethereal people....

...Which is exactly how three-dimensional space once was populated for our species, and that is a mystery. In other words, while the technology of the place we call the Internet may remain a functional mystery to all save a chosen few of us, the rest of us could not care less. How Columbus charted the course and workings of the Santa Maria is a fine bit of esoterica that might interest us if we were all naval historians. For the moment, however, we are far too busy living in the world he opened up to care a fig about the particulars of how he got here or the theories about how he knew he could. Jim Barksdale and Bill Gates already stand in about the same place as Columbus does now, and they're both still alive and charting. What matters is not, in other words, the intricacies of accomplishment, but the mysterious place itself and the fellow creatures that are "in" it.

The Internet is not the Garden of Eden, and for all my talk of ur-folk, I don't mean to suggest that it is. I do mean to suggest, however, that virtual space is mysterious because it is essentially imaginary. It is, in fact, the only "place" where, like Alice, we can as adults actually, physically, be in our imaginations; and that is a mystery. I mean to suggest also that virtual space's culture is basically an oral one that depends on images and "conversation" rather than literacy as we have known it for the last five or six centuries. I mean also to suggest that, because of all these characteristics and properties, cyberspace is medieval, or it transports experience back to a perceptual paradigm that is medieval.[24]

For a people bereft of moorings, filled with nostalgia, driven by a sense that somewhere back in time we lost truth, sickened by consumerism, uprooted from natal beginnings and isolated from one another by schedules and fear, disillusioned about the worth of progress, persuaded of life beyond the reason's ... for such a people, what environment could possibly be more cordial than the one we have just described? And to the extent that god-talk is both the concern and the solution for many such people, what better place could ever be imagined for that conversation than the virtual one? And as if that weren't enough, there are some other things as well that further enhance the Internet's attraction for god-talkers.

A century and a half ago Sir Arthur Helps observed that "if you would understand your own age, read the works of fiction produced in it. People in disguise speak freely."[25] Little did Sir Arthur, who died in 1875, know about the freedom of true anonymity. He hadn't even met it yet. Anonymity's name is not fiction, but cyberspace. And with the anonymity of screen names that can be changed or multiplied at will, there is the anonymity of equally flexible autobiographies. Everyone in cyberspace is who he or she claims to be for as long as his or her claims can be sustained. The resulting "feel" is that of my childhood's closet — one of invulnerability and, more particularly, of emotional safety that flows into community with all the dreams and sorrows and histories that inform the place. And over and over again it is community that Internet god-talkers themselves cite as the reason for their own participation and for the swelling numbers of newcomers who are joining them.[26]

Dr. Dale Lature, whose area of academic expertise is electronic media as it relates to theology, expands upon these connections routinely in his writing and work, much of which — naturally — occurs on-line first.[27] Referring to what he calls a "validation" of his own legitimacy as a seeker from others on the Internet, Lature says, "I recognized a common journey [i.e., with other Internet god-talkers] and my own rightful place in articulating that journey.... [This] would not have happened in face-to-face gatherings because, for one thing, there were no such gatherings that could have taken place, and also because I would not have felt as uninhibited as I did in the pseudo-anonymity of on-line discussion."[28]

Lature is both ordained and a theolog, meaning that he by training and pastoral position should already have more than enough access to community and god-talk outside the academy. Yet he later adds that "the World Wide Web structure invites us to go out and seek our fellow sojourners on the path to truth and life."[29] Lature's recorded experience and his conclusions about it seem to be the norm rather than the exception across all the levels of theological expertise.

This is not to say, of course, that cyberspace does not have its detractors in this regard, men like Clifford Stoll, whose *Silicon Snake Oil* has become the bible of the nay-sayers. Stoll argues that computers and the Internet isolate us from one another, drying up our urge to engage each other face to face and substituting an unreal for a real sociality.[30] "I think not," says Lature. "It looks to me like people are flocking to on-line meetings due to a lack of such in their real, face-to-face, social lives."[31]

Regardless of which man's evaluation is correct, there's little question that the numbers are with Lature and that the communities are genuine relationships in the minds of their constituents. It doesn't take many visits out on the net, either, to discover the rich variety of experience available under the rubric of community. There's everything from literally thousands of prayer groups — sorted by faiths or by the nature of the need or by age and/or sex or by profession or by simple personality and natural affinity — to thousands of theological chat rooms sorted on pretty much the same bases to thousands of "official" sites established to inform the seeker and sustain the persuaded of a multitude of different faith systems — everything from Gallup's worship to Lature's socially empowered theologizing, in other words.

Undeniably, part of the appeal of the net for god-talkers is also the emotion of serious, timely, intellectual engagement. This is true not only of engaging people, but also of engaging texts. The CD-ROM, for example, has provided unprecedented access, as we have said, to core documents in theology and ecclesiology. Even more exciting, however, is what happens when the two forms of electronic text availability — the CD-ROM and the World Wide Web — are used in concert. Logos Research Systems[32] has pioneered in this, as in much other cutting-edge work in electronic religion texts.[33] Since mid-1995 users who already own the CD-ROM-based Logos Library System (LLS) of religion texts (users may select which of the many available texts they want by "unlocking" them) have been able to download off of the Internet additional Logos-readied texts, unlock them electronically, and insert them into their LLS, all without ever leaving the comfort of home or office. Yet even that wonder of ease, immediacy, and selection has paled before the hyperlink facility that Logos released a year later in mid-1996. With this capability, readers/users can "hit" hyperlinks or "hot-spots" embedded in their LLS CD-ROM texts and automatically link instantly to specific related Web pages. The two in tandem, in other words, provide previously unimagined timeliness and richness of sources with efficient integration of information and a maximum economy of effort and dollars.

For god-talkers, whose conversations presumably center on eternal issues, the notion that timeliness is important seems almost paradoxical. Mark Kellner, whose book *God on the Internet*[34] has become a kind of classic in the electronic god-talk business, is fond of citing, in this particular regard, a front-page story that *New York Times* religion reporter Gustav Niebuhr posted early in August 1996 entitled "Christians Split: Can Nonbelievers Be Saved?" It dealt with the Rev. Richard A. Rhem, an ordained cleric of many years in the Reformed Church of America and pastor of a thousand-member RCA church in Spring Lake, Michigan. Several weeks prior to the Niebuhr coverage, Rhem had been censured by a regional church authority for heresy, and Rhem's congregation had voted to secede from the RCA in loyalty to him. The pastor's "heresy" was in believing and teaching that, as he told Niebuhr, "the scope of God's mercy extends beyond the Christian community."

What is interesting to Kellner is not yet another controversy, of which we all have seen more than enough, but the fact that quite literally within a twenty-four-hour period copies of the story were glutting the Internet complete with cross-referencing to related church and doctrinal texts and events. (I gratuitously received several such postings myself, so I share some of Kellner's amazement.) Additionally, chat rooms — *informed* chat rooms — opened immediately to debate not only the issues, but the repercussions, the most judicious response, the proper support structure to be offered, prayer groups keeping vigil, etc., etc.

The Rhem affair, as it's now being called, was one of our first clear examples, and definitely our most dramatic one to date, of just how exponentially the Internet has increased response time and thoroughness of information in America's god-talk. It was an indication, as well, of just how quickly the myth of denominational integrity or isolation can be eroded in a global conversation.[35] One other thing that the Rhem affair did as well was to highlight the pleasure many god-talkers find in locking theological horns with their peers and their betters.

On the net and in the chat rooms with their noncorporealness and anonymity, somehow even the timid and apologetic seem free to challenge what they don't understand or, understanding, don't accept. Increasingly, clergy are discovering that the electronically able can instruct and pastor on the net with a directness and compassion (both giving and receiving, by the way) that do not always accrue to face-to-face or pulpit-to-pew encounters. Several seminaries are likewise noticing this phenomenon and offering Internet courses for all comers. They are reporting as well that the net classes are generally made up of both clergy and laity and that the conversation among the participants is far more "theological," instructive, and pastoral than is that between the participants and the electronic faculty.[36]

In the midst of such largess of opportunity and sources, it is sometimes hard to be temperate much less judicious, but the truth is that change, especially paradigmatic change, is almost always destructive of things as they are and of lives built on the old ways. This is especially true in matters of faith and belief where the deeply personal issues of identity and worldview and meaning all are tied directly to the systems undergoing the radical restructuring.

The Rhem affair, for example, showed us just how superficial as a loyalty denomination can be when the faith as a whole is opened up for general discussion. "I have concluded," observes Lature, speaking as an "Internet theologian," "that denominations are good for cooperative effort and economic backing for education, but deter us when they become buffers between members of the theological community that have common concerns and causes."[37]

Mark Kellner, from his position as authority on theology and the Internet certainly, but also as a student of communications history, sees the potential for this and even greater danger as unavoidable. Theology on the Internet, he says, can only "generate more and more schism" in all of America's faith systems.[38]

And Jay Kinney, publisher of *Gnosis,* a widely respected journal of mystical and esoteric spirituality and religions, is even more outspoken. "What strikes me," says Kinney, "is that it [i.e., the Internet] has the potential for taking interreligious dialogue and theological discussion out of the hands of the church hierarchy and the elites, and turning it into a street brawl."[39]

Strong words, especially from Kinney, but perhaps more dramatic than appropriate or applicable. A brawl is an amorphous explosion of discontent lacking cohesion among either its perpetrators or the goals toward which they move. Brawls, moreover, are the despair of the disenfranchised and an end unto themselves. Our streets, by contrast, are filled with the ever more broadly informed and, therefore, of the ever more deeply enfranchised theologically.

There is much talk recently in many quarters about reformation and much citing of Reformation with the "r" capitalized as the prototype for what we are presently passing through.[40] What must give us pause in such comments is the full knowledge that what ever else it was, the Reformation was a street brawl in real time, one that went beyond talk and destroyed lives as well as systems, one that for decades expunged unity and compassion as well as error from human experience.

None of us can actually conceive of the possibility that such upheaval might await us in the new millennium; but each of us can recognize that the circumstances of our technology and of institutional religion are indeed analogous to the ones that ignited the Reformation. We can, in other words, discern points of significant similarity between that catastrophic time and our own; and we can certainly learn to better respect our new conversational license because of the cautionary stories of history. To do less would be foolhardy; but to do more, it seems to me, would be to misread what's actually happening — to overlook or deny a process that goes to issues far deeper than an internecine conflagration, for that is exactly what the Reformation was. The Reformation was a family affair, a street brawl, and, finally as it escalated, a civil war. Our closing millennium is, interestingly enough, none of these.

Dr. Craig Dykstra is vice-president for religion at the Lilly Endowment, one of this country's largest funders of religious research. It is Dykstra's opinion, as it is that of most other observers, that we are indeed in a period of tumultuous change, but rather than run the danger of evoking more history than the facts will bear, he calls our situation one of "fundamental transformation." Ours, says Dykstra, "is the time between the times, a time of the boundary between a passing age and a new one not yet born."[41]

I like those words because they catch the mystery in which we stand; because they deny the possibility of an absolute parallel with what has been; because they suggest with hope that there is a kind of grandeur ahead of us and that we are involved here with something far beyond religion and yet totally entwined with it. Dykstra's words intimate what I too believe.

Nostalgic, home-sick and God-sick, empowered and informed and enfranchised, constantly in contact with one another, we are a new kind of god-talkers, the egalitarian ones the Reformation may legitimately claim as its kin but not as its progeny. And what we are at last doing, I think, is separating theology from formal religion from religious institution. I think also that the world will never be the same again once we're through. For that I both thank God and find the need to offer one last story as proof text.

Interlude

A<small>NY JOURNALIST</small> whose beat is covering an industry for a specialty publication will tell you very earnestly that the anathemas of the job are trade shows. They last too long — three to ten days, not to mention the prep and follow-up time that wraps each of them. They are too frenetic — eighteen-hour days of wall-to-wall (or stall-to-stall) product promotion. They are too many in number, yet a sizeable core of them are truly significant.

In the book industry, which I cover, "trade show" means the American Booksellers Association's annual convention, or the Christian Booksellers Association's EXPO, or the American Library Association's semi-annuals (not to be confused with the Public Library Association's), or the Religion Booksellers Trade Exhibit (not to be confused with innumerable shows for just Roman Catholic material alone), or the Christian Booksellers Association's International (always held in this country), or at least five major international shows that are never held in this country (the one in Frankfurt alone attracts over a million people and occupies nine buildings), or some ten regional bookseller association shows, state library shows, etc., etc., etc.

The list is probably impossible to list, come to think of it. It certainly is impossible to attend, even if one were willing in this day of laptops to live in a suitcase and never see the fires of home. So one cordons off the shows that look either possible or absolutely necessary each year and goes from there. It is an exercise in educated guessing that sometimes backfires, but that as a rule works surprisingly well. Despite all the hazards of a system that is on the face of it excessive and fundamentally intuitive, the hard news and pivotal ideas and accurate product assessments seem to rise to the top and make their way successfully into reportage. And usually most of us enter into that time of postshow wrap-up feeling pretty good about ourselves and the job that we've managed once more to pull off against all odds.

We also, truth told, usually feel pretty good about the experience of each show once it's in wrap. We've seen friends and colleagues, many of whom we see only at trade exhibitions. Always we've made some new contacts that will expand our network of information sources and outlets. And, let's face it, most of us are addicted to the rush of being the first to identify and broadcast a new idea or nugget of business gossip; and a good trade show can furnish an attentive journalist at least a half-dozen such heady thrills in half as many days.

But that's all professional or, if there is any distinction to be made, personal. Not by any stretch of the imagination could it be called spiritual. Not even in my clearly demarcated part of the world as a religion observer could a trade show ever be said to leave behind it some kind of spiritual residual per se. Every once in a great while, however, a show will offer up, almost gratuitously, a blinding moment of epiphany that will never appear in my coverage of the show, but that will forever after affect my private life. Certainly walking into the Pantheon was such an epiphany — or theophany. And I have had one other, far less dramatic, but equally formative trade show experience that is pertinent here. This one happened not as an aside to a show, however, but on the exhibition floor itself.

The Christian Booksellers Association — CBA, for short — is the professional organization of retailers who serve primarily

America's huge Protestant Christian population. Historically the greatest emphasis in product selection and market position for these merchants has been on Evangelical and conservative Protestant materials rather than on more general ones. Over the fifteen or so years that I have been covering the CBA shows, however, I have watched a gradual expansion of those narrow criteria to include more liberal and mainstream Protestant points of view and, most remarkable within the last few years, to incorporate more and more Roman Catholic and Orthodox Christian product and exhibitors. There have even been for quite some time several Jewish exhibitors, most of them from the ranks of converts to Christianity like the "Jews for Jesus" organization.

It is, therefore, no startling surprise anymore to see sales banners with Hebrew letters on them at a CBA trade show, no shock to look down an aisle and see a yarmulke ahead of me in the crowd, no real jolt even to pass a shofar or two propped against a display table as booth decoration. This dulling by previous exposure is the only reason I can offer for my having been on the floor of a recent CBA show for at least thirty minutes before it dawned on me that something new had been added.

Whether it was the bobbing knot of booksellers surrounding a display — they had their order blanks out and were writing, a gesture that always rivets my attention — or whether, as I would like to think, my journalistic instincts responded before my conscious mind did to the presence of discordant product, I can't say. I can say, however, that beyond the chattering, order-writing clump of seven or eight retailers crowding his booth, and more or less pinned to his own display wall by them, stood one genuinely confused Jew.

There was no question he was a Jew. Not only did he wear a yarmulke and the uncut beard of the Jew, but he wore as well the dark, keen-eyed, high-foreheaded face of the Jew. More than that, between him and his customers as well as hanging in multiples on the display racks behind him were the discordant product: *tallith,* prayer shawls! Prayer shawls like I had never seen before in my life, and certainly in far greater quantity.

Two or three of them were beautiful. I don't use that word very often, but in this case there is no other that conveys the kind of religio-aesthetic mix that was hanging in front of me, a combination of stunning material quality and excellent workmanship with a soft, almost humble, unity of parts with purpose. Some of the other talits were handsome, certainly, while the remainder ran the gamut from adequate to gaudy with one or two being something I could only describe as downright bizarre in decoration and material; but they all were Jewish prayer shawls. Of that there could be no question. They all had the head band, they all had the *shema* or a Hebrew prayer incorporated into them, they all had the *zizith,* or tassels, at their four corners. They all were right by the book, in other words. I was fascinated.

Fascination, however, was not enough to get me into that stall. Even if it had been, I would not have intruded. One of the first lessons one learns in my business is never to get between a man or woman and his or her customers at a trade show, not if you ever want to be welcome in that booth again. Instead I stepped back far enough so I could check the names and store addresses listed on the convention badge of each retailer who was placing an order. Sure enough, every one of them was from a CBA bookstore (I even knew one of them casually) and every one of those stores was a traditional and reasonably conservative one, so far as I could tell.

The happy but trapped Jew still pinioned against his wall looked up long enough to nod at me. I smiled back, shrugging my shoulders in a kind of "I-give-up-you-tell-me" gesture to which he tossed his head ever so slightly in a "come-back-later-and-I'll-tell-you" invitation. I went away.

I went away by about two aisles, in fact, before I passed another stall with a smaller crowd and a very definitely Asian exhibitor who was also selling talits, this time presumably ones of Taiwanese manufacture. But they still were prayer shawls, they still were Jewish, and they still were selling to Protestant Christian retailers. To make a long story short, I found a third stall of talits while I was biding my time, waiting for the first merchant to clear his booth so I could accept his invitation to talk. A colleague told me later that she had found a fourth booth, but I never went looking to confirm that. Instead I killed an hour and went back to my original sighting.

The floor itself was beginning to empty for lunch, and my Jewish exhibitor was perfunctorily straightening his stock when I returned. "Do you have a minute?" I asked him, and he laughed. I knew immediately from the laugh that we had read each other's body language accurately. "It beats me," he said in heavily accented English, and offered me a seat on one of the two stools behind his sales counter.

As our interview progressed, it turned out that his "It beats me" was not true at all. I have rarely talked to a more articulate — albeit in a second language — man, or to one with a more clearly defined history of just exactly what was going on and with whom. It was the why that bemused him.

What was going on, he told me, was the first industry-wide evidence of a phenomenon that had begun slowly in perhaps the early part of the mid-1990s. By 1995, it had grown to such proportions that his Tel Aviv-based company had moved him from Jerusalem to an office in this country to try to capitalize on the burgeoning market for talits among American Protestants, primarily among charismatic and fundamentalist ones. Moreover, he said, the sales for talits had developed a predictable sales pattern; they were peaking in the weeks before Easter, Pentecost, and Christmas with lesser but still demonstrable activity before Advent, Lent, and All Saints, in that order.

As for the reasons behind such an abrupt assumption of Jewish liturgical habit by Christians, my new source was very clear as well. The shift to Jewish prayer shawls was, he said, due to a number of very prominent and powerful preachers — he listed three in particular — who had begun to suggest, or perhaps insist, from their pulpits that their congregants begin the discipline of routinized, scheduled, deliberate prayer as a foundational spiritual practice. "And," he said, the eyes flashing now, "in their praying, these pastors are saying, the Christian peoples must do what their Jesus told them to do. They must 'enter into their closet when they pray.' The *tallith* the pastors are saying, are closets — that is, that Jesus was a Jew and the *tallit* was His closet. About this last I don't know, of course" — and he shrugged his shoulders.

I was stunned briefly in that distorting way that makes all the noise and activity around one arrest momentarily while the brain struggles to right itself from so unexpected an experience. I had come back to this stall expecting a good story certainly, but hardly an insightful one. Truth be told, the notion that Jesus' closet was a talit, while it may be bad etymology, is still brilliant exegesis.

The passage in question is one of the most familiar in Christian scripture. It comes from Matthew 6 and says:

And when you pray, you shall not be like the hypocrites. For they love to pray standing in the synagogues and on the corners of the streets, that they may be seen by men. Assuredly I say to you that they shall have their reward (v. 5). But you, when you pray, go into your closet, and when you have shut the door, pray to your Father who sees in secret; and your Father who sees in secret will reward you openly (v. 6).

The problem for me — the initial shock — was that I had never taken those words literally, or at least not as literally as one has to do to transpose a closet into a prayer shawl. And transposition had certainly taken place. For what it's worth — I went immediately and looked it up — the Greek original says "into your closet" as in "into your room" or "treasury" or "storehouse." No talits anywhere or even a suggestion of one, not that that fact is in any way relevant, because it truly is not. In fact, the farther in time I have gotten from my talit experience, the more I have come to appreciate just how irrelevant the matter of etymology really is in this particular instance.

The truth is that both the closet and prayer in it are directed in Christian scripture. They are taught first as the alternative to the ferocious sins and boredom of religiosity and second as the prescribed environment for the most central prayer of the Christian faith. Consider the closet passage in its entirety:

And when you pray, you shall not be like the hypocrites. For they love to pray standing in the synagogues and on the corners of the streets, that they may be seen by men. Assuredly I say to you that they shall have their reward (v. 5). But you, when you pray, go into your closet, and when you have shut the door, pray to your Father who sees in secret; and your Father who sees in secret will reward you openly (v. 6). And when you pray, do not use vain repetitions as the heathen do. For they think that they will be heard for their many words (v. 7). Therefore be not like them. For your Father knows the things you have need of before you ask Him (v. 8). In this manner therefore pray: Our Father, Who art in Heaven, hallowed be Thy name... (v. 9).

The most-beloved and most-used liturgical text in Christian practice pivots around a closet, in other words; and if in a time of standardized construction the place of that prayer must change from the privacy of irregular walls to the tenting of prayer shawls, it matters not at all. What matters is that the communion and petitions of each worshiper's faith first be solitary and that in their privacy of place these exercises of the individual heart stay ever mindful of their connectedness to the general principles of monotheistic faith: divine, familial love: *Our Father;* the assertion of belief: *Who art in heaven;* the use of reverence and awe: *Hallowed be Thy name;* the declaration of greater qualities; *Thy Kingdom come;* a readiness to submission: *Thy will be done on earth as it is in heaven;* the hope of expectant request: *Give us this day our daily bread;* the two-edged practice of a reciprocal and truly frightening repentance: *And forgive us our trespasses as we forgive those who have trespassed against us;* and the security of ecstatic praise:... *For Thine is the kingdom and power and the glory forever and ever. Amen.* Whatever happens after that *Amen* happens as a result of the whole.

Beyond the accommodation of some gifted pastors to changing ways, however, and far more commanding of my attention was another consideration. For me as for my merchant friend, the why of it all was the story's bemusing center. In a time of spiritual ferment and dwindling participation in organized religion, some of the most influential clergy of America's fastest growing religious subgroup — charismatic, pentecostal, fundamentalist Christianity — had begun to urge the most literal of all possible returns to solitary prayer as key to faith and spiritual understanding. Why?

Right on the face of things, it seemed to me as I left the show that day, such a position as the pastors' justifies more and more disestablishment of formal religion. It certainly encourages the decentralization of religion's institutions. It emphasizes the authority of the inner over the outer experience. By association, it substitutes theology for doctrine and accepts the private interpretation and/or extension of that theology as safe practice. In short, as a position the pastors' teaching on *tallith* and their referencing of it back to Matthew 6 were either incredibly foolhardy or absolutely prophetic. Either these men were trying to put themselves out of business or else they had seen and were preparing for a reformation in the role and definition of religion in America. And the more I have thought about the matter since, the more persuaded I have become that the latter is the case.

Eleven

With Constantly Changing Tools

═══   ═══

$\mathcal{M}$ANY HISTORIANS persuasively argue that the Great American Experiment could never have happened had it not been for the Reformation. The religious intolerance that followed the Reformation not only produced the persecuted who became our Founding Fathers; it also produced much of the emotional history that informed their sense of just exactly how social and cultural enlightenment should be applied to running a New World.

The dedication of powerful American rationalists like Jefferson and Madison, Franklin and Adams, to the principles of natural law, to Lockean economics, and to Rousseauean social theory approached the fanaticism of religious belief anyway. All of them products of their own intellectual age, these men and their influential contemporaries saw three things as immutable: rationality as the always-appropriate approach to assessing and deciding anything; the individual as the first and most inviolate unit of society; and a constitutional republic as the only defensible form of government for free people. From these things they fashioned the body and mind of a new political order. The spirit, however, arose from something a bit less cerebral than enlightened thought. It rose up from the blood of contemporary and near contemporary martyrs.

Woven inextricably into the daring new model and, as we now know, integral to its success was the right of every citizen to religious freedom and, by extension, to religious privacy. But while the privatizing of religion may have been born in North America and allowed to mature here, it had been conceived in Europe — in Geneva and Zurich, in Germany and Scotland, in Gunpowder Plots and Thirty Year Wars. The imperative forged in those experiences and then carried, like treasure, across an ocean was the absolute political disestablishment of any specific religion coupled with an almost theocratic assumption of its role as genius of the state.

In much the same way that religious Reformation enabled a Bill of Rights and a Constitution of These United States, so one can argue that our present religious upheaval would not be happening now had there been no 1776. Obviously the events of politics have created us as contemporary Americans, just as the Reformation created our early settlers. Far beyond that bit of the obvious, however, the Reformation-born tenet of absolute religious freedom and its sequela of inviolate religious privacy defined the range and rules of America's spiritual polity and — perhaps even more significantly — nurtured the diversity within which the current tumult is occurring and out of which it has come.

Because there can be for us no single paradigm, no established revelation, no official set of eternal verities . . . Because what we as a polity effect must be effected through constantly shifting "spiritual coalitions"[1] and fluid alliances . . . Because how we persuade each other and allow ourselves to be persuaded must be, first and foremost, rationally defensible . . . Because we hold the rights of the individual as a trust to be broached only under extraordinary circumstances and then only after considerable public debate involving more coalitions and shifting alliances...Because our history of sanctuary to the misused and downtrodden has been an actual as well as a theoretical one and because, even in our gravest violations of respect for human diversity we have managed to chastise and attempt to correct ourselves...Because of all our legacies of freedom and empowerment and the ironic restrictions they have laid upon us...Because of all these things and many more, we have come at the end of the twentieth century to the disruption of business as usual—or at least to the disruption of god-business as usual—in America. And that has ramifications for every other part of our life as a people.

Religion holds a group together. Next to blood and maybe even beyond it, religion has been within recorded history the great cohesive agent in life, the one around which to-the-death loyalties are formed. When differing peoples—even those of differing bloods—have shared a common religion, they have been one people. Specifically, they have been one in the irreducible, ineluctable way of those who hold as givens a common set of goals, a shared history and system of values evolved out of it, a reciprocal understanding about the meaning and purposes of living and of how to conduct it, and a unifying system of rituals and texts to validate experience and lift it up out of the banal and the prosaic. All of which really is to say that people are one when they share a sacred story. And so long as we Americans shared a story, things stayed more or less in equilibrium, even during those times when we had to tweak and tinker a bit with our labels.

At first, it was the Protestant Christian story that told us who we were, or who at least we should strive to be. But the susceptibility of our natal times to rationality and a pervasive intellectual enlightenment early added deism to Protestantism. Almost as quickly, European affairs added Roman Catholicism to our mix, so that the story we held in common had to become simply the Christian one. Americans were "a Christian people," we told ourselves and the world.

Then European affairs intruded again, and we became home to another story, one we recognized as part of ours and could therefore accommodate to. We became "a Judeo-Christian country" and were content with that term for the ties that bind us — content, that is, right up until modernity brought the acceleration that burst even that gracious label.

Latinos brought in ritual and a social history that made their liberating Christian story almost more distinct from mainstream Judeo-Christian practice than Christianity had originally been from Judaism. African Americans began the halting process of incorporation into America's mainstream, and the religious praxis they brought with them was likewise a "foreign" one, filled with experiential reinforcements and informed by a vastly different American and Christian spiritual and social history.

With the coming of a petroleum-based economy and global markets, Muslims became neighbors and business associates or just the folks down the street whose story was more difficult than Judaism's had been to integrate into our standard one. But eventually we became comfortable with seeing ourselves as "a monotheistic culture"; and some of us — more and more of us everyday, in fact — have even begun to be comfortable with referring to ourselves as "people of the Book" in honor of that small part of the story that is held in common.

The globalization first of wars and then of markets brought those of Asian heritage and descent among us and gave us thereby our first intimate association with nontheistic religion and our first tentative introduction to nonsectarian spirituality. At that point, the tensions patent in such diversity, accentuated by the active presence of the information glut and the social changes we have already looked at in detail, carried the day. There were no longer any labels big enough nor any more pretensions credible enough to fuse us. There was no longer a common story, except....

...Except, of course, that there was. It just wasn't in a specific religion any more, but in our dedication to the place of religion and religious practice in the well-ordered life, be that life private or public. We at last really did become (and have remained) by any set of definitions "a religious nation."

The result of social insistence upon religious observation in a political system of protected disestablishment is, as we Americans have known for decades, first of all the creation of a religion of the public square, that is, the establishment and continued evolution by consensus of the religious civilities of public and political life. The second, and currently far more pressing, result is an urgent, an almost undeniable, need on the part of every believer and would-be believer to determine his or her own place in the mix.

When privatized religion occurs in a time of cumulative literacy, democratized theology, and public religiosity, in other words, it must of necessity demand of its adherents answers to at least two pertinent questions: (1) just exactly what do *you* believe? and (2) how does that set of beliefs interact and interface with the beliefs that are operative in the culture at large? The pursuit of those questions and their answers are a work of "seek and ye shall find," and we became "a nation of seekers" in the process. But of those two questions that defined our search, the first one is a matter not of religion, but of the far greater issues of theology;[2] just as the commonality among seekers today is one not of shared story, but of intimate absorption with the variations of story.[3]

The notion that theology is different from, much less that it is greater than, religion is a fairly recent one in the long tale of history. Only within the last two hundred or so years probably would it have seemed reasonable to make either that separation or such a judgment. Historically theology — which basically was a Christian product in the first place, thereby making for it a fairly foreshortened history — would have been the doctrine of a religion, and religion would have been the realization of a theology.[4] That probably is no longer even perceived as half true by many, many Americans. Rather, religion is more often seen by most of us, when we are forced to think about the matter, as a particularized elaboration of some nebulous but very real, general, and universally applicable theology.

There is today, in other words, the tacit assumption of a universal set of theological possibilities that each expression of religion, be it a sect or denomination or broad tradition or just simply an individual struggling, comes in time to select from and then ritualize, hallow, and inculcate in ways peculiar to itself. A religion is defined, in this way of looking at things, by that part of the common pool from which it chooses to draw down and by the methods with which it chooses to do the drawing,[5] while theology as such is unchanged by the process. Thus, like a huge sow with many nursing piglets, theology is impervious to the variety of meals she is serving from one common menu.[6]

One of the immediate consequences of this way of seeing things is that "religion" ceases to denote an integer and becomes, instead, the uncomfortable and ill-fitting name for three very different things.[7] Clearly, "religion" can, and still does, denote the corporate embodiment and implementation by a group of people of a systematized doctrine that rests on sacred texts, claimed revelation, and transmitted history.[8] Used in this traditional context, however, "religion" now has an almost academic rather than a respectful or affectionate ring to it. The implication and tone of its use have subtly shifted to ones of dispassionate observation or critical assessment. The same principles of religious equality that have protected us have also militated this kind of impartial public representation. As a result, they seem as well to have instilled as matters of good manners and good sense a kind of emotional distancing or disengagement from the peculiarities of established doctrine and the specifics of denominational particularity.

Far more frequently, however, and even more pejoratively, "religion" also connotes a public agency[9] and, specifically, a useful and/or useable,[10] sociopolitical rather than a divine one.[11] Moreover, being publicly observant of a particular religion, under this rubric, becomes indecorous, if not downright suspect, conduct.[12]

By contrast "religion," if it would be socially acceptable, must connote, as it has indeed come to do among us,[13] an internal and spiritual praxis that is self-aware about its own beliefs and conventions as well as very candid and honest about its confusions — that prays in secret, if you will, and does not presume to reward itself openly. The proofs of faith, in this model, are perceived by the individual and observable to others in the moral generosity and grace of the life lived, not in the loudness by which belief is professed.

Established, public, and private religion all still exist,[14] then, but the one held in secret quietness has become the valid one, and closeted considerations of general theology have become its source. More specifically — and perhaps most cynically — theology has been marked off as the proper exercise ground for private rather than for public faith, the unspoken prejudice being that theology is too pure and potent a territory to be trampled by the sordid politics of public religion or of ordained and vested interests.

Inevitably of course, theology must come into direct contact with religion in all its connotations, not just its "pure" one of private faith. Just as surely, private faith in a democracy must eventually give rise to some public and some institutionalized effect, whether the individual citizen-believer wants that to be true or not. Interestingly enough, moreover, the area where all these things meet each other and interact we increasingly refer to as god-talk.

There is, as we have observed throughout this essay, a kind of leveling or benign irreverence in the colloquialism of "god-talk" as a term. That characteristic alone might be enough to make it more comfortable and appropriate than some others for describing conversations that stir politics and institutions and personal passions all together in one unholy mix. But there is in our selection of "god-talk" as the label of the day something else as well. There is a realization of a shift in our American way of seeing the life of the spirit and the nature of our unity.

"God-talk," with its lower-cased "g" and its flip insistence on conversation, disestablishes in two syllables the primacy of any one point of view and buys, at least temporarily, impunity from every hierarchy of authority. It abstracts in one brief utterance the whole range of possibilities inherent in theism and thereby suggests as well the possibilities of nontheism. It radiates a tolerance for and a cultural loyalty to holy or sacred search that have not been with us so intensely since the days of the Grail.[15] There is, in other words, in "god-talk" the kind of affection of usage and tenderness of approach that no longer accrue to "religion" or, if they ever did, to "theology." There is a coalescing peopleness, a unifying humanness, a connectedness that is, in and of itself, much of the bulk of the god-talk which the very term itself seeks to name.

We have looked in detail at the environment of this extended conversation we know as god-talk. It has been the purpose of this essay from the first to demonstrate that that environment is, in fact, our own quotidian one. We have looked as well at the conversants and recognized in those participants our ordinary selves, just as we have claimed their communal yearnings, history, and skills as our own dearly acquired ones. Lastly, we have looked, as it were, through these things and into the concepts and concerns that are the recurring themes and driving questions of the conversation itself.

Not all of these issues have been created equal, however, in the abundance of their spiritual concerns, in their historic uniqueness, in their relative urgency, or in their potential for precipitating change. Instead, some of them, emerging out of today's god-talk, seem in aggregate to be not only more substantial, but also downright prophetic, at least in terms of near time. It is these last chosen few that we still must summarize if we are to call our parsing honestly done.

— Twelve —

From One to Many
and Back Again

═══   ═══

*W*HATEVER ELSE IT IS, god-talk is first and foremost a folk
medley of hope in America, home of the hopeful. We can
say many things in summary about what our god-talk has become
and postulate with considerable equanimity several sound theories about what it is likely to become in our near future. Always,
however, we have to begin the discussion here, with hope. The
spiritual optimism that pervades our god-talk is its hallmark —
the belief that beyond morality and politics and social ills and
all distress there is the possible subjective life and that it is both
good and inalienable.

A fierce sense of community and a generosity of person as well
as of goods are and have increasingly become the *sine qua non*
for admission into serious god-talk.[1] So too the belief in family
and human affection as sacred duty, sacred privilege, and sacramentalizing opportunity are preexisting givens. A desire to move
toward simplicity and a need to ritualize the ordinary occupy and
will occupy much of the more practical portions of god-talk just
as a quiet demand for spiritual elegance and a sacred aesthetic

seem increasingly to be informing expectations at both an applied and a theoretical level.

Reverence and an unflinching tolerance for what others revere with a sworn unwillingness to discriminate (except for one's own private use) among all the honored options are dominant — if not *the* dominant — rules of conversational good manners in god-talk today in America. Side by side with them in the protocol of the game are two other icons of our new congress: an ever more militant demand for the clear-eyed, well-argued integration of faith with cutting-edge scholarship; and an inviolate respect in both faith and scholarship for mystery and its place in the human experience.[2]

Religion, the schizophrenic first cousin of faith, is less and less a part of god-talk these days and more and more a part of cerebral talk — a conversational element in the planning of the good society, the living of the good life, the creation and nurture of the good family. The traditional institutions of American religion — especially the Protestant Christian ones — began some time ago to accommodate to these changes[3] and to reconfigure themselves.

The parachurches like Youth for Christ, Young Life, or even ones like the Billy Graham Evangelistic Association and televangelism's 700 Clubs and PTLs, whatever else they are, are adaptive behavior at its shrewdest.[4] In much the same way, the megachurch — the Willow Creeks of today's suburbia — are incredibly astute and effective responses to what can only be called vividly postmodern, ahistoric[5] definitions by religion's constituency of what religion should be and must accomplish and has to provide.[6]

The old understanding of faith and religion as the two inseparable faces of Janus is gone, having become as antique as the old god himself and perhaps as faintly charming. Gone with the old gods as well are the old paradigms. Denominational religion and hierarchial religion give more ground every day to independent congregations and interdenominational community churches, even to interfaith ones.[7] And what is most obvious in its Christian expression by virtue of sheer numbers and volume is just as operative in other established faiths as well.[8]

The common denominator behind much of this readiness of realignment is the American conviction that private faith — which we have in such rich supply — must find corporate expression and communal exercise to be real. The interdenominational or even the interfaith union gives us a means through which to realize and effect the universal theology of hope, faith, and brotherhood that we hold however diversely in common. It worships and expresses and is active in the name of The God we reference as ground zero in our daily god-talk without requiring that any one of us declare, like Quakers in meeting, either the particulars or the certainty of God.

Those particulars and certainties — our privatized theology privately forged — may be shared, and are, in intimate conversation with trusted others or in deeply candid books or even in seminars, rallys, and retreats. What they may not be is systematized and dogmatized and organized for us by somebody else, except perhaps indirectly and then only by an exquisitely courteous sensibility. Most certainly they may not be — in fact, cannot credibly be — scrutinized for flaws or inconsistencies by those in a different divine/human relationship....

...Which ultimately is the definition of theology in our time. The divine/human relationship as perceived by the two participants and as a definition of both rather than one of them. A deeply private matter that is formed in the closets of life, that relationship may allow itself to be informed by systematized thought and shared experience just as it allows itself public exercise and enjoys its participation in god-talk. But faith in America today and the god-talk that is its most audible expression are still a constellation of millions of shining parts, each an integer in its own right and each the luminous guardian of its own light.

Notes

Chapter One: From Greece to Berkeley

1. Every time a discussion about any part of god-talk gets to this magic spot, somebody always blows a whistle and wants proof. Usually the whistle-blower is a moralist, I have discovered, but no matter. Neither I nor any other right-headed individual I know is contending that our behavior as a people evidences a consuming passion for the will and ways of God. Far from it. One of the defining characteristics of the religious experience in this country, as it is observed and reported by those of others nationalities, is our near complete separation of belief from action. More ink has been spent here than will allow for more. One of the most succinct and instructive summaries of these interrelated issues, however, may be found in Martin Marty's excellent commonplace newsletter, *Context*, February 15, 1996, 3, 4.

Professor Marty opens his overview by noting: "We citizens of the United States rank higher than those of other industrialized nations in almost all measurable measures of religious belief and practices. But...," and he proceeds to discuss George Gallup, Jr.'s, notion of the "three critical 'gaps' in America's religious experience": The Ethics Gap, The Knowledge Gap, and The Church Gap. The second of these, of course, speaks as well to my own, earlier point, namely, that of our theological innocence. Professor Marty defines The Knowledge Gap as "the often vast difference" discussed by Richard Morin in the *Washington Post Weekly Edition* (November 6–12, 1995) "between Americans' stated faith and their lack of the most basic knowledge about that faith."

Gallup himself updated these perceptions in his January 1996 issue of the Princeton Religion Research Center's *Emerging Trends*. Expressing amazement "at the low level of Bible knowledge" prevalent among Americans, Gallup concluded that "people's stated opinions don't always translate into behavior" in this country since "religion does not appear to be creating a more loving society. Something is wrong with the way religion is being practised. . . . People want the fruits of faith but not the obligations."

It would seem fair to say that nothing has changed appreciably in the time since either Gallup, Morin, or Marty made their respective assessments, except for the fact — the very encouraging fact — that Mr. Gallup seems to have arrived at a more positive possible interpretation of the data. Writing once more on the contradiction between Americans' claimed dedication to religious faith and our apparent moral breakdown as evidenced in our private and civil conduct, Gallup posits "two key reasons that could be offered as explanations for the religion/morality paradox" ("Levels of Religious Commitment," *Emerging Trends,* June 1996, 5). The first suggests that the American dedication may be a function more of breadth than of depth. The second is the telling one here: "A second explanation for the paradox," Gallup writes, "could be that religion is actually having a pronounced effect on the climate of morality, and that the situation would actually be worse if religious conviction on a significant level were not present in our society."

2. This restriction to America is an uncomfortable one for me in many ways. Space necessitates it, of course; and my own limitations probably would require it, even if space did not. What bothers me about such an unnaturally narrowed focus, however, is the fear that American readers may find implicit in what follows some sort of notion that what is happening in this country is, in real time, restricted to the American experience. Absolutely nothing could be farther from the truth. One of the most emphatic statements I've read lately was the opening paragraph of the May 27, 1996, issue of *Netfax* (the fax-only newsletter of Leadership Network): "We are living in the midst of two major shifts in human history. Both are not limited to the United States but are occurring world wide. One is the shift from the Industrial Age to the Information Age and the other is the shift from the modern to the postmodern world. Both shifts are 'in process' and one reason we are experiencing such dissonance and apparent chaos is that we are in the 'in-between' times."

This same point is being made over and over again by international observers as well. It was brought poignantly home to me most recently by Czech President Václav Havel when he argued that in the modern world as a whole we all have lost what he calls our "transcendental anchor" (as reported by Philip Berman, "Search for Meaning," *Chicago Tribune Magazine,* April 7, 1996, 22).

The other "restriction" here that wants commenting upon is that of theology itself. With this as with almost every other concept overviewed in this book, there is a complexity and subtlety of issues that far exceed the working requirements of a general understanding. That is to say that within academic scholarship there are very carefully drawn lines of demarcation between theology and religion, lines that blur in popular discourse and that I, for that very reason, will either blur or appear to ignore myself in the first few chapters of this book. That does not mean, however, that the distinctions are not exquisitely important and central to my thesis. It simply means that the argument I hope to develop here will expose gradually, rather than assume, the lines of distinction as part of its movement.

Chapter Two: In the World of Overload

1. Over the years, I have been singularly blessed by the guidance and generosity of media colleagues. It was, in this case, Kim Campbell of the *Christian Science Monitor* who suggested to me that many of the cultural factors to be discussed in this essay actually are "the environment of the conversation" that is god-talk. A former book editor for the *Monitor* and now working the religion beat, she holds a particularly compatible perspective, and I am grateful for her insights.

2. Before somebody rises up in protest, let me defend this last addition to my litany of literacy's sources that have theological impact. Chris Seay in addressing the "Gen X Forum," a significant conference of Christian church movers and shakers that was sponsored by Leadership Network in Colorado Springs March 7–9, 1996, made the point more emphatically than I ever could. "One-half of the music in CD stores talks about God now," he told that leadership group. "*Music is life to this generation* [emphasis his]. The world and this generation are desiring a dialogue with a church that won't listen. Be authentic . . . get away from manuscripts."

Far more than the Baby Busters generation is involved here, however. There is a growing crossover of traditionally "Christian" (i.e., Evangelical Protestant) pop music into the world of commercial audiences.

Christianity Today, in an article by Steve Rabey entitled "Pop Goes the Gospel" (May 15, 1995) used as the deck for the piece the words: "Contemporary Christian music secures an unprecedented secular market push" (15).

And not to argue the point to tedium, but one has to consider as well the lyrics of much of the "secular" radio fare so popular among office-working Boomers these days. Consider, for example, Joan Osbourne's "One of Us" that, at the time of this writing, seems to barrel out at me at every turn of the dial: "If God had a face, what would it look like and would you want to see, if seeing meant that you would have to believe?" Etc., etc., etc., every *e*, *t*, and *c* among them being a theology-laden squiggle.

One can of course also find superb overviews and musical bibliographies that address this subject in an objective, more commercially oriented way. See, for example, "Movin' to the Global Beat" by Paul Adams and the reviews following it in *Napra Re View*, June 1996, 96–127.

3. One of the more militant examples of exodus-with-religious-motivation away from the use of trained professionals is in the home-schooling movement. Gayle White, religion writer for the *Atlanta Journal-Constitution*, has estimated that by the end of 1997 the number of home-schooled children would approach two million. White cites the National Home Education Research Institute as saying that "religious reasons influenced some 85 percent" of those who are home-schooling. Those parents are also "likely to be fairly well-educated and middle-class." Contrary to popular perceptions, they will probably, but not necessarily, be Protestant Christian, since home-schooling groups presently exist for Jews, Muslims, Mormons, Roman Catholic Christians, and Unitarian Universalists as well (*Publishers Weekly*, July 15, 1996, 27ff.).

4. For a detailed discussion of the book as crib and cradle for ideas, see "It's All About Content" (*Publishers Weekly*, June 24, 1996, 28–30) in which giants of the American information and entertainment industry like Larry Kirshbaum of Time-Warner and Tom Dooley of Viacom talk with Jim Milliot about the book's unique role in our present society.

5. In all this cataloguing of commercial media, it is important to note that TV is probably the one that most successfully crosses back and forth over the lines that distinguish one medium from another and is the one that most nearly melds their various messages into a cultural or

social *zeitgeist*. For example, Tom Brokow, NBC's news anchor, turned the religion cover stories of *Time, Newsweek,* and *U.S. News and World Report* for Easter 1996 into a "Nightly News" commentary that lifted the stories from single pieces of coverage of a Christian holy time into the larger context of significant, interpretable event.

That shoe can fit the other foot as well, of course, as when in 1994, *T.V. Guide* created quite a flap by doing its own cover story on "Does TV News Snub God?" and drove the networks scurrying for broader and more responsible coverage. Admittedly as well, the present climate of concern with religion and spirituality has the kind of marketing and therefore economic ramifications for television that make such an article in a popular journal a smart, as well as a cautionary move. Peter Jennings, ABC's news anchor, recently told an audience at Harvard Divinity School that "I get more mail about religion than with any other subject we deal with" (as reported in "Peter Jennings Speaks at Harvard on Media and Religion," *Religion Newswriters Newsletter,* November–December 1995, 2).

Perhaps the most authoritative observer of TV's role as mixer and formulator, however, is Stephen Carter, William Nelson Cromwell Professor of Law at Yale University, frequently cited social critic, and author of such bestsellers as *The Culture of Disbelief* and *Integrity.* Carter is quoted in *Religion in Public Discourse: The Role of the Media* (Stewart M. Hoover, Principal Investigator, Center for Mass Media Research, University of Colorado, Boulder, 1994, 68) as having called TV "a major context in which religion is constructed in American life."

Nor is TV's melding into discernible *zeitgeist* confined to hard news coverage. In fact much of it, according to David Briggs of the Associated Press, occurs now within the context of TV dramas and so-called "faith-friendly" series like CBS's *Touched by an Angel* or *Promised Land* as well as in some of the medium's situation comedies (Briggs, "Prime Time Religion," Associated Press, May 6, 1995). One recent example of this latter and most unlikely phenomenon occurred on May 20, 1996, when another CBS product, *Dave's World,* aired a segment built entirely around the emotional issues (sometimes humorous in real-life as well) of faith as acted upon within the intimacy of an individual family. In urging church-going upon Dave, Beth (Mrs. Dave) at one point tells him that "we owe it [religious practice] to our children." She explains this position by saying that "faith is something that belongs just to me" and is, therefore, an inviolate gift and unmovable tool for later, adult living.

The case for the movies as theological sounding boards is even more obvious. In this regard, for example, see the discussion of *Pulp Fiction* in "Staring into the Heart of Darkness" by Ron Rosenbaum (*New York Times Magazine,* June 4, 1995, 44).

6. One of the great testimonies to the power of this medium and to its affinity for theological matters is not just the dramatic growth in the number of religion stories carried now in major secular magazines. The appearance within the last two or three years of so many successful "secular" (i.e., commercial) magazines with a "theological" focus must also be added to the mix. Consider, for instance, the stature of *Common Boundary* or *Body, Mind and Spirit* in this regard.

7. The use of "commercial" as a qualifier of media here is not an idle or capricious one. Stanley Hoover, longtime student and respected chronicler of the relationship between religion and the media in this country, is most explicit about the difference in public respect for commercial religion coverage and the coverage of the very same events and issues when carried in religiously owned or operated organs. Hoover has found that "a high percentage of newspaper readers expect religion coverage, and most do not turn to 'religious' sources for news which fits this interest" (*The Religious News Service–Lilly Study of Religion Reporting and Readership in the Daily Press* [School of Communications and Theatre, Temple University, 1989]).

Awareness of this public dependency is particularly keen at the moment within commercial newspaper circles as well. Ralph Langer, senior vice president and executive editor of the *Dallas Morning News,* told Michelle Bearden in a recent interview that "for us to not adequately cover religion is tantamount to not covering the Cowboys in the Dallas market" ("The Media Gets Religion," *American Journalism Review,* December 1995, 20.) And even among that most commercial of all commercial newspaper types, the tabloids, Ron Rosenbaum reports that "the great tabloid stories are the ones that raise theological questions" ("Staring into the Heart of Darkness," 36).

8. Here one caveat: Stanley Hoover has noted in *Religion in Public Discourse* (68) that while broadcast is the "most public, pervasive, and 'democratic' of all the media," it has had no tradition of religion news to parallel that which has long held sway at the nation's newspapers" (71).

9. Mark Jurkowitz of the *Boston Globe* in a very fine overview of increased media attention to, and incorporation of, religion calls our current level of frequency a "theological boomlet," which expression

seems to me to cover all the bases quite nicely (as run in the *Durham Herald-Sun*, April 27, 1996, B1).

10. Part of this supremacy has to do with more than just the importance of books as motherlode or even as market indicators in and of themselves. It has to do with the greater, relative objectivity of sales figures and sales patterns as opposed to narrative answers given by respondents to demographers and questionnaires. Mark Chaves, a professor of sociology at the University of Notre Dame, summarized this disparity for the *Atlanta Journal-Constitution* (January 21, 1995, E-6). Remarking upon a study that he and fellow professor James Cavendish had just completed of the overreportage discrepancy between how many Roman Catholics told a 1991 Gallup survey that they attended weekly Mass and how many actually did attend as documented by church registries, Chaves observed, "I don't think it means people are liars. It's a well-known phenomenon in survey research that people overreport what they think is socially desirable behavior." It is a universal weakness, and nowhere more so than in dealing with religion.

Having shared that unavoidable caveat, however, does not mean and should not be taken as meaning that I or any other observer of the scene could ever read the landscape with any accuracy on the basis of any one form of assessment alone. It simply means that all available indicators of human activity — sales figures, audience patterns, survey answers, sociological studies, narrative observations — all of them, taken together, keep each other honest. Each compensates in some way for the limitations of the others. In that vein, this seems as good a place as any for a little aside, not about statistical research in religion, but about the human beings who do it.

While George Gallup, Jr., certainly needs no encomium from me, I do think his story is an illuminating one and probably fairly representative of the motivation that informs the field. Over one summer, just prior to his beginning formal study for the Episcopal priesthood, the young Gallup came to realize, he says, "that research (my father's field) gave me much of what I was looking for in the ministry. . . . It could give voice to the voiceless." And thus he chose, rather at the eleventh hour, to enter demography instead of the priesthood as a career.

Disagreeing with the position that religion, being a private matter, should be kept private and never be scrutinized as an aggregate, Gallup gives three reasons for what he does as America's premier demographer of religion. The first is sociological: "The spiritual or religious element in American life is a key determinant in our behavior. ... If you want to understand our society, you need to understand the religious dynamic." The second is practical: "If ministers want to minister to people, they need to know what the challenges are, what they have to do. Surveys can help." And the third is religious: "If there is a God looking over us, and I believe there is, then to bring us closer to God, we should do everything possible to examine the relationship between God and humankind" (taken from a chapter by George Gallup, Jr., in *Empowering Your Church through Creativity and Change: Thirty Strategies to Transform Your Ministry*, Marshall Shelley, ed. [Moorings, 1995]).

11. As contributing editor in religion to *Publishers Weekly*, the international journal of the book industry, and as editor-at-large to *Publishers Weekly's Religion Bookline*, I deal every day of my professional life with religion books and the religion sections and/or implications of other books not specifically about religion as such.

12. This is a fairly broad assertion on my part, I realize. I have already argued it at length, however, in *Re-Discovering the Sacred: Spirituality in America* (Crossroad, 1995) and don't wish to bore my readers by repeating those validations. Suffice it to note just a point or two here, referring interested readers to *Re-Discovering* for further discussion:

According to *American Bookseller*, the professional journal of America's retail book trade, Baker and Taylor, the country's largest distributor of books to libraries, reported a 96 percent increase from 1990 to 1991 in sales of books from their top religion publishers (Sandee Brawarsky, "Getting Religion: The Market for Books Exploring a Variety of Faiths Continues to Grow," June 1992, 26). So far as I know, that was the first "hard" (i.e., quantified), in-print report of what many industry observers had been sure of for three or four years — i.e., the strong resurgence of public interest in religion.

Shortly after the *Bookseller* report, Pat Peterson, at that time head buyer for the Barbara's Books in Chicago, offered Lynn Garrett, *P.W.*'s religion editor, her own analysis of why books seem to be the best barometer in religion. Calling the increase in sales of religion books "a natural consequence" of cultural shifts, Peterson explained that "fewer people are affiliated with formal religion, so they don't have a place to turn for help, and they go to the bookstore." I must have heard that same explanation, or some variation on it, a thousand times from booksellers and librarians in the four years since Ms. Peterson first articulated it.

Perhaps, however, Mary B. W. Tabor, columnist for the *New York Times*, really gave the most all-encompassing explanation when she chose the historical one. Tabor opened her July 31, 1995, feature "Of Grace, Damnation and Best Sellers" in the *Times* by saying: "For as long as humans have written, they have been publishing works (stone tablets, books, CD-ROM's) that wrestle with the notions of Good and Evil, and man's efforts to forge a spiritual life between the two."

Chapter Three: From "Who Is Man?" to "Who Am I?"

1. This newest generation of adult Americans is checking in at 41 million strong. Technically composed of those born between 1965 and 1980, the Busters are also referred to as Generation X, 13th. Gen, The Repair Generation, Gen-Xers, Twenty-Somethings, The Free Generation, and/or The Confused Generation. By whatever label, they are just now emerging into fully enfranchised adulthood, and their impact on society in general and on theology in particular will be enormous.

Like every human generation, Busters most condemn and seek escape from the defining characteristics and habits of the immediately preceding generation that bore them, in this case, the Boomers. As a principle of human behavior, quiet rebellion is already impacting their approach to religion. Thus, for example, two Busters out of three told a 1996 Gallup poll that they expect to be more religious than their parents; and approximately four in ten were confident that they will spend more time than their parents have in helping others (*Emerging Trends*, April 1996, 3).

Since the chemistry of generational conflict has always been notoriously unstable and explosive, there's every reason to assume that it will remain so, of course. But of this, more later. Suffice it to note here that Dieter Zander, an authority on Busters and Buster theology, probably said it best when, in his own low-key way, he noted that "being a buster is more attitude than age" ("The Gospel for Generation X, *Next*, May 1, 1995, 3).

2. Acceptance, as a working premise, of an unprecedented religious ferment abroad in the world today is one of those underlying assumptions that I mentioned earlier. It is, however, so central as underpinning to the concerns of this book that a sampling of the validation available beyond my own assertion might not be amiss.

For example, writer Philip Berman (*The Search for Meaning, Journey Home*) in his popular-press essay for the *Chicago Tribune Magazine* entitled "Search for Meaning—Why the Pursuit of Happiness Has Not Made Us Happy" begins his commentary by saying, "we are in the midst of a massive spiritual and religious revival" (April 7, 1996, 21.)

Or consider this from an academic essay entitled "The Bible in Public Discourse." The writer is Richard Lovelace, professor of church history at the highly conservative Evangelical Christian Gordon-Conwell Theological Seminary, who pretty much nails the matter down by saying, "Any political landscape with this much God-talk going on may be divided, but it is religiously alive. In fact, I would suggest that we are in the midst of a bull market in religion" (in *Christianity and Civil Society*, ed. Rodney L. Petersen [Orbis Books, 1995], 69).

Just as an aside, the economic metaphor of the bull market seems to be fairly pervasive in describing the current state of religion and theology in this country. Thus Gallup opened the March 1996 issue of *Emerging Trends* published by the Princeton Religion Research Center with the words: "The Dow-Jones Industrial Average isn't the only index that is bullish: The final figures are in for last year and show that organized religion in America is at a ten-year high mark."

Literally dozens of similar (though perhaps less colorful) observations arriving at the same conclusion are on the record and range along the whole spectrum that stretches from academic and professional to popular and lay sources.

3. The "sixty years" parameter was nicely memorialized in 1996 by *Life* magazine when it ran a celebratory series of retrospective collections called "*Life*—60 Years." The photo-essay for July 1996 (76–80), prepared by Eleanor N. Schwartz, opened with the words: "Few subjects have captured *Life*'s attention so keenly as religion. Man's infinite forms of worship and the rites by which he has sought divine intervention have inspired many of our photographic essays over the years." What follows after that is very arresting and well worth taking time out to look up and ponder, if one has not already done so.

4. This is not a condemnation, nor even a pejorative description, of the shift that has taken place. Far from it. I personally have become increasingly convinced of the so-called "holiness of information" premise that welcomes as divine gift and far future the obvious burgeoning of cognitive powers and resources in our time. While many able men and women are presently working and writing about information the-

ory, George Johnson's *Fire in the Mind: Science, Faith and the Search for Order* (Knopf, 1995) stands out in my recently read bibliography as the most reverent yet hard-nosed and "informed" presentation of information as entity. Johnson, who is science writer for the *New York Times,* grew up and now lives in New Mexico, where the combination of nuclear facilities like Los Alamos, of the Tewa pueblo, of this country's oldest Roman Catholicism, and of the Santa Fe Institute think-tank has lent him an exquisite sensitivity to the poetry as well as the neutral brawn of information.

5. The fact that for the sake of brevity I have limited my comments to the "new" disciplines does not mean that I can thereby hope to include even all of them, but rather only a few of the major ones. By "major," I mean those that seem to me to have been the most obviously formative ones in terms of our presently emerging theology. Nor does the fact that I have chosen to deal *only* with "new" mean that new theories in older, established disciplines — as, say for example, in literary theory and criticism — have not also impacted postmodern theology and religion. They have. But they have also usually continued to appear as ongoing extensions of their respective originating matrices rather than as discrete new members of the academic and theoretical world. Perhaps as a result of this as much as of any other factor, their impact has not, however, been as wrenching, formative, discrete, or visible and seemed to me, therefore, to lie beyond the limited scope of a condensed overview like this one.

6. Basic Books, 1981.

7. Little, Brown, 1991.

8. Oxford University Press, 1989.

9. Basic Books, 1992.

10. Simon & Schuster, 1994.

11. At times they've also seemed to be miles apart in their respect for each other's methods and conclusions as well, but that is a different matter.

12. Fools, as we all know, rush in where angels fear to tread, a maxim never more wisely employed than in dealing with the wily Descartes. Readers may want to look at some of his other "errors" in a relatively recent study of them by the same name, Antonio R. Damasio, *Descartes' Error: Emotion, Reason, and the Human Brain* (Grosset/Putnam, 1994).

It's important as well to remember how many times Descartes has stood his ground against the jeering years and been found right. His insistence that images come into our eyes upside down and are converted to right side up by the brain got him in hot water for a while. His equally bizarre notion that we see because the universe is filled with an intangible, ubiquitous substance (which he called *plenum*) that presses in upon all of us and along which light travels in order to arrive at and enter our eyes was laughed out of court for three and a half centuries. Only recently has physics begun to reconsider not the *plenum* part, which remains patently absurd to us, but the "pressing" part of the Cartesian theories of vision.

13. There are sure signs everywhere, of course, that we are feeling significant pain over the loss of this particular piece of Cartesian assurance, but the morning I was actually writing this section on Descartes, the mail brought me an especially amusing additional example. In that mail I received the new sales catalog for Plough Press, the book publishing arm of the Bruderhof Communities. The front cover of Plough's catalog was not filled with images of books, as one normally expects, but with huge graphics that read "We Are What We Think" and then added in highlighted type: "About." In these days since Schrodinger's cat, Descartes would have found the subtlety of that adjustment quite delicious, I suspect.

14. For an absolutely exquisite example both of how subtly pervasive these ideas are, especially in periodical presentation, and of how almost unavoidable, see *Time*'s cover story for March 25, 1996, "Can Machines Think?" by Robert Wright (50–56). But see particularly the sidebar of that story (55) by Garry Kasparov, whom *Time* heralds as "*still* [emphasis mine] the chess champion of the world" after his fearsome but successful contest with "Big Blue" or, if you prefer, IBM's top-of-the-line computer. Kasparov's sidebar title would make even the most stalwart a little bit queasy: "The Day That I Sensed a New Kind of Intelligence." More sober-sided and far more direct about its own repercussions is Julian Dibbell's "The Race to Build Intelligent Machines" (56–58) of the same issue. There the boxed flag for Dibbell's article reads: "Two Approaches, Top Down and Bottom Up, Represent an Almost Theological Schism in Computer Science." "Almost" seems to be the only possible exaggeration in those words.

15. Nor is this any great surprise to the general reader of popular books in the mind sciences or to their writers. Both groups were, from the beginning, aware of just how closely many of the ideas in these studies cut over toward the business of God. A cursory look at the books'

titles and subtitles exposes that relationship very quickly. Consider, for example, MIT's 1995 release by Paul Churchland, *The Engine of Reason, The Seat of the Soul: A Philosophical Journey into the Brain.* Or look at the subtitle of Hofstadter and Dennett's broadly popular *The Mind's I,* which was reissued in paperback by Bantam Books, serialized in *Book Digest,* and chosen as a selection for three book clubs including Book-of-the-Month Club: *The Mind's I: Fantasies and Reflections on Self and Soul.* Or how about Crick's *Astonishing Hypothesis,* reissued in paperback in 1995 by Touchstone and subtitled *The Scientific Search for the Soul,* etc., etc.

16. This figure, which is consistent with other surveys, is drawn from *Emerging Trends,* March 1996, 2: "Belief in God or a universal spirit is unusually high in America, with levels of belief ranging from 94 percent to 99 percent over the past five decades. Currently 96 percent of Americans say they are believers."

Chapter Four: Out of the Mouths of Physicists into the Ears of God

1. One of the most dramatic, as well as cogently argued, examples of this coming together of personedness and agency is to be found on pages 154–55 of Frank Tipler, *The Physics of Immortality* (Doubleday, 1994). I look at Tipler and his Omega Point theory within the text that follows. Suffice it to say here, therefore, that Tipler concludes this portion of his thesis by saying: "The Omega Point in Its immanence counts as a Person."

2. As we will see shortly, some of these god-talkers are professional scientists, some are professional theologians, most are just informed members of neither camp. Indeed, it is in public places like the Internet that I have chanced upon some of the most clear-eyed but effecting mini-essays on the god(s)-problem currently being written.

I think immediately of a public meeting on Ecunet during 1995 and 1996 entitled "Science, Monotheism and Religion." My best guess as a "lurker" was that everybody participating on-line was in the "informed laity" category, but it was the burden of the discussion that most held my attention for the weeks that I eavesdropped. The principal and recurring concern was with the way in which social consciousness forms and is formed by structures. Would it, for instance, be possible to conceive of a unified theory of everything in a nonmonotheistic worldview? Would a Western-born unified theory be capable culturally of polytheistic corollaries? Does not the suppression of many possibilities in favor of a centralizing unity in religion (monotheism), in politics (king, emperor, pope, head of state) and in science (order, GUT) create fascism (...or did it not create the fascism of our history?), etc., etc.

These are sophisticated questions; and while I have reiterated them, I have not in any way conveyed the detail of bibliographic referencing that accompanied the arguments. This was not a battle of untrained foot soldiers. It was, instead, deadly serious and absolutely self-conscious.

The bulk of the truly brilliant, sustained god-talk as it relates to the "new" sciences (our focus *du jour* in this chapter) is going on in books, however; but we must note that not all of it is in books that lie within the parameters of the secular marketplace and therefore within the scope of this study's central text. These books are themselves "new" in that they are just now emerging as a major subcategory of religion publishing.

Produced by religion publishing houses, especially by those from within the Christian tradition, and written by believing professionals for marketing primarily through religion stores or direct sales mechanisms to religion professionals and/or believing laity, these books are not designed for broad popular appeal. Rather, their purpose is to inform and/or help theologians inform the faithful about the unavoidable interchange of concepts between the new physics and traditional or classical theology. There are several bibliographies now available of the recent books that have most impacted theology and/or dealt most directly with the interface between the two fields of science and theology. One of the most comprehensive and useful is "Science and Religion Meet across the Great Divide: New Books Forge Links between the Scientific and the Theological" by Henry Carrigan in *Publishers Weekly's Religion Bookline,* April 15, 1996, 2, 3.

As Dr. Carrington indicates in his bibliographic overview, a number of religion publishers have also initiated "science and theology" book programs designed specifically for their own clergy and theologians as continuing education tools as those professionals try to deal with the cacophony of too many hypotheses doing battle with too many traditions. A particularly excellent example of this kind of program, should the reader want to try a sample, may be found in the "Theology and the Sciences" series, Kevin Sharpe, series editor, of Fortress Press, which is the professional publishing arm of the Evangelical Lutheran Church in America.

And one further note might be added here, in that academic or university presses have from time to time made significant contributions to this area in popular or fairly wide-ranging ways. One thinks, in this regard, for example, of Fr. John Polkinghorne's 1993 Gifford Lectures, which were published by Princeton University Press in 1994 as *The Faith of a Physicist* and have had a broad theological effect in recent time, albeit with a fairly select readership.

3. The blurring, we must remember, can be very beneficial to all parties. My own favorite expression of this is St. Augustine's very personal one: "O God, help me to believe more so that I may understand more."

4. To maintain a balanced picture of our particular time in history, we need to stay mindful of this continuous interdisciplinary activity that characterizes it. For example, it was Roger Penrose, whom we treated in chapter 3 with reference to his work in the field of human mentation, who partnered with Stephen Hawking in developing the theory of singularity on which so much of our present understanding of everything from black holes and anti-matter to Hawking's history of time depends. Hawking and Penrose, by the way, have yet another collaborative effort recently out in this same window, *The Nature of Space and Time* (Princeton University Press, 1996).

But lest we think that this kind of interdisciplinary crossover is peculiar to our time rather than to the highly creative mind, we should remember that, for instance, René Descartes was, first and foremost, one of the West's most brilliant physicists. He and his peers called their field of expertise "natural philosophy," however, a charming but telling indication of just how tied their time still was to discursive investigation over demonstrable experimentation.

5. Carl Sagan, one of the best-loved of the early popularizers of science, reflects on this ongoing process in his newest work, *The Demon-Haunted World: Science as a Candle in the Dark* (Random House, 1996) when he writes of science as "a profound source of spirituality" because its revelations of "the intricacy, beauty and subtlety of life" lead to "that soaring feeling, that sense of elation and humility combined" that for Sagan is indeed "spiritual."

6. From time to time, it's necessary to keep one's sense of perspective lest one fall off these dizzying heights. In 1992 HarperCollins published a book by Gerhard Staguhn, *God's Laughter: Physics, Religion and the*

Cosmos. While the book was a fine piece of work — it was reissued
in trade paperback in 1995 by Kodansha — its title is my reason for
mentioning it just here. There is an old Jewish proverb which holds that
God laughs every time humans think. There is a contemporary corollary
that says God has laughed to the point of divine soreness of late.

7. My emphasis here on Buddhism is not intended as a slight of any
of the other great faith traditions coming to us from the Far East. The
simple fact is that Buddhism is the most visible of those traditions in
this country, because for largely geopolitical reasons it has the greatest
number of followers resident within our shores.

The Eastern tradition with the second largest number of American
followers is, of course, Hinduism, which has influenced contemporary
god-talk, but in less profuse ways. Hinduism in general and some of its
practices and doctrines, like yoga and reincarnation in particular, have
fired the American religious imagination by giving it a new vocabulary
of possibilities and symbols as well as a new regimen of physical disciplines. Few books, for example, have had greater impact on popular
theology than Paramahansa Yogananda's *Autobiography of a Yogi* (Self-
Realization Fellowship) that was first published here in 1946 and has
maintained steady sales ever since.

The restricting problem seems to be that Hinduism with its many
avatars can hardly be called an "unpersonned" theology. As a result,
it both clashes with our popular predisposition toward monotheism
and fails to offer any useful insights into the "more spiritual" (i.e.,
less personned) supreme being whom more and more Americans seem
increasingly to envision when they say the word "god."

8. The ability to see process as an agency of God and therefore as
a source of further awe and wonder is not given to all. The very implication of "mindless process" is indeed the offense of Darwinism for
many conservative Americans. I have rarely found a clearer or more
even recital of that offense than that which Alvin Plantinga published
in *Books and Culture* (May/June 1996 issue).

In an extended essay entitled "Dennett's Dangerous Idea" and based
on Dennett's new book, *Darwin's Dangerous Idea: Evolution and the
Meanings of Life* (Simon & Schuster, 1996), Plantinga writes: "Darwin's dangerous idea, says Dennett, is really the idea that the living
world with all of its beauty...was not created by God or anything at
all like God, but produced by blind, unconscious, mechanical, algorith-
mic processes.... The idea is that mind, intelligence, foresight, planning,

design are all latecomers in the universe, themselves created by the mindless process of natural selection." Having established the problem, Plantinga first notes that Dennett regards it as dangerous "because if we accept it, we are forced to reconsider all our childhood and childish ideas about God" and then counters from the Christian perspective by saying, "Christians, of course, believe that God has always existed; so mind has always existed, and was involved in the production and planning of whatever there is" (16).

9. Tipler's earlier book, *The Antropic Cosmological Principle* (Oxford, 1986), coauthored with John D. Barrow, a British astrophysicist, also received strong critical endorsements from his fellow professionals as well as from appreciative lay readers.

10. October 1994, 89–109. See as well the Tipler interview in *D Magazine,* where Tipler is, if anything, even more specific in stating his at times idiosyncratic definitions of some theological terms.

11. The term "Omega Point" is, fittingly enough, taken from the work of a theologian who was also a paleontologist, Pierre Teilhard de Chardin. A Jesuit priest trained in physical science, Teilhard began in the 1920s to lecture on evolution as it impacted on Roman Catholicism. Unfortunately, his superiors were having none of it or of him, and he was "exiled" by the Jesuits first to China and later to the U.S., where he died in 1955. Teilhard's greatest work — again, enormously popular — was *The Phenomenon of Man,* posthumously published but composed in or around the late 1930s. The Omega Point, for Fr. Teilhard, was the far future, the place/time into which All Knowing will coalesce, a naming that plays to the "I am the Alpha and Omega" of John's book of Revelation, of course, and that correctly reflects the mystical, poetic tone (as opposed to factual and experimentally supported) of *Phenomenon.* What Tipler has done is attempt to correct that perceived imbalance by applying cutting-edge math and physics to Teilhard's poetry.

12. This is a slight exaggeration on my part. Part of the success in a broad market of *Immorality* is that Tipler uses only 340 pages of text to present in what he gently regards as "general terms" the supporting ideas of his theory of far future. Pages 341–95 of *Immortality* are the supporting notes for that text. The remaining 122 pages are entitled "Appendix for Scientists" and offer the trained professional a far more specific and explicit look at Tipler's formulae.

13. It must be noted here that not everyone — theologian, scientist, layperson — is going to agree with Tipler's use of theological terms or

his implied definitions of many of them. The operative factor here is that Tipler is articulating a synthesis that involves new definitions and new applications,...that is, in short, impacting theology by denying part of its traditional sense of itself.

14. *Immortality*, 109.

15. Of this company, I am the first and leading case in point. The significant thing, however — and I must say so again and again — is not so much whether or not lay readers understand the intricacies or the proofs of the science presented, but that the very asking of these questions and the presentation of their often disparate conclusions is what is impacting popular understanding. The problem with this — actually, there are several problems, so better to say: the immediately apparent and powerful problem with this — is that being equally as naive in theology as in the sciences, most of us are rudderless in both oceans.

Neither science nor theology uncovers its principles by means of majority vote, yet almost all Americans feel compelled to vote at least about the latter, if not the former. It is a dangerous situation, but it is also one filled with private angst for seekers after spiritual truth and religious validity. Perhaps it is my awareness of the angst, more than anything else, that has driven me to write this book.

16. In all this talk of "new" disciplines we must not forget the ongoing attraction for the American public of some of the older "new" sciences. Evolution and Darwinism, for example, have surely never lagged for a moment in their role as objects of book-length fascination; and one of the surprise "hits" of late 1995 for the book world was David Berlinski's *A Tour of the Calculus* (Pantheon, 1995) that took off to both critical acclaim and popular sales.

17. Stephen Hawking's incredible resiliency and productivity as well as his tenacity enhance this public stature. One compelling proof of the presence of all three qualities is the fact that in addition to his 1996 book with Penrose, Hawking also published in November 1996 *The Illustrated 'A Brief History of Time'* (Bantam, 1966). There were at least two reasons for this. First the original *Brief History* has sold over nine million copies since it was first issued by Bantam in 1988; and second, Hawking wanted to add a new introduction and update the book's treatment of wormholes and time travel to conform with our more recent knowledge.

18. This situation began to change dramatically for the mind sciences after Oliver Sachs's books began to people the field with sympathetic

protagonists. There has followed a whole catalog of first-hand accounts by patients and sufferers whom the mind sciences have both studied and helped. This new subcategory of books has become so sizeable and successful, in fact, that in March 1996 a review in the *New York Times Book Review* assigned it a label. Such books are now called "autopathographies," though one hopes with some bit of tongue in cheek.

19. Books, in particular, have been an especially cordial medium of transmission. An extended list of the successful (if by that term one means, as I do, solid penetration of the market as well as outright bestsellers) popular books in the new physics and mathematics would itself constitute a small book. For our purposes, a cursory glance at only a few of them and the theological questions they raise will suffice as exemplary of three possible authorial approaches. N.B.: A more detailed overview of several dozen of these books, particularly of those with the greatest implication for theology, may be found in "The New Religion/ Science Dialogue" by Henry Carrigan, *Publishers Weekly*, June 2, 1995, 25–27.]

Almost as spectacular as Frank Tipler in terms of public attention is John Gribbin. An astrophysicist by trade, Gribbin is a bestseller in every sense (*In Search of the Big Bang* [Bantam, 1986], *In Search of the Edge of Time* [Harmony, 1992], *In the Beginning* [Little, Brown, 1993], and with his wife Mary, *Time and Space* [Dorling Kindersley, 1994]). But it was not until his 1984 now-classic *In Search of Schrodinger's Cat* (Black Swan, London, and Bantam Books, New York) that Gribbin's popularizing studies began to visibly impact theology. Then in 1995 from Little, Brown came Gribbin's sequel, *Schrodinger's Kittens and the Search for Reality: Solving the Quantum Mysteries*.

Kittens is one of the, if not the, clearest, most detailed, and most daring explications to date of superstring theory for a popular readership. Like Tipler, Gribbin divides his text to admit two levels — lay and professional — of proof comprehension; and like Tipler he is not the heralded darling of all of his fellow scientists. Unlike Tipler, however, Gribbin is not arguing his own theories. Rather, he writes as a beautifully informed and totally at-ease-with-his-materials reporter who is simply overviewing the whole block for us from the helicopter of his greater knowledge. The result is a strange authority that is at once dispassionate in its objectivity and almost erotic in its understated possibilities. His, in other words, is a potent contradiction that struck a very responsive note in the reading public, not to mention a number of full-bodied chords in popular theology.

Gribbin positions string theory, just as his subtitle suggests, squarely in the middle of the fray about what reality is and about the place that agency plays in it. He pulls no punches when dealing with what Einstein called a "spooky action at a distance"; and even an agnostic reader would have to come away wondering about whether or not there is something more miraculous about miracles than even the religious have ever allowed.

Kitty Ferguson's popularizing *The Fire in the Equations: Science, Religion and the Search for God* was first published in Great Britain by Bantam Press in 1994 and reissued a year later in this country by Wm. Eerdmans. Ferguson's is a lucid explication of twentieth-century physics that exercises an almost exquisite sensitivity to the theological implications and ramifications involved.

Oddly enough, Kitty Ferguson, who produced two other very successful books in popular science before *Fire* — *Black Holes in Spacetime* (Grolier/Franklin Watts, 1991) and also from the same publisher in 1991, *Stephen Hawking: Quest for a Theory of Everything,* which was reissued in 1992 in paperback format by Bantam Books — began life as a musician. Only after years of a full career as a conductor and singer did she turn to her other great passion, science. Like Gribbin, she is a friend as well as biographer of Stephen Hawking; and like Gribbin hers is a wide-ranging, all-incorporating overview for intelligent lay consumption. But perhaps because of her training in music or perhaps because of something so simple as personal disposition, Ferguson exposes with a cool balance and a greater directness than he not only the logical consequences of contemporary physics and the grandeur of their scope but also the fullness of their resonance with received tradition. Undoubtedly it is this latter quality that has so endeared her to readers. Undoubtedly it is also this latter quality that has made Ferguson's work a powerful tool for those cumulatively literate Americans who yearn to see doing theology become an acceptable activity among thinking people.

Another writer/scientist, City University of New York professor of theoretical physics Michio Kaku takes a third approach. Kaku makes a simple but useful distinction between the physics "of the very small" (quantum mechanics) and the physics "of the very large" (relativity) (*Beyond Einstein,* 9) While Gribbin is to some extent more concerned with the physics "of the very small" and Ferguson with an integrating overview of both, Kaku has more or less cornered the popular market recently for the physics "of the very large" with two books that established his position as a major popularizer. Their titles and subtitles perhaps tell their own tale best. *Hyperspace: A Scientific Odyssey through Parallel Universes, Time Warps, and the 10th Dimension* was published by Oxford University Press in 1994, and in October 1995 Doubleday followed *Hyperspace*'s success by rereleasing in an undated and revised edition Kaku's 1987 classic, written with Jennifer Trainer Thompson, *Beyond Einstein: The Cosmic Quest for the Theory of the Universe.*

Like Ferguson, Kaku is no fool about the theological consequences of the new physics; and his is an increasing sensitivity to issues that seems to have matured as his own presence in the market has grown. In the very opening chapter of *Beyond Einstein*, he speaks of the affinity of physics and theology for one another, and even of the affinity between theologians and scientists as seekers, noting especially their common bond as professionals having constantly to engage the great questions. (*Beyond Einstein*, 11). It is in concluding *Hyperspace*, however, that Kaku returns to this subject most definitively in two closing essays entitled "Science and Religion" and "Our Role in Nature" (330–34). Here the voice and tone are much more clearly those of the seasoned theoretical scientist. Here Kaku separates with a surgical nicety the sociological function of religion and what he calls the "God of miracles" on which it must depend from the "God of order" and from the potentiating reality — "almost approaching a religious awakening" — of the discussions and investigations and queries we as creatures are being empowered to conduct ... which brings us back to the body of my main essay and its *leitmotif* (or perhaps its full-chorus assertion) of the interplay between the popularized new branches of physics and god-talk.

20. Most readers will already know, but it's still wise to mention again, the fact that a good deal of the early popularizing and many of the scientists who engage in it were originally motivated by the need to fight a P.R. battle for pure science. Informing the voting public intellectually was not nearly as important to them as was persuading that public of the emotional and practical wonders to be enjoyed as a result of their continued funding for some endangered projects and Federal divisions like super cyclotrons and NASA.

Chapter Five: In the Middle

1. *Beyond Einstein* (Doubleday), 9.

2. I am interested here, as previously, in keeping our attention focused not on the whole field, but only on a few examples of the newer expressions of these sciences and especially upon these that are most aggressively informing popular theology right now. This inevitably means, as I have already noted, that this essay is far removed from any claim to be exhaustive. Hopefully some readers, having seen the forest covered in this chapter, will want to investigate in greater depth the proverbial trees that compose it and will find in the notes that follow some useful suggestions for doing so.

There is another complex of difficulties involved here as well. In setting up so crude a label as "the middle sciences," one loses many of the useful, traditional distinctions within the physical sciences. We will lose as well — and perhaps with charges of cavalier mayhem — the distinctions between humanistic disciplines and scientific ones. In addition, in treating the mind sciences in an earlier chapter rather than here, I have, in essence, already violated my own self-appointed category for reasons that I trust will shortly seem valid. Despite all these caveats, however, I still can think of no more economical, or even logical, way to proceed than via the sciences of the middle.

3. I once heard a speaker (whose name is lost in memory and therefore is not attributable) make this very same distinction on the basis of cosmocentric as opposed to anthropocentric disciplines. That labeling, while it is clear enough, seems to me to lack the Goldilocks-and-the-three-bears charm of small, large, and middle. If one is being a little free and loose with categories anyway, charm has a good deal of redemptive value.

There is something beyond charm involved here as well, however. There is a kind of unarticulated tradition of empathy between humanity and its middle sciences, especially with biology and all its spin-off disciplines. When NASA announced in August 1996 the discovery on Mars of archebacterial life, *Time* magazine reprinted in hard-copy as its closing essay for the issue of that momentous week an article, "So You're a Human Being. Isn't That Special?" by Nathan Myrhvold that had appeared a few days earlier in the on-line magazine *Slate*. Myrhvold comes nearer than anyone I know of to capturing the subtle sizing and symbiosis to which I refer: "But the hubris that makes us insist on a special role for humans and Earth didn't disappear [i.e., after Galileo]. Among the sciences, biology became its refuge. . . . However, the dogma being shattered [i.e., post-NASA announcement] is based fundamentally on ignorance. Biology has rested precariously on a single data point—life on Earth" (August 26, 1996, 64).

4. John Lobell, *Joseph Campbell: The Man and His Ideas* (The Joseph Campbell Foundation, P.O. Box 413, San Anselmo, CA 94979-0413, 1993), back cover.

5. This is a broad claim and one that, because of its wide sweep, needs a bit more comment. I have made it, please note, in terms of the modern thinker who has most changed the syntax and frames of reference of postmodern popular god-talk. Billy Graham, for example, has deeply affected popular theology as well and with an intensity of impact that probably no one could be said to have exceeded and very, very few could be said even to have equalled. (After all, it was Billy and not some Jungian Campbellite who was on the cover of *Time* for May 13, 1996!) Graham has not, however, brought about theological changes so much as he has championed theological positions that are conservative of earlier god-talk. As such, his positions seem to me to have served more as denials of the challenges of men like Campbell than as syntheses of new with former interpretations of fact.

When one speaks of the conservatory impact of Graham, however, or of other, popular religious leaders like him upon our theology, one must also take note of another piece of the puzzle. I have strenuously avoided the "trickle down" and "rising up" language of Reaganized economics because of their unsavory implications in the minds of many. Yet, like most successful expressions, both these terms clothe a large core of truism. Jung's ideas diffused (note that I still did not say "trickled down") into the general culture through mediums that by their very nature and in their era were open to a more affluent and/or more intellectually turned American and through means that by and large are experienced privately or individually. Graham's ideas, on the other hand, have diffused into the culture via mediums that are more populist in framing and in costs and that are communally experienced and reinforced. Both are potent modes of entry for any type of thought, whether it be active or reactive; and neither means alone could have succeeded in influencing our culture as dramatically or as rapidly as have the two together. We will return to this point shortly when we consider the place of nostalgia in present-day god-talk.

6. Just because we have taken his name so many times in vain already, the reader may be amused to read the following words which are the opening sentence of an essay on "Understanding Mythology" by John Lobell in *Joseph Campbell: The Man and His Ideas* (16): "The modern interest in the study of myth is first seen in Giambattista Vico (1668–1744) who opposed René Descartes's (1596–1650) attempt to extend mathematical and scientific methods to the understanding of human beings." Alas, poor René, we do not use you kindly these days.

7. Lobell, *Joseph Campbell: The Man and His Ideas*, 14.

8. Campbell began publishing in 1943 with *Where the Two Came to Their Father: A Navaho War Ceremonial Given by Jeff King* (Princeton University Press). That book was followed a year later by *A Skeleton Key to Finnegans Wake* (Harcourt, Brace) We should note just here as well that Campbell's first, passionate engagement of the material ideas that were to be his life's work was through Native American civilization. His was a progression that was to become almost the prototypical pattern for thousands of seekers who would follow him through the indigenous to the universal.

It was not until 1949, however, that Campbell broke into the world of high visibility. That year he published *The Hero with a Thousand Faces* (Bollingen Series XVII, Princeton University Press). A study in perfected detail of the archetypal hero journey, *Hero* was to become that rare thing — a classic, a scholarly work of excellence and insight, and a commercial bestseller. (By commercial success one can honestly mean just good, solid sales. Rarely does one mean, as I do here, that a book has stayed on the national bestseller lists for years, yet *Faces* was on the *New York Times*'s lists up until 1988 and has continued to enjoy "good, solid sales" ever since.)

Ten years after *Hero, The Masks of God*, which was to occupy almost ten years of Campbell's publishing life, quite literally burst upon the scene. *Masks*, a four-volume work published by the Viking Press from 1959 through 1968 and now available in paperback as well, immediately found its place with a readership of the already predisposed. The shifts that were to give forth in our present religious, spiritual, and theological upheaval had already begun. Thousands and thousands of Americans had already begun their search for a credentialed authority that could legitimatize their sense of some ecclesial offense as well as their earnest desire to serve the truth rather than its shadow.

In 1969 Campbell further obliged this seeking audience of the newly megaliterate with *Flight of the Wild Gander* and, in 1972, *Myths to Live By,* both from Viking. In 1974 came *The Mythic Image,* a richly imagistic study that rewove or perhaps reunified Eastern and Western mind-sets (Bollingen C, Princeton University Press). In 1983 the *Historical Atlas of World Mythology* was published. A work of five parts in two volumes, much of it appeared after Campbell's death in Honolulu in 1987 of cardiac arrest. (Volume 1, *The Way of the Animal Powers,* first published by Alfred van der Marck in 1983, was republished by Harper in 1988 when that company released volume 2, *The Way of the Seeded Earth.* Both titles are now available in both hard- and softcover editions.)

Campbell's work, obviously, was gargantuan. His contribution to god-talk among nontheologians, however, was not so much that of new ideas or concepts as of an objective, academically credible defense of ideas that had been circulating for decades. From the fiction of Tolstoy (N.B.: "The Three Hermits," etc.) to the romanticism of the West's early nineteenth century to the theoretical and didactic arguments of New Thought, the ideas were there. They simply lacked the validation and defensible purchase that Campbell, by his comparative approach, gave them for ordinary, god-fearing people. Thus, as I have already noted, part of the fulcrum that rendered Campbell's contributions so powerful was the genius of the times themselves. All things were in confluence, and he was but one of them.

9. Lobell, *Joseph Campbell: The Man and His Ideas,* 9.

10. The videos are presently available both from Mystic Fire Video in Livonia, Mich. (800-446-9784) and the *Signals* catalog (800-669-9696) as well as from most video stores and booksellers.

11. This statement, while accurate, needs to be tempered lest it become more sweeping than I intend. Campbell recognized the distinct divisions between, and hallmarks of, Eastern as opposed to Western cultural, mythologic, and religious experience. In fact, volume 2 of his masterpiece, *The Masks of God,* is *Oriental Mythology,* while volume 3 is *Occidental Mythology.* In the divisions between East and West, similar is not identical, or, at the very least, "identical" is buried under more and more layers of "similar" the farther one moves in time and distance from humanity's early history or sites.

12. This has, to date, been less true for American Muslims. Islam's historic position is that the Qur'an was directly dictated to the Prophet

and cannot, therefore, even be read outside of its original Arabic and still remain the holy book of the faith. That is, the Prophet was the conduit for, not the composer of, the text contained in the Qu'ran. Because of this stringent physical tie between original vehicle and divine truth, there has, up until recently, been little or no significant push on the part of Muslim laity to join America's other two major traditions in text analysis. This situation seems now to be changing a bit, however.

There are two or three translations — or as Muslims prefer to call them, paraphrases or interpretations — both print and electronic, available on the American market for the use of believers in study, if not in worship. At least one of them, however, published by Ahmadiyya Anjuman Ishaat Islam Lahore, USA, with corporate offices located in Columbus, Ohio, is purportedly now being used officially, though not exclusively, for more than study by the Nation of Islam. Additionally, Touchstone, a division of Simon & Schuster, reissued in December 1996 *The Koran Interpreted: A Translation by A. J. Arberry,* a reprint of a forty-year-old classic that has become a favorite of non-Muslim, Western readers who want primarily to understand Islam, rather than to themselves become devotees.

13. Judaism has always provided for the inclusion, to some arguably greater or lesser degree, of the faithful and devout from traditions other than itself under the provisions of the Noachide Covenant (Gen. 9ff.). In this it has exercised a far greater inclusivity than Christianity or Islam (and can point to history as its proof of that generosity of spirit).

Additionally, one of the minor, but interesting, sequela to lay absorption with texts and questions of religious inclusiveness has been a slender but steady trickle of books about the Noachide Covenant. There has also been a mini-resurgence of the Noachide Movement, a relatively small body of disaffected Christians seeking to reposition their faith as a modern expression of Judaism rather than as a separate religion.

Like Judaism and Christianity, Islam recognizes Noah. Indeed, Noah is seen as the first prophet in the line of seven of whom Mohammed is the last. There is no resultant, religious inclusivity, however. In mainstream Islam, any such idea is tempered by the Muslim doctrine of *jihad,* or "striving" with other faiths in the cause of Allah. Judith Miller in her stunning, authoritative study *God Has Ninety-Nine Names* (Simon & Schuster, 1996), coins and employs the terms "Islamist" and "Islamicism" to differentiate politicized Islam from theological Islam. One of the benefits of such a distinction is that by separating the two, one can acknowledge the existence of holy as well as of profane or theocratic uses of *jihad*. What such labels of distinction cannot meaningfully do is change the fundamental principle of exclusivity that undergirds *jihad* in any presentation.

14. This assessment is a fairly brash one on my part and is one that we will return to later in the body of the larger essay. For the moment, however, it still seems prudent to offer some justification or explanation. Words of inclusivity obviously abound. They have abounded for centuries, in fact.

In 1965 Vatican II issued a very specific document, *Nostra Aetate* ("In Our Time"), that defined the relationship of the church to non-Christian religions. According to His Holiness John Paul II writing in *Crossing the Threshold of Hope* (Knopf, 1995) that "very rich" document "authentically hands on the Tradition, faithful to the thought of the earliest Fathers of the Church. From the beginning, Christian revelation has viewed the spiritual history of man as including, in some way, all religions, thereby demonstrating *the unity of humanity with regard to the eternal and ultimate destiny of man*" (italics his). The pope continues by saying: "The Church sees the promotion of this unity as one of its duties" (78), and concludes his comments about this unity by saying that Christ's ways of reaching humanity are many and varied as well as His own and that He "came into the world for all these peoples. He redeemed them all" (83).

This posture of "many ways to arrive at Christian salvation" does not, at a lay level of understanding, however, address the real question. It does not explain why Christian salvation is the *desideratum*. It is all well and good that Christian theology is persuaded that God can effect salvation through many faiths and even in ways unknown to those of other faiths who are being accepted, but why should that be the place of the "Christian" god? This central question, while it has been circled, has not yet been engaged. Additionally, so long as there is a proviso for Yahweh or Jehovah or Allah to act salvifically, the majority of us may be relieved, but as yet none of us has an answer to the question of whether or not they three are all the same.

15. More to the point, at my last count (in 1996), there were still some seventy-four volumes of Jung's own work in print and readily available in bookstores; and I suspect that even Viking/Penguin no longer knows exactly how many copies of their *Portable Jung* have been sold since it was first issued in 1976.

16. Jung's book by this very title of *Memories, Dreams, Reflections* was published by Random House in 1961 and has been available from Vintage in paperback since 1965.

17. His work in alchemy (Bollingen Series XX, Princeton University Press, 1967; also available since 1983 as a Bollingen Paperback) remains one of the most spectacular *tours de force* in religious studies in modern times.

18. Wade Clark Roof is perhaps the most knowledgeable and most frequently cited observer of the religious temperament of the Boomer population. In his bestselling *A Generation of Seekers* (HarperSan-Francisco, 1993) Roof explicates brilliantly the causative relationship between Jung and the contemporary state of spirituality in America. In this discussion (69ff.), Professor Roof also gives considerable credit to Abraham Maslow as well as Jung. Because of Roof's own stature as an analyst in this field, if for no other reason, serious readers will want to explore Maslow's considerable influence as well and will find Roof's *Generation* to be a solid introduction for positioning his work.

19. Watts died in 1973, but he never left his place of central importance for Westerners seeking to understand the new and incontrovertible discoveries. Most recently, Charles Tuttle, Inc., has republished a series of his lectures on Eastern religion as *Buddhism: The Religion of No-Religion* (1996) with an introduction by his son, Mark. The same house has also rereleased *Myth and Religion* (1996), a series of Watts lectures on the Judeo-Christian tradition, or, more precisely perhaps, challenging the evolved religions and doctrines of that tradition to address some very specific parts of themselves that are discordant with contemporary understanding and just possibly in violation of their originating revelations. As if to further emphasize the importance of all media in this age of media expansion, Tuttle also rereleased in late 1996 two tapes of Watts's public "performances" (that's exactly what a Watts lecture was, by the way) under the title of *Zen Clues: Subtle Keys to the Mystery of Life*.

20. *The Sacred and the Profane* (Harcourt, Brace, 1959) was followed by half a dozen seminal works of which *Myths, Dreams and Mysteries* (Harper, 1960), *The Quest: History and Meaning in Religion* (University of Chicago Press, 1969) and *A History of Religious Ideas* (University of Chicago Press, 1978–85) were probably the most influential.

21. Jung in particular, as one might expect, has had a highly able and very articulate line of spiritual as well as intellectual descendants who have proved especially adept at the application of his principles.

Of these none has been more influential at the popular level perhaps than Thomas Moore, whose Jungian-based trilogy of *Care of the Soul* (HarperCollins, 1992) has been a publishing phenomenon from the very first, a kind of testament beyond contest to our current absorption with spiritual practice. In paperback format, which was not even released by Harper until 1993, *Care* had been on the *New York Times* bestseller list for 131 weeks at the time of this writing in July 1996. And Moore's subsequent volumes — *Soul Mates: Honoring the Mysteries of Love and Relationship* (HarperCollins, 1994) and *The Re-Enchantment of Everyday Life* (HarperCollins, 1996) have sold, quite literally, millions of copies as well.

There have been other scholars in the middle sciences — there is an unintentional tendency on the part of many of us to assume, erroneously, that popular authors in the field of spirituality are not, by the very reason of their subject and their popularity, scholars. Moore, for example, who credits Jung as his intellectual progenitor, holds degrees in music, philosophy, and theology, not to mention a Ph.D. from Syracuse University in religion.

There have been other scholars in the middle sciences who have managed to achieve and maintain a similar kind of public presence and influence on a more theoretical or abstract basis than Moore's. In comparative religion itself, for example, consider Huston Smith. His public presence is due in no small part, of course, to Bill Moyers and the power of television. (The Smith/Moyers connection led to the five-week PBS series *The Wisdom of Faith,* which first aired in 1996 and is available through *Signals* and *Parabola Magazine* at 800-560-MYTH on videotape.) But since 1958 and the publication of his *The Religions of Man* (HarperCollins), Smith has produced a steady flow of academically respected, popularly pursued books about the uniformity within diversity of humanity's religious practice. Of particular relevance and impact here are his highly influential *The World's Religions,* published in 1986 and available since 1991 as a Perennials paperback as well, and in 1994, HarperSanFrancisco published an updated, expanded edition of *Man* under the title of *The Illustrated World's Religions.*

22. Specifically, I am referring here to *Lucy: The Beginnings of Humankind* written with Maitland Edey (Simon & Schuster, 1990) and *Ancestors: The Search for Our Human Origins* (Random House, 1994).

23. Once more it would be a violation of my own travels in these broad fields if I did not at least mention by name that great popularizer

who was, additionally, one of the very first to understand the didactic power (as well as, I always suspected, the perceptual and incorporating limitations) of television. Jacob Bronowski's *The Ascent of Man* bowled the world over in 1976 when it ran as a series on the BBC and, in this country, on PBS and when it appeared in book form from Little, Brown and Co.

24. Shanks has become best known in the world of popular theology and archeology perhaps as the founding editor and guiding intellect behind the magazine *Biblical Archeological Review*. I shall never forget nor quite forgive my surprise one day in 1993 at a professional meeting when I was discussing the effects upon popular theology of men like Shanks. Afterward, a staff member of Eastern National Park and Monument Association, a firm which despite its unwieldy name is one of this country's largest distributors of magazines and books, came up later and told me that the second fastest-growing magazine on Eastern's list was *Biblical Archeological*. "Proof enough for anybody," she said, of successful penetration of the popular market by Shanks's kind of very focused, but very intensely perceived scholarship.

25. Pellegrino gives graphically detailed descriptions, based on recent excavations, of the courses and devastating results of flood after flood in the Middle East during the Stone Age, for example (*Return to Sodom and Gomorrah* [Random House, 1994; reissued in paperback by Avon in 1995]). I cannot imagine that, having read his work, any imaginative soul could ever hear the psalms, especially the roar of the creation psalms, again without a holy awe considerably removed from the quietude that is more typically gleaned there....

> The voice of the Lord is over the waters, the God of majesty thundereth, the Lord over the sea!
> The voice of the Lord shattereth the cedars; the Lord breaketh the cedars of Lebanon.
> The voice of the Lord spreadeth flames of fire; the voice of the Lord shaketh the desert, yea the desert of Cades.
> The voice of the Lord maketh the oaks to reel and strippeth the forest, and in His temple all sing: "Glory! ... "
>
>   —Psalm 28 (as taken from *The Psalter of a Short Breviary for Religious and the Laity,* 4th ed., the monks of St. John's Abbey (Liturgical Press, 1949).

Those psalms, like the forests of the original psalmist, are stripped bare of both myth and historicity to assume actuality in Pellegrino; and the post-Pellegrino reader wants to cry out "Glory!" in concert with a thundering majesty that he or she knows can be apprehended like an heirloom rediscovered, and gathered into oneself like a peace obtained.

26. Yale University Press, 1972. Ironically, despite its totally objective point of view, *A Religious History* was chosen by the *Christian Century* as "Religious Book of the Year" in 1979.

27. The author of at least three dozen books currently on the market, Marty has chosen a route of influence that is a bit unusual. He is a devout Lutheran and a pastor as well as Fairfax M. Cone Distinguished Service Professor of the History of Modern Christianity at the University of Chicago. Most of Marty's "popular" writings come from the pastoral side of his training. Oddly enough, however, it is his professorial writings, most of them directed to professional readerships, that have managed to affect popular theology. They have, by and large, been distilled by other thinkers and then themselves popularized. The most influential Marty work has probably been the recently completed five-volume Fundamentalism Project, edited with R. Scott Appleby under the sponsorship of the American Academy of Religion and published by the University of Chicago Press. Volume 5, *Fundamentalisms Comprehended,* was released in 1995 and was the culmination of a brilliant analysis of fundamentalism as a religious mind-set or distortion present in all faiths.

28. Simon & Schuster, 1992, with Touchstone paperback publication in 1993.

29. Barna, who is head of and works from the Barna Research Group, is the author of many books offering statistical analyses of religion in this country. His recent volume, *The Index of Leading Spiritual Indicators* (Word, 1996) has been of special interest to Evangelical Protestant Christians for its insights into changing Roman Catholic/Protestant relationships, into the overt evidences of religious commitment that affect the institutional future of that segment of American religion, and into the assessment of those "values" that culturally and historically are as much American as religious.

30. Subtitled *American Faith in the 90's* (Collier, Macmillan, 1989), the book was hugely popular and is still cited by author and speaker after author and speaker as the authoritative, predictive source on the subject. More information about Gallup's work, including a com-

plete listing of his available books, newsletters, lectures, and reports is available from the Princeton Religion Research Center, P.O. Box 389, Princeton, NJ 08542.

Chapter Six: Of Micro and Macro

1. This statement is not a condemnation and might even become a defense, were there sufficient room here to develop it. My own husband is a physician, and over the years we have both become more and more sensitive to the superficiality of thought and lack of realism that lie behind much of the criticism of the "cold" objectivity and emotional removal sometimes required by his profession.

2. It would seem incomplete or perhaps simplistic not to at least mention as a footnote here that economics, while absent in my exemplary scenario, is very much present in real ones. The economics of moral, spiritual, and theological precepts and practice is the stuff of many books, none of them, alas, this one.

3. It is the religio-moral obligation to act that I hear creeping into more and more venues these days. While this is an informal observation rather than a documented fact, I am fascinated by the rhetoric in which the arguments are being couched. For instance, as an active Episcopalian, I was pleased as well as faintly surprised in June 1996 by a line of argument published in my own church's official organ, *Episcopal Life.* In *EL*'s "Forum" section, which was dedicated that month to the question of assisted suicide, one of the ordained presenters, the Rev. Lawrence Falkowski, took the position that "attempts to keep a person alive regardless of the physical and psychological consequences may actually become an act of aggression rather than an act of caring and kindness." He's right, but the waters he churns are not for casual bathers.

4. I know; I contributed to their deaths in 1991 with a book entitled *Confessing Conscience: Churched Women on Abortion* (Abingdon Press) that continues to sell both in print and in audio format. Yet the book, which was an attempt to forge some common ground among believing women, fell and falls as far short of its intended mark as any book ever could.

5. Of the many American commentators and thinkers who are presently wrestling with the issues of morality and religion and the inter-

workings of the two, few are more in the public eye than Stephen L. Carter. Certainly very, very few are more respected or — and surely there is a relationship between the two — more devoutly rational in their positions. Carter, in his 1996 bestseller *Integrity* (Basic Books), cites figures to substantiate this very point of the electorate's withdrawal from the public debate of these deeply felt issues. Citing the *New York Times* and the *L.A. Times* as sources, Carter reports that only 5 percent of American voters considered abortion a decisive issue in 1995 and that, according to a 1992 poll, only one voter in nine even wanted our presidential candidates to talk about it (261, n. 21).

6. Here again we are on ground that Stephen Carter has tilled very effectively. He certainly has exposed quite clearly the public or civic implications of religion and the necessity, within a democracy, of a common, moral ground, something he refers to as "the religion of the public square." Carter's major exposition of these issues may be found in his 1994 bestseller, *The Culture of Disbelief,* also from Basic Books.

Other writers, of course, have also engaged our civil or public morality. Some, like Carter, are trying to spell out their own versions of what it should become while others are more occupied with what it should return to. One thinks immediately, for example, of William Bennett, whose *The Book of Virtues* (Simon & Schuster, 1992) and all of its sequela have been consistently on the country's bestseller lists. There have also, especially for the Bennett books, been any number of books playing off of the "virtue" theme and format; and imitation still remains the surest sign of success in the book business, as well as the greatest compliment.

7. The most lucid, complete and sympathetic presentation of Darwin's offense that I have ever read is to be found in Bishop Jack Spong's *Liberating the Gospels: Reading the Bible through Jewish Eyes* (HarperSanFrancisco, 1996), 8ff.

8. *Emerging Trends,* the official publication of Princeton Religion Research Center and Gallup International, devoted its lead report in April 1996 to the question of how many Evangelicals there are in the U.S. today. (The finding by Gallup was that fewer than one American in five now holds the fundamentalist beliefs of the early nineteenth century.) The bulk of this lead essay treats of the impact of Darwinism upon the history of Christian denominationalism in America. In particular, it argues that the splintering of denominationalism caused by liberals breaking off from mainstream Christianity shifted in nature to

the breaking off of conservatives after William Jennings Bryan's rout by Clarence Darrow at the Scopes trial. Gallup's is an important overview for students of American religion.

9. One of the religion writers who most impresses me on a routine basis these days is Terry Mattingly, religion writer for Scripps-Howard. In his column of May 15, 1996, Mattingly outlines exquisitely this particular descent into hell.

10. While many American religious bodies have jousted recently with the issue of homosexuality and the given order, much of their agitation seems to have been defused and/or focused by the more juridical proceedings of the Episcopal Church in its trial for heresy of Bishop Walter Righter. The court found, in May 1996, that no doctrine governing homosexual ordination existed within the Episcopal Church and that, consequently, no heresy could have occurred. Although that decision has hardly put an end to the matter within either Episcopalianism or American religion in general, it does seem to have served as a highly public, credible statement of acceptance and as a proof text for many, many people of all faiths that this issue too is going to be absorbed eventually into the fabric of our communal life.

11. This list is so vast that it seems almost irresponsible to reduce it to the "dozens of others" phrase that space dictates. Moreover, the writers named here are all megastars. For a broader overview of their stature, see *Time*'s cover story for June 24, 1996, "Faith and Healing" (58–69) and in particular David Van Biema's contribution, "Emperor of the Soul."

Just as Van Biema shows, despite the fact that Weil's *Spontaneous Healing* (Knopf, 1995) was a *New York Times* #1 bestseller and Dossey's books like *Healing Words* (HarperSanFrancisco, 1993) and *Prayer Is Good Medicine* (HarperSanFrancisco, 1996) are always on lists all over the country, it is still Deepak Chopra who stands the tallest in this land of giants. His *Ageless Body, Timeless Mind* (Harmony Books, 1993) rode the lists for almost a year, and that was before he was on *Oprah*. His 1994 *Seven Spiritual Laws of Success* was on the lists even longer and still appears from time to time, having sold at last count something like a million and a half copies.

Having said all that, however, one must add that it was Weil, not Chopra, whom *Life* chose to feature with a full-page portrait for their September 1996 cover story, "The Healing Revolution" by George Howe Colt (34–50). Beyond the photographs, however, readers may

want to pay particular attention to Colt's summary of what is quite literally, as he establishes, a revolution. His separation of homeopathic from
allopathic medicine and of the proper sphere of each offers as concise
and pertinent introduction as I have yet seen to why and how alternative medicine is being accepted, if not applauded, by the scientific and
medical communities.

12. George Barnam, *The Index of Leading Spiritual Indicators* (Word,
1996), 28.

13. Cecil Hellman, in commenting on Bonnie Blair O'Connor's book
Healing Traditions: Alternative Medicine and the Health Professions
(University of Pennsylvania Press, 1995), is quoted by Martin Marty
in *Context* (May 15, 1996, 3). Citing the fact that the *New England
Journal of Medicine* estimates that in 1990 we Americans made 425 million visits to unconventional healers as opposed to the 388 million we
made to primary-care physicians, Hellman is quoted by Marty as saying:
"Medicine has partly filled the void created by the decline of organized
religion.... Much of the moral discourse of the age is now couched in
medical (or pseudomedical) terms. Sickness, for many people, has replaced sin.... The 'sinful life' has been supplanted by the 'unhealthy
lifestyle.' "

14. Syndicated religion columnist Clark Morphew devoted his February 17, 1996, column to the documentable connection between religious
practice and good health. Morphew's coverage is especially to be cited as
remarkable, however, because of the objectivity with which he presents
the nonsectarian nature of that correlation.

15. Perhaps the thing that most strongly attests to Americans' separation of mind as distinct is the ubiquity of the phrase "body, mind,
and spirit" in everything from magazine titles to advertising copy. It is a
tripartite conceptualization of ourselves that our forebears would have
found befuddled and perhaps perverse as well.

16. Viking, 1993.

17. Even more interesting, the advances of psychiatric medicine have
not yet elicited an even minimally effective response from religion publishers and the publishing houses that traditionally are the means, along
with the lectern or pulpit and podium, by which such direction is
transmitted.

Religion publishing in America's three monotheistic faiths of Judaism,
Christianity, and Islam generally divides its product into three large categories: lay, curricular, and academic and professional. The first — lay

books and information products — are, as their name suggests, the ones that convey directly to the believer or the seeker the theological view and sureties of a formalized theology or established religion. The second — curricular books and products — obviously are of concern to houses that are the official and/or underwritten publishing arms of an organized religious tradition, denomination, or establishment. As a category, curricular products have also gained in importance recently in the editorial programs of free-standing or institutionally independent religion publishers like Thomas Nelson, Inc., or Focus on the Family. This will undoubtedly continue to be true in our present climate of movement away from the particular and specific and toward the inclusive and multiperspectived in religion. As one would suspect, professional and academic products are designed for the use of religion professionals, be they ordained or appointed or simply employed. Although this last type of materials frequently did not pull its fair share of the fiscal load for many religion publishers in the past, it is gaining in market share and increasing in profitability, primarily because of an expanding interest in professional and academic issues on the part of educated laity. But more of this later.

The point to be made here is that psychiatric medicine, unlike the bulk of our new sciences, has up to now provoked almost no sustained treatments from any of these three traditional categories of religion publishing. This omission is most obvious and most inexplicable in the publishing of academic and professional materials. One of the small but consistently well-done areas of recent academic and/or clerical publishing in religion has been in those fields in which cumulative literacy has unleased a horde of theological ramifications, but not in psychiatry. And much as I have cast about in my mind for some explanation for that singular silence, I have yet to find one that seems feasible, much less adequate.

18. One of the things that is often conveniently overlooked by Western Christians is just how exploitative of the environment Christianized societies have been. Eco-theologians and proponents from other faiths are quick nowadays to point out this history and even its scriptural bases, starting with the traditional Christian, exploitive interpretation of God's instructions to Adam and Eve to go forth and occupy the earth as its overlords. Jewish thinkers who share the same early scriptures, and especially those in the eco-kosher movement like Arthur Waskow, are even quicker to point out the sharp differences between Christian and Jewish or Muslim applications of those early texts.

19. Carson's success rests as well upon her *The Sea Around Us* (Oxford University Press, 1951).

Just as an aside, it is worth noting here that Jane Goodall, one of those who has followed the Carson tradition most closely in terms of personal popularity and professional effectiveness, has also produced a sinewy book of eco-spirituality. Written with Phillip Berman, *Reverence for Creation: The Spiritual Ties That Bind Us* is to be released in 1998 by Warner Books, who paid a seven-figure advance for the privilege. The reason? According to Jamie Raab, Warner v-p and senior editor, "A lot of spirituality books seem half-baked; this one seemed profound."

20. Although books have been a major means of popularization for eco-spirituality and related concerns, they have certainly not been the only ones. Televised series like those by Jacques Couteau have made substantial contributions, as have magazines like *Common Boundary, Parabola,* and *Shambhala Sun* that, while not focused on environmental issues, have nonetheless managed to present in a favorable light the theological and spiritual sensibilities that are cordial to them.

21. Most notably, see his *Dreams of the Earth* (Sierra Club, 1988).

22. Fox's *Creation Spirituality* (HarperSanFrancisco, 1991) perhaps created more stir than any book in its field in the early 1990s. *Natural Grace* (Doubleday, 1996), which Fox coauthored with Rupert Sheldrake, expands those first articulations and further integrates the effects of cumulative literacy with the values and intentions of an intense spirituality.

23. With a subtitle of *Ecology and the Human Spirit,* the title was published in 1992 by Houghton Mifflin.

24. An in-depth overview of these books and some real insight into why I speak of them as being lucrative as well as culturally correct may be found in "Keeping Faith with the Earth" by F. Lynne Bachleda for *Publishers Weekly,* February 14, 1994, 36–40.

It seems wise to mention one more time the presence in many other parts of the world of tensions beings discussed here only in their American presentation. So intense has been our new, postmodern awareness of the interface between human spirituality and human space/context that it has been almost poetic in its power and its subtlety. It has also been very catholic as well. For example, the Parliament for the World's Religions first met in Chicago in 1893. When it met for the second time upon the occasion of its centenary in 1993, the parliament's primary business, any observer could have concluded, was less the theological well-being or political unity of the world's established faiths than it was the composing and eventual endorsing of a document known as "The Global Ethic," which basically was and is an ecological position paper. I am not exaggerating; I was there and watched. Interested readers may also study the document itself: *A Global Ethic: The Declaration of the Parliament of the World's Religions* (Continuum, 1993).

25. Foremost among the gentle and more persuasive presenters of the bond between ecology and theology for Americans of disparate religious allegiances has been the Buddhist monk and teacher Thich Nhat Hahn, published in this country predominantly by Parallax Press. In exile from his native Vietnam, he lives now at his community of Plum Village in France and travels from time to time here where his books and conversations enjoy a broad popularity.

26. The first, great tidal wave of surprise for white America about all of this was probably Vine Deloria's *God Is Red* (Grosset and Dunlap, 1973), but there have certainly been dozens of other powerful inundations since.

27. In this regard see particularly the recent catalogs of Christian mainline denominational houses like Westminster John Knox Press (Presbyterian Church USA) or the Pilgrim Press (United Church of Christ) and of independent religion publishers like Wm. B. Eerdmans Publishing.

Chapter Seven: About the Many Uses of "Once upon a Time"

1. In his discussion of nostalgia as an element of Baby Boomer religion in *Generation of Seekers* ((HarperSanFrancisco, 1993, esp. 251), Wade Clark Roof makes a distinction between the role of memory and the role of nostalgia. While I would be very hesitant to differ with Roof on almost any point he might choose to make, I do think that at an effectual level the yearning back toward what is remembered is just as repainted by time and subsequent experience as is the yearning back toward that which has only been known through transmitted story and artifact. I suspect, also, that Roof and I are suffering a semantic, rather than a substantive, difference on this point, and that what I am calling nostalgia, he would call yearning, saying that it can originate from either nostalgia or memory.

2. The degree of sophistication we have achieved in dealing with the wrenching dislocations of rapid technological change is brought home to me most emphatically every time I see the ecologists' L≥C formula. As a formula it means that in order to survive, an organism's learning capacity must be greater than the rate of change going on around it; but what it really means to me is that we've been there and done that long enough and often enough to reduce the agony to symbols.

3. This translation obviously happens, as I am about to suggest, because so many of the pieces and parts that made up our culture originally were religious in nature, causing their subsequent separation from religious expression to be essentially impossible. Having said all of that, however, there are always those exceptions that keep generalizations honest. Elaine Storkey's *The Search for Intimacy* is such a case in point. First published with great success in Great Britain in 1995 by Hodder and Stoughton, the book was published in this country a year later by Wm. B. Eerdmans. Even laying aside references to tea breaks and vicars, no one probably would take Storkey's treatment of cultural disjuncture and lost intimacy to be of American authorship. But anyone, I submit, American or otherwise, would recognize, as being worthy of even the most inveterate Yank, the inherent ease with which Storkey makes the connections between cultural and religious angst.

4. For a real taste in a popular presentation of just how absolutely true this was, see Hugh Hewitt's *Searching for God in America* (Word, 1996), especially the earlier papers included in his "Selections from America's Spiritual Treasury" (179ff.).

5. Stephen Carter's *The Culture of Disbelief* (Basic Books, 1994) undoubtedly makes and sustains this argument more ably than any other piece of contemporary popular literature. Carter's presentation of Alexis de Tocqueville's insights into the immutable tie between democracy and a commonality of moral understanding is especially persuasive and illuminating.

6. I have treated these reasons (and especially those that have been causative in contemporary religion) in my earlier *Re-Discovering the Sacred: Spirituality in America* (Crossroad, 1995), where the reader will also find citations to several other book-length studies of them as well.

7. This statement was truer in the years from 1992 through early 1996. The closer we move in time to the millennium itself, the more radically religious and/or sectarian (or just plain hysterical?) some of these connections are becoming. See, for example, *Beginning of the End*

by John Hagee (Nelson, 1996) that played around just below the line for weeks on the *New York Times* bestseller lists. Based on our history of prior calendar rollovers, however, one must assume that there will be a righting of tone after 2001 C.E.

8. The most suggestive and best articulated précis I know of to date on the place of nostalgia in all religion and of the interplay of place and center in that mix is in Karen Armstrong's *Jerusalem: One City — Three Faiths* (Knopf, 1996), 8ff.

9. The growth of Buddhism and, concomitantly, of Buddhist publishing in this country was one of the major religion stories of the first half of the 1990s. Exclusively Buddhist houses like Parallax Press and Snow Lion Publishing posted gains in the three digit figures, sometimes annually. Older houses like Shambhala that emphasize Buddhism and regard it as the core of their publishing program did almost as well and sometimes better. There was, also and just as dramatically, a shift by commercial publishers like HarperSanFrancisco to quickly acquire and incorporate Buddhist materials into their lists. The emphasis in all of this publishing excitement was upon Buddhist meditational and centering exercises and methods.

10. Always I hear in my head, when I make this kind of statement, the cries of the sectarian, bemoaning the impurity of "religious stew" and "salad bar faith." I am reminded immediately thereafter of the stories and anecdotes — really confessions of faith — that as a secularist covering religion, I hear in the course of my work for *Publishers Weekly*. The one that seems most apropos here, for instance, involves the writer Jane Redmont. She is the author of *Generous Lives: American Catholic Women Today* (published in 1992 by Morrow in hardcover and issued a year later by Triumph Books in paperback) and is presently at work on a manuscript about Christian prayer that is under contract to HarperCollins. Those titles would certainly indicate a strong, longstanding Christian connection. Not so, Redmont told me during the course of an academic afternoon we shared one day on the Berkeley campus. In fact, she said, "I came to Christianity through Buddhism." And hers is not an unusual story.

11. Basil Pennington with his *Centering Prayer* (Doubleday/Image) wrote the classic text in this area three decades ago; but it was the Benedictine monk Fr. Thomas Keating, who reintroduced the ancient principles to contemporary popular audiences. His 1994 *Invitation to Love* (Continuum) deals primarily with centering prayer, and his sub-

sequent books — *Intimacy with God* (Crossroad, 1994), *Open Mind, Open Heart* (Continuum, 1994), etc. — continued to expand and enlarge upon his methods and principles. Keating, by the way, was one of the subjects of Hewitt's *Searching for God in America* series in 1996, and a transcript of the Keating interview may be found in Hewitt's book by the same name (Word, 1996).

12. There have been so many excellent and skillfully beautiful published examples of this that I hesitate to mention any of them singly. One thinks, for example, of the work of Sue Bender whose *Everyday Sacred: A Woman's Journey Home* (HarperSanFrancisco, 1992) has been a consistent bestseller in the years since its publication and has endeared Bender to literally hundreds of thousands of Americans. Frederick Buechner, himself equally beloved and a constant bestseller, has home and a religiously ladened longing for it as an almost fixed motif. The most recent expression of the Buechner treatment, *The Longing for Home* (HarperCollins, 1996), deals even more directly than usual with the soul's ties. Certainly John Updike in *In the Beauty of the Lilies* (Knopf, 1995) addresses the central theme of religious evolution in and through the home about as directly and clearly as anyone ever has or could. The list goes on, being almost inexhaustible.

13. There are two important points here that urge me toward more elaboration than is probably actually needed by any informed reader.

First, the gender history of woman in Western society is a study by class or social stratum as well as by era. There has never been such a thing as a universally agreed upon "woman's role." The point that is of significance here, however, is that what many of us think of as the traditional characteristics of that role — the at-home mother and the cult of domesticity — were never operative for lower-class women, nor were they admired by other times. King Solomon, for example, in his complete description of ideal woman, has her selling linens and buying fields with the best of them. Such wheeling and dealing was part of woman's life, just as rebellion against domesticity and into social and political causes was Victorian upper-class woman's answer to having had that public forum closed to her by affluence and social changes. Nor were things all sweetness and light *intra-familia* in "the old days" among the affluent. The curious might want to check out a few texts like *The Family, Sex and Marriage in England: 1500–1800* (Harper Torch, 1983) by Lawrence Stone for some pertinent commentary on just how bad things could be in some cases.

Second, the conversation, both lay and academic, about America's "Golden Age" has been increasing markedly of late. Whatever else that talk may do, it certainly seems to be forcing the general American mindset toward a more realistic assessment of our present circumstances, the subjects of our nostalgia and the bases of our goals. There have been numerous fine studies of this recently, but Michael Elliott's *The Day before Yesterday: Reconsidering America's Past, Rediscovering the Present* (Simon & Schuster, 1996) is an especially apt and useful one for elaborating and illuminating the golden-age phenomenon in the context that I have employed it here.

14. I do not mean to imply here that the transmission of spiritual vigor is conducted by only one sex. Clarissa Pinkola Estes, for example, celebrates more efficaciously than anyone I know the way both sexes convey to children the art and powers of the soul (See *The Faithful Gardener* ([HarperSanFrancisco, 1996]) while at the same time defining the primal and primally feminine. Her *Women Who Run with the Wolves* (Ballantine, 1992) was on the *New York Times* bestseller lists for ninety-two weeks and has sold in excess of a million copies to date.

15. My favorite example of this phenomenon of returning is *The Telling*, primarily because of the prominence of the women involved and the success the book itself enjoys. Published by HarperCollins in 1993 and edited by E. M. Broner, the book's full title is *The Telling: The Story of a Group of Jewish Women Who Journey to Spirituality through Community and Ceremony*. It features on its cover the faces of several of its coparticipants/writers: Gloria Steinam, Letty Cottin Pogrebin, Bella Abzug, Phyllis Chesler, to name a few. (Grace Paley was in the group, but for some reason missed the cover.) The book is exactly what all of that verbose subtitle says it is — the story of a group of highly visible and highly successful women who met at each other's homes over a number of years to explore together, and ultimately to reclaim, their Jewish faith. Their work as a community of feminist religious seekers led them to unconditionally embrace some of their heritage and to adapt other parts of it. (The book contains within it, for example, another book, *The Women's Haggadah*, a *haggadah* written by Broner and Nomi Nimrod and used by the group in conducting its feminist seders.) Theirs is a potent "telling" that Christians would probably refer to as "witnessing" or "professing." By whatever name, it celebrates a powerful process at work within contemporary American god-talk.

16. The use of the word "glut" is deliberate and accurate, if not euphonious. So extreme has been the growth of the market for these materials that *Publishers Weekly* has had to run two major overviewing features (an unheard of event!) on it within the last four years: my own "In the Company of Mighty Women and Powerful Words" (April 12, 1993, 31–32) and "A Celebration of Women's Spirituality" (January 8, 1996, 28–30) by LaVonne Neff.

17. While I hear bookseller after bookseller talk about the strength of their sales in this area, the theological ramifications were brought home to me by another bookseller, Debra Farrington. Farrington is the manager, not of a general bookstore in which the sales patterns in women's spirituality have been so well documented, but of the stores of the Graduate Theological Union at Berkeley. Her stores, in other words, serve a consortium of eight seminaries on the GTU campus and, according to Farrington, "Anything in women's theology and spirituality is going to sell...*anything!* It's our most predictable, steady genre and has been for quite a while."

For a detail-specific overview of the situation, the reader may want to see *Saving Work: Feminist Practices of Theological Education* (Westminster/John Knox Press, 1995) by Rebecca Chopp. Chopp is professor of systematic theology and dean of faculty and academic affairs at Emory University's Candler School of Theology, positions that certainly lend her the authority with which to interpret the present trend.

18. This is not a slam of men alone. There are, at the time of this writing, already several look-alike organizations, primarily for women: Heritage Keepers, Keys for Abundant Living, Women In Faith, etc., etc.

19. There is so much popular interest in the Virgin that one can hardly keep up with the books that are being published into the hunger. Curious readers will find a mini-overview of some highly successful recent ones in *Publishers Weekly,* August 14, 1995, 40. Readers curious in a more theological way will want to see *Mary through the Centuries: Her Place in the History of Culture* (Yale University Press, 1996). Written by the renowned scholar/theologian Jaroslav Pelikan, *Mary Through* has ridden the current wave of popular interest to a considerable success of its own, having been a selection of the Book-of-the-Month Club, the History Book Club, and the Readers' Subscription all three. A more remarkable feat, however, may lie in the fact that the book is basically an examination of how Jews and Muslims as well as Christians have depicted and venerated Mary throughout the centuries.

20. There is a whole developing and expanding subgenre of religion and spirituality books growing not only out of this severance, but also out of the trauma presently being suffered by thousands of adult Americans as a result of our almost ironic return to working at home and to the home office. Predicted more than adequately in Faith Popcorn's *1991 The Popcorn Report* (Doubleday), the changes in the relationship between home and work have had all the spiritual ramifications she anticipated.

　　Writers like Laurie Beth Jones (*Jesus CEO,* 1993; *The Path,* 1996 [Hyperion]), Carol Osborn (*How Would Confucius Ask for a Raise?* 1993; *Solved By Sunset,* 1995 [Random House/Harmony Books], etc.), Alan Briskin (*The Stirring of the Soul in the Workplace* [Jossey-Bass, 1996]), and dozens of others deal with the place of faith and private inspiration in the work place. Additionally, many periodicals — especially those related to organized religious bodies — have turned their attention to the issues involved in these changing patterns of work. *U.S. Catholic,* for example, published a special issue in September 1996 on "The Work of Human Hands," which it promoted heavily with full-page ads and mailings long before the issue's actual release.

　　Readers wanting to know more will find that books dealing with the consolations of faith for the downsized and with spiritual practice for the adult working at home were featured by Lynn Garrett in her August 12, 1996, overview of forthcoming religion books for *Publishers Weekly* (32) and extensively in the issue of September 1, 1996, of *Publishers Weekly's Religion Bookline.* In addition, Doubleday periodically releases a newsletter, *Currency,* that précises its new and bestselling titles in this area by authors like Dr. Peter M. Senge, poet/lecturer David Whyte, etc.

　　21. This seems to me to be almost mawkishly present lately in Christmas books and Christmas marketing, though such an observation may be too obvious to be a very telling one.

　　22. I think here of more than just spiritual practice (for routinized but meaningful work is indeed good spiritual practice) and the reenforcement of ethno-religious identity through food and domestic custom. I think also of books like *In Memory's Kitchen: A Legacy from the Women of Terezin* (Jason Aronson, Inc., 1996) which makes available for the first time the favorite traditional recipes, painfully recorded on scraps of paper and hidden away for later generations, of the women who were to die for their Jewishness in Czechoslovakia's most notorious concentration camp.

23. One remarkable example of this may be found in the decision by Rodale Press, one of America's premier publishers of garden and domestic craft books, to open a religion/inspiration line. The new imprint — DayBreak — launched its first list in the spring of 1997 and, according to Dudly Jahnke, Rodale's trade marketing manager, is a natural consequence of "the compatibility between religion and spirituality and what we traditionally do at Rodale."

24. Two points need to be made. First, my omission of Orthodox Christianity and the Orthodox Christian church is deliberate here, but it is also temporary. The coming together of the three large divisions of Christianity is definitely in process; and I will be dealing with this rapprochement within a matter of a few paragraphs. In general, however, the popular, and some would say cavalier, assumption of the outer trappings of Orthodoxy per se has not yet happened, with one exception — icons. Just how far that assimilation is going to go and whether or not the public's fascination with icons will extend to incorporate more of Orthodoxy's outward evidences are both questions on which the jury is still out at the time of this writing.

Second, in American Roman Catholicism the home has played a political or politico-religious role that is unique to our experience and that reinforces to some extent this identification of church with home and especially — all politics being local anyway — of the parish church with home. A pertinent in-depth study of this phenomenon may be found in John T. McGreevy's *Parish Boundaries: The Catholic Encounter with Race in the Twentieth-Century Urban North* (University of Chicago Press, 1996).

25. Many of these appointments had their origin in Christian experience prior to any divisions within the faith. As the push toward reabsorbing these accoutrements into Christian practice increases, it is becoming more and more customary as well as euphemistic for Christians to refer to all of them as "historic" rather than as Roman.

26. I must reemphasize two things here. First, as I will note shortly and discuss in great detail in a later chapter, worldwide there is presently a movement toward the coming together of many faith traditions, as well as of the many divisions within each of them. (For example, the major Protestant churches of Scotland began an "initiative" in February 1996 that is designed to move them toward formulating a plan of union.) Second, while this movement toward greater unity is hardly

limited to American or even North American society, what is about the American expression of the shift is its intensified, emotional component.

27. Frequently the most memorable examples of this kind of shift are anecdotal. That is certainly true here. I was stopped one morning on the floor of the 1995 Christian Booksellers Association's annual trade show in Denver by a bookseller whom I had never met before. The show, called CBA International, is a huge one that services almost exclusively the Evangelical Protestant bookstores whose professional organization sponsors it. I was not surprised, therefore, to see from the bookseller's convention badge that he was from a very conservative Christian store. I was surprised, however, not by what he had to say, but by the earnestness with which he said it. "You don't know me," he began, "but I just wanted to say to somebody in the media who would think it mattered that I have come to this convention for twelve years and I have sold Roman Catholic materials in my store for all twelve of them. But I would never have felt comfortable in saying so here until this year. Now just look," and he gestured toward the convention floor. "There's at least ten Roman Catholic publishers and suppliers showing now and — what I really wanted to tell you — I got a letter two weeks before the show from XYZ [and he named a prominent Evangelical publishing firm] inviting me to come by and see a new line of Roman materials that they are trying to establish!"

He couldn't have been more gleeful if the pope had suddenly taken up immersion and laid aside infallibility.

28. This is no small concern, by the way; and several studies lately, including some 1996 Gallup ones, show Americans arguing for greater union among Christians on this very basis. And practicality does not always mean fiscal reality. There is a political reality as well. One of the most outspoken explications of this phenomenon is by the much-respected theologian, writer, and teacher Peter Kreeft of Boston University. Kreeft's *Ecumenical Jihad: Ecumenism and the Culture Wars* (Ignatius Press, 1996) argues that the three monotheistic faiths must soon realize that they are closer to each other than they are to their nonobservant cultural and social compatriots who are humanistic and secularized. In positioning the book for the market, the publisher pulled no punches, declaring even in its ad copy that "Kreeft issues a wake-up call to all God-fearing Christians, Jews and Muslims to unite together in a 'religious war' against the common enemy of godless secular humanism, materialism and immorality. Aware of the deep theological

differences between these monotheistic faiths, Kreeft calls for a moratorium on our polemics against each other so that we can form an alliance to fight together."

29. While there are numerous evidences of this intention scattered across the whole of John Paul II's papacy, the most concrete is certainly his May 30, 1995, encyclical, *Ut Unum Sint,* That They May Be One. Brief overviews of *Ut Unum* from the two communions involved may be found, among other places, in "The Pope's Ecumenical Advances" by Jennifer Reed (*St. Anthony Messenger,* September 1995, 19) and "Pope Issues Call For Christian Unity" (*Christianity Today,* July 17, 1995, 56).

30. "Conservative Ecumenicism?" Terry Mattingly, Scripps-Howard News Service, August 16, 1995.

31. Readers desiring to see this document in its entirety, as well as some excellent commentary by those who assisted in its formation will want to look at *Evangelicals and Catholics Together: Toward a Common Mission,* ed. Charles Colson and Richard John Neuhaus (Word, 1995), xv–xxxiii.

32. Numerous articles and book-length treatments resulted from the ETC instrument. One of the most complete and well-sustained essays about the document and about what greater alignment actually involves may be found in Norman L. Geisler and Ralph E. MacKenzie, *Roman Catholics and Evangelicals — Agreements And Differences* (Baker Books, 1995).

33. *Christianity Today,* May 15, 1995, 53.

34. *Christianity Today,* July 17, 1995, 56. There is no intention here of suggesting that movement toward greater unity of Orthodox and Roman Catholicism is without history. Discussions, at some greater or lesser levels, have been ongoing for years. For a summary of this dialog, readers may want to study *The Quest for Unity,* edited by John Borelli and John H. Erickson and jointly published in 1996 by St. Vladimir's Seminary Press and the United States Catholic Conference.

35. There were at least a dozen and a half U.S. publishers producing the *Catechism,* but the one that is most frequently cited and that has been most successful in terms of gaining and holding market share is Liguori Publications.

36. This pattern of sales may have had more than nostalgia or curiosity driving it, of course. For example, *Christianity Today,* the premier journal of Evangelical Protestantism in this country, in its issue of December 12, 1994 (28–33), ran an article, "Do We Still Need the

Reformation?" by Alister E. McGrath. Much of McGrath's argument
has to do with the new *Catechism;* and in publishing it, *C.T.* chose to
block off and highlight a fairly emphatic quote from McGrath's text:
"This volume [i.e., the *Catechism*] must be in the hands of every evangelical concerned with the future of evangelical relations with Roman
Catholicism" (33).

37. *Crossing* was published by Knopf, but many other publishers of
every size and persuasion have aggressively entered the marketing of
what some ruefully call pope-a-mania materials. There has been everything from biographies of His Holiness to reprints of his earlier work to
critiques of his papacy to compilations of his thoughts, all of it doing
well. There has even been at least one successful companion for Protestants to *Crossing* published by Paraclete Press in 1996, *A Reader's
Companion to 'Crossing the Threshold of Hope,'* edited by Charla
Honea. And for those who still can doubt the man's singular "pull"
upon the public's heartstrings, the record-breaking crowds at his recent
visits should be definitive proof.

38. More than just "on the lists," *Simple Path* topped *Publishers
Weekly* religion lists for the first six months of 1996 before settling
down to a respectable fourth place position.

39. It's equally impossible these days to go into a bookstore or library
without being almost literally hit in the face by the so-called "culture
war" books that address these policy issues, all too often in an ar-
gumentative or confrontational way. For an overview of some recent
major ones, see "Battle Plans for the Culture Wars," by Gayle White
(*Publishers Weekly,* July 11, 1994, 34–36).

40. The patness with which I write this sentence gives even me pause.
The truth is that none of us can presume to define "family" values with
any confidence. This is especially true now in view of the 1996 boycott
actions by the Southern Baptist Convention and the Assemblies of God
against Disney, that most "family" of family oriented media corpora-
tions. My definitions, therefore, are offered with considerable humility
in the face of the impossibility of the task and with no claims of being
exhaustive.

41. Jaroslav Pelikan spoke to this point rather sanguinely not too long
ago when he wrote that "every president has invoked the language of
the Judeo-Christian tradition and the metaphors of the Bible to carry
out his leadership function of instructing and inspiring 'a city set on a

hill,' as Ronald Reagan called the United States, quoting Matthew 5:14" ("Believers-in-Chief," *New Republic,* September 4, 1995, 30).

42. One of the most complete and lucid summations of this whole process is contained, unusually enough, in a book review by Richard A. Baer, Jr., of Isaac Kramnick and R. Laurence Moore, *The Godless Constitution: The Case against Religious Correctness* (Norton, 1995). Entitled "Our Faithless Forefathers," Baer's essay *cum* review may be found in *Christianity Today,* August 12, 1996, 42–46.

43. There is far more going on here than just books and chatter, of course. In an August 9, 1996, feature captioned "Pop Culture Steps in to Quench Thirst for Morality," *USA Today* reporters Ann Oldenburg and Patricia Edmonds give some startling statistics about the morality/value phenomenon in everything from toys to Christian music ($750 million annually), as well as books. So great is the present public hunger, they say, that even Dr. Ruth (Westheimer, that is) has changed her tack and entitled her next book *The Value of Family*—all of which, the reporters concluded, must mean something is going on.

44. The best "naming" is happening at the moment in fiction, rather than in nonfiction. The narrative form, being less specific and more suggestive, is cordially inclined toward matters of nostalgia, it seems. For a particularly successful example of this celebration-in-story of American and family values, see any of the titles in Jan Karon's Mitford series. Originally published by Chariot/Lion, an Evangelical Protestant publishing house, the first two of the Mitford books did so well that Penguin picked them up in paperback and then became the originating publisher for subsequent volumes.

There are those who prefer a good old-fashioned directness in their naming, of course; if you are in that number, check out *1939: The Lost World of the Fair* by David Gelernter (Free Press, 1996), which, while partly fiction, nails down in a nonfiction way the specifics of what we lost when we abandoned what Gelernter refers to as "the American religion, the 'civic religion' which has always been characteristic of this country."

The best example of the fictive naming of pure morality (i.e., morality stripped of "American" and "family" as descriptive adjectives) is in books like *The Celestine Prophecy* by James Redfield, which, by the way, was on *Publishers Weekly*'s bestseller lists for over two years! Love it or hate it, the book is pure morality, and any honest observer would, in my opinion, have to say that its success is due to the fact that it offers an accessible Ten Commandments that is updated and free of sectarian paraphernalia. It and its sequel, Redfield's *The Tenth Insight,* have triggered hundreds of small-group reading discussions and on-line chat rooms. One such chat room on the Ecunet system concluded at one point that *The Tenth Insight* was "a Christian parable...probably a gnostic Christian gospel."

Readers interested in other examples of moral and religious tenets presented in the nurturing environment of fiction will want to investigate the bibliography offered by Matthew Gilbert in "The Metaphysics of Fiction" (*Napra ReView,* May 1996, 32–41).

45. The lead article in *Atlantic Monthly*'s August 1996 issue (37–57) was "Welcome to the Next Church" by *Washington Post* reporter Charles Trueheart. An intensive study of the present state of religion, and especially of Christianity, as it approaches the next millennium, the piece treats this whole nostalgic complex in detail and in relation specifically to how god-talk and the church of the next thousand years must begin to recognize and address it. "What used to happen naturally, at least in the small-town America we mythologize," writes Trueheart, "today needs a little more deliberateness."

46. Though this is the last in my list of specifics, there's a strong part of me that thinks it may hold first place in terms of influence upon all the rest. There are any number of treatments of this issue, of course, but an especially fine one is Page Smith's *Re-Discovering Christianity: A Search for the Roots of Modern Democracy* (St. Martin's, 1994). Smith argues that egalitarianism, which is patent in American Christianity's understanding of democracy, fits poorly or not at all with capitalism and creates an ongoing contrariety of massive proportions.

47. One of the most arresting doctoral dissertations I've run across in a long time is "American Acropolis: The West End of the Washington Mall" by Richard Allen Hyde of the Church Divinity School of the Pacific (GTU) in Berkeley. Hyde argues "that the three memorials at the west end of the Mall (the Lincoln, Vietnam War Veterans and Korean War Veterans Memorials) particularly deserve to be called 'a sacred place,' for there the American people come to three 'temples' that were self-consciously designed to preserve memory and foster appreciation of sacrifice."

All of that very insightful rhetoric aside, the presence of a civil religion in American affairs is an informing one. In a review of Ronald Thiemann's *Religion in Public Life: A Dilemma for Democracy* (Georgetown

University Press, 1996), religionist Margaret O'Brien Steinfels defines that "religion" as "a non-Christological civic piety derived from Protestant Christianity" and says that "Abraham Lincoln was its most artful practitioner" (*New York Times Book Review*, July 7, 1996, 21) Hers is probably as clean a definition and choice of exemplar as anyone could ever want.

48. For a very reasoned and even presentation of this posture, see Ralph Reed's *Active Faith* (Free Press, 1996). And for a different, but equally balanced, view of things, see Dennis Prager's *Think a Second Time* (HarperCollins, 1995). (N.B.: Appearing with Tom Snyder on CBS's *Late, Late Show* on April 8, 1996, Prager made a distinction between "holy" and "moral" by saying that premarital sex is moral, but not holy. "Politics and politicians," he said, "must be moral, but are not required to be holy.")

49. In his April 11, 1996, column, Scripps-Howard reporter Terry Mattingly adds an interesting twist to this problem. He reports on the findings of the Media Research Center's third annual "Faith in a Box" survey of television's treatment of religion, quoting the report's principal writer as having found that "nebulous faith in some higher power" is fine; it's when a character shows a clearly defined religious commitment that he and/or she are portrayed as "strange" and "almost always turn out to be intolerant, violent wackos." The subtlety of this distinction between generalized religious profession and overt, sectarianly argued action is an important one for the Evangelical who, because of the faith/works connection in his or her credo, is always going to come out on the short end of the public image stick.

On the other hand, all is not lost. The Barna Research Group, Ltd., in 1995 surveyed Americans about the major faith groups in this country in terms of whether or not the respondent thought the tradition had a positive or negative influence. The results, released February 5, 1996, showed that when asked about Christianity in general nearly nine in ten Americans (85 percent) see Christians as having a positive effect on our society. Six in ten (58 percent), when asked about Judaism in general, see Jews as having a positive effect. Interestingly enough, only 13 percent of Americans think that atheists have a positive influence upon our society.

50. My omission of the "Protestant" restrictive adjective is deliberate here. The number of "Evangelicals" is falling rather precipitously in this country. According to George Barna, research shows only 7 percent of Americans holding Evangelical beliefs in 1994, a drop from 9 percent

in 1993 and from 12 percent in 1992 (*Virtual America* [Regal Books, 1994], 113). In a February 24, 1995, news release, the Barna Research Group, Ltd., reported that "although evangelicals get a lot of media attention, they represent only about 6 percent of the adult population. This is a 50 percent decrease in magnitude since 1992" (2). Barna's figures are consistent with those reported by other demographers, though all agree that there is some room for discussion about just exactly what an "Evangelical" is and therefore about who should and should not be counted.

By whatever set of definitions being used, however, it is still true that many of Evangelicalism's characteristics and tenets are being taken up by disaffected Roman Catholics, leading to a recognition that it is quite possible to speak, as here, of Evangelical political activity or even Evangelical religious sympathies without meaning Protestant religious practice. The fact that this is something of a doctrinal and historical hodge-podge seems to bother no one, least of all those engaging in it.

51. This one was, in its origins, valued for its religious, rather than its sociopolitical, benefits. Reporting on religion's "Ten-Year High" worldwide, George Gallup wrote: "The U.S. is unique in that we have at the same time a high level of religious belief and a high level of formal education. In fact, formal education in this country generally traces its origins back to colonial times and early days of the republic when colleges were founded to train ministers and schools were started up to teach children to read the Bible" (*Emerging Trends,* March 1996, 5).

52. In this list of evils, I have studiously avoided including religious pluralism both because it seems to me to not be so much destructive as confusing to most people (and even enlightening, for many) and because historically it has not, as I have suggested in the body of this essay, been an American bugaboo. Paul Galloway of the *Chicago Tribune* summed up the history part of this quite nicely when, using several sources, he debunked some of the pet assumptions of the "Christian Right" that fly in the face of the facts. The founders' goal was pluralism, Galloway's authorities argue, citing as examples facts like our being the first Western nation to deliberately omit crosses and other overtly Christian images from its flag and national symbols. They cite as well our 1797 treaty with Tripoli, an Islamic nation, that was negotiated by George Washington and, following the Senate's ratification, signed by President John Adams, "As the government of the United States of America is not in any sense founded on the Christian religion" ("U.S.'s Christian Founda-

tion Formed on Shaky Evidence," as carried in the *Herald-Sun,* July 1, 1995, C-2).

On a less narrative basis, Kosmin and Lachman in their magisterial *One Nation under God: Religion in Contemporary American Society* (Harmony Books, 1993) likewise question the actual divisiveness of pluralism. "Yet, amid talk of moral pluralism," they write, "8 in 10 Americans agree 'mostly' or 'completely' that absolute standards of good and evil apply universally, and 94 percent would welcome stronger family ties" (280).

53. One of the most useful points made by Richard Baer in his "Our Faithless Forefathers" is his discussion of this very point. The deistic Jefferson's eighteenth-century concepts of reason guided by the senses as an effective tool for apprehending the moral law of nature and of nature as qualitative as well qualitative simply do not obtain today, making for an almost irresolvable conflict between original descriptive intent and the present-day applicability of it.

At a more personal level, I attended a July 1994 press conference during the Christian Booksellers Association's International Convention in Denver at which William Bennett, Os Guiness, Michael Horton, and Jim Wallis spoke. Cal Thomas was moderator. It was he who set the tone and drove home for me even more graphically this hiatus between older and newer ways of viewing. Thomas said in his opening remarks about the need for government intervention in moral matters: "Why is that necessary for government to do? Because the founders understood that men and women were basically flawed on the inside — and that if they would not be constrained from within by the presence and power of God whom they worshipped, then they needed to be restrained from without by the presence and power of the state in order to conform them to a standard that would, because of self-evident truths, [i.e., *Jefferson's Natural Law*] promote the general welfare, etc., etc." (a printout of this conference may be found in *Modern Reformation,* September/October 1994, 24–27).

54. Next to the pope (and, some observers would add, Mother Teresa), the most admired spiritual leader in the world today, including in this country, is the Dalai Lama. While Buddhism and the Tibetan Buddhism of which he is the appointed leader are profound systems of perception and disciplined praxis, they are not theistic in the usual sense of that term. They are, however, almost entirely spiritual. Perhaps the sequela of America's increased intimacy with Buddhism that has most

affected god-talk in this culture is a forced, popular awareness of the logic and, at times, even the efficacy of this approach.

His Holiness the Dalai Lama, in an interview granted to Jean-Claude Carrière in late 1995, goes to some lengths to elaborate upon this very point. Entitled in its published form "Beyond Religion," the interview opens with His Holiness's saying, "Many think that spiritual and religious activities are really just one. Religious leaders, here and there, loudly proclaim that they own the territory of the spirit, that it is their fief. By the same token, to hear them talk, anyone who rejects religion is *ipso facto* rejecting all spiritual experience" (*Shambhala Sun*, November 1995, 18–23).

His Holiness proceeds to discredit the "need" for religion and outline, instead, the place of mind and spirit, remarking in one place that of course humanity can survive without religion: "Figure it out: There are more than five billion of us on the planet. Three billion have no sort of religion." It is, as he suggests, a point no intelligent person should naively ignore in making personal decisions about faith and practice.

There is a second point to be made here. For purely numerical reasons, it does not belong in the body of my argument just yet, and probably also because it treats only one aspect of this particular part of contemporary god-talk. It does need to be mentioned, however. I refer to the potentially ameliorating effect of Islam upon the inability or reluctance of many Americans to integrate private faith, public stances, and organized religion into a coherent, moral whole.

Islam's presence in American culture is not yet sufficient to influence that process very much, if at all. (Louis Farrakhan and the Nation of Islam may be the one exception, depending on how one defines N.O.I.'s place within the larger faith tradition.) As Islam's influence grows, however, and as its numbers increase, the Muslim integration of these three spheres of expression under the principles of Sinai is bound to receive more and more attention.

Islam incorporates both a Law and a Way, each of which deals with morality. While *Shariah* (Divine Law) outlines and codifies actions as obligatory, recommended, permitted, disapproved, and forbidden, the Way deals with the heart as the center from which such voluntary compliance comes. The result is known as "Spiritual Chivalry" and is the kind of clean, clear, integrated morality that is becoming increasingly attractive to many Americans. A detailed explication of this part of Islam may be found in *God's Will Be Done*, volume 2 in a five-volume series: Laleh Bakhtiar, *The Moral Healer's Handbook: The Psychology of Spiritual Chivalry* (KAZI Publications, 1994).

Additionally, there is also a considerable push underway to accomplish much the same thing as Islam does out of motivations that are closer to the Dalai Lama's principles of a-religiosity. To many the efforts may seem to be only a playing at semantics, but there is a growing number of voices speaking out for a return to Virtue (capital "V" intended) or Character as different from any value as we usually employ that word. That is, value is somewhat idiosyncratic, or may be, and is definitely susceptible to cultural and political influences, whereas virtue — or at least the four classic Aristotelian ones of prudence, justice, fortitude, and temperance — are a kind of moral horse sense that doesn't require any religious commitment or offer a conflict with any. This line of thinking has at least become visible enough in the public arena to have constituted a *Newsweek* cover story by Kenneth Woodward ("What Is Virtue?" June 13, 1994, 38–39).

Oddly enough, as a line of thinking it is also very, very close in its near avoidance of religious validation to what virtue's great popularizer, William Bennett, has argued, however inelegantly and opportunistically (see "The Man of the Minute," Michael Kelly, *The New Yorker,* July 17, 1995, 26–30).

55. One of the most enjoyable as well as complete ways I know of for arriving at a working knowledge of contemporary spirituality is through the magisterial collection Frederic and Mary Ann Brussat, *Spiritual Literacy: Reading the Sacred in Everyday Life* (Scribner, 1996).

Interlude

1. Among the most remarkable, utile, and insightful recent studies of current theology, in my opinion, is Harvey Cox's *Fire from Heaven: Pentecostalism, Spirituality, and the Re-Shaping of Religion in the Twenty-first Century* (Addison-Wesley, 1994). It is that rare kind of book that fills me with the urge to strike all the people I care about on the hand and say, "Read this! Now!"

One of the multitude of points that Cox makes brilliantly and with stellar economy is this sense, in what he calls primal religion and I have begun to privately think of as closet religion, of genderless God. Describing a recent trip of his own to Italy and Sicily to visit Christian congregations, Cox ruminates upon a sermon and says: "This is where the most fundamental revolution is going on because what is being altered is nothing short of what might be called 'the gender of God' " (201). He concludes, as have many of us in the populism camp, that " 'God-the-lover'...may already be courting the hearts of unlettered men and women...albeit unnoticed by theologians" (202).

Chapter Eight: Up from the Belly of Time

1. Perhaps the popular thinker who most needs mention here is Marshall McLuhan inasmuch as he predicted the experiential religious revival that we are indeed passing through. A brief but thorough overview of McLuhan's writing on this and related ideas may be found in Ian Cotton, *The Hallelujah Revolution: The Rise of the New Christians* (Prometheus Books, 1996), especially in chapter 2, "How Green Is My Vicarage."

2. Tricky word "transcendent," because it has a theological nicety and a lay utility that often seem at loggerheads. As Campbell used it and as popular usage appears to employ it, seeing the transcendent is possible only because it is also immanent in the theological sense of that word.

3. While using the word "tragic" may appear to be editorializing on my part (and probably is, at least to some extent), I mean by it to assign a kind of heroic proportion to what is happening, one that lies far beyond "odd" and "poignant," though they too appertain. The tragic element here is a kind of literary one that matches in its descriptive parameters the fourth and last of Campbell's major mythological periods, The Way of Man (see Lobell, *Joseph Campbell: The Man and His Ideas,* 26–28).

4. The major demographers all report essentially identical statistical profiles here. Approximately 90 to 93 percent of American adults believe in some supernatural being that they define on a sliding scale of personal involvement and established orthodoxy as anything from a Spirit to a Higher Being to God to God the Father. About 80 to 83 percent of those Americans claim Christianity, again on a sliding scale of orthodoxy and personal involvement. Only about 3 percent of Americans claim atheism, the rest choosing either agnosticism or privacy. Beyond the obvious validation of ours as a Christian polity, the second most telling fact may

be the extent to which it is also Christianized. Thus the 1994 Harris poll (the most recent national research firm to my knowledge to have asked such questions) found that approximately half of the 17+/-% of believing Americans who declined to profess Christianity still claimed belief in the resurrection of Jesus Christ and in the Virgin birth, an astonishing allegiance to doctrines that are, at the very least, very specifically Christian and, ironically, are contested by a sizeable proportion of American self-professing Christians.

5. Reporting in *Religion in America: The 1996 Report of the Princeton Religion Research Center,* George Gallup describes the phenomenon by saying, "We want the fruits of faith, but less, its obligations" (8).

6. There is a deliberate vagueness in my use of "a dozen years" to date this phenomenon. The so-called "spirituality movement" in American culture is commonly dated from ca. 1965. At some point, its visible presence and general appeal became so great that its practices and principles began to find a place within the larger culture and, of importance here, to actively affect religious understanding and practice. That slide from subculture to main culture to institutional culture was so gradual as to lack any remarkable events by which to date it. Most theorists would, however, agree that the bridge in each case was, in large measure, the self-help movement which swept the country from the late 1970s onward, carrying spirituality on its ample back as it came. Certainly by the mid to late 1980s (my dozen years or so ago) Hazelden books were showing up in church study groups, just as recovery groups were showing up in churches and synagogues. Melody Beattie, Sue Bender, Keith Miller, Anne Wilson Schaef, and at least another dozen writers within the same field became not only household names, but theological ones. Once that had happened, the popular refinement of the distinction between spirituality and religion was well on its way to established fact. The complementary relationship between the two, however, has not as yet been nearly so forthcoming.

7. The stripped-down, denuded aesthetic austerity of American Protestantism has become not only its hallmark, but also the source of far bitterer and more acerbic comments than mine here, ones like "Protestantism? Oh, you mean four walls and a sermon." The popular presence of such cracks (which quite literally were unheard and unheard of fifty years ago) speaks volumes about the increasing emphasis by seekers on sensual richness in worship.

8. Just what exactly does make a space sacred is a little trickier. Perhaps, as some have suggested, the number of such places is indeed limited, the ancients having found the bulk of them long before our coming. Perhaps they are the result of natural energy fields that, like the dowser's art, presently lie beyond our ability to identify and define them scientifically. Perhaps they are places of unanalyzed and currently unanalyzable acoustical peculiarities. Nobody knows and most of us, including me, aren't terribly comfortable even pursuing the matter for very long.

There has been, however, a consistently expanding flow of books about the nature, identification, use, and doctrine of sacred space over the past few years, some of which have greatly diminished my own prior and probably arrogant set of sureties about them. One of my "picks" of this crop is actually a 1992 reprint of a 1976 release, *The Silbury Treasure: The Great Goddess Rediscovered* by Michale Dames (Thames and Hudson). And skeptics in particular should try John Edwin Wood's *Sun, Moon and Standing Stones* (Oxford University Press, 1978).

9. We should reemphasize here that the sweep of popular absorption has engaged not just physical space per se, (as evidenced, for example, in the impressive sales of books like Judith Cornell's *Mandala* (Quest, 1995), but has engaged even more enthusiastically and particularly the rituals that sacramentalize both overt and covert space and give it its spiritual utility. For a superb overview of the role of ritual, readers should see Debra Farrington's "Hungry for Ritual" in *Publishers Weekly's Religion Bookline* (August 15, 1996, 2–3). A seminary bookstore manager, Farrington furnishes a well-worded and at times beautiful analysis of this complex subject.

10. Though it is probably very obvious, care demands that we remind ourselves from time to time that ours is also a very Romantic period of history. Thus the medievalism of which I speak is most definitely a romanticized, rather than a historical, one. Marshall McLuhan foresaw this shift, and interested readers may want to look again at his predictive insights, an affirming number of which are now fully effected fact.

11. Lumping all of these "forms" of sacredness and ways of creating nonlocative spaces in which to engage it is a convenience for the sake of brevity that is almost as distorting and unfair to the reader as it is painful for me.

The arts in general have, from time immemorial, been the offspring as well as the servant of the gods. Christianity's oldest branch, Orthodoxy, for example, has traditionally seen its ancient liturgy as having been constructed around the five senses specifically so that the worshiper might "know/feel" God: the visual beauty of vestments, decorations, icons, etc., appeal to sight; incense appeals to smell; music appeals to sound; the Eucharist appeals to taste; and kissing icons, crossing oneself, passing the peace, lighting candles all appeal to touch.

For an overview of the changing role of the arts in postliterate Christianity, interested readers may want to see *The Landscape of Praise* by Blair Gilmer Meeks (Trinity Press International, 1996). For an overview of the same issue in religion in general, of the growth of sales in books about that area, and of the expanding place of poetry in particular, see my "Through Art to Adoration" (*Publishers Weekly*, September 11, 1995, 34–36). For an especially incisive discussion of the changing role of one art — music — in private or individual spirituality and/or religion, see "The Virtual Sacred: Finding God at Tower Records" by Katherine Bergeron (cover story, *The New Republic*, February 27, 1995, 29–34).

12. There has been considerable coverage in both academic books and popular periodicals over the last two or three years of the growth of both these hybrid systems as well as of better known ones like voodoo. My favorite recent example of the popular power of these faiths, however, is not in such factual overviews, but in a *New York Times* report (August 8, 1995) by Rick Bragg about a whole crack-infested neighborhood in New Orleans that for two hours one Wednesday night invoked Ogoun La Flambeau, the voodoo god of war and fire, to come among them and drive out the criminals from their midst. The fascinating thing about Bragg's coverage is not that the event happened or that he covered it, but that the priestess who conducted the service was a Maine-born white and, as Bragg notes, many of voodoo's followers in New Orleans "seem to be white people — nose and tongue piercers, middle-aged intellectuals and men with foot-long ponytails — who enjoy the religion's drumming and cultural aspects."

13. See Bachleda, "Keeping Faith with the Earth," *Publishers Weekly*, February 14, 1994, for an overview of the connections involved here and of recent texts that address them.

14. The authoritative recent volume on Pentecostalism is certainly Harvey Cox's *Fire from Heaven* (Addison-Wesley, 1994), a delight to read whether one is interested in Pentecostalism or not. The same religious energy that informs Pentecostalism, however, also informs many other divisions of Christianity, several of them mainline denominations.

United Methodism has its Aldersgate; Episcopalianism has whole parishes changing their names to include the word "charismatic" in some
way or other, etc., etc. Randall Balmer in his *Mine Eyes Have Seen the
Glory: A Journey into the Evangelistic Subculture of America* (Oxford
University Press, 1993) does a good job, especially in his introductory essay, of overviewing this shift among some of America's Christian
mainstream.

15. Pentecostalism is also the fastest growing segment of Christianity
worldwide. With 410 million adherents globally, Pentecostalism is gaining close to 20 million new members every year. The threat to Roman
Catholicism of Pentecostalism in Latin America is so great, for instance,
as already to have necessitated at least one papal visit (see "John Paul
Goes to War," *Newsweek,* February 12, 1996, 39); and the so-called
"Toronto Blessing" has swept through far more than Canada, trigger-
ing no small amount of official agitation in this country among mainline
Protestants who apparently share the pope's level of concern about their
own faithful.

16. This particular quote is taken from "Re-Imagining the Church,"
Ruth Nicastro, *Journal of Women's Ministries,* Spring 1994, 14. The se-
riousness, scope, and history of the Minneapolis conference can hardly
be more than suggested in the present essay. I would be derelict, however, if I did not use note space to urge upon every reader *Wisdom's
Feast: Sophia in Study and Celebration,* new edition, by Susan Cole,
Marian Ronan, and Hal Taussig (Sheed & Ward, 1996). The authors
have been intimately involved in Sophia scholarship and Sophia liturgy
for many years and in this new edition chronicle with surprisingly un-
empassioned succinctness the role they and their work played in the
events leading up to the Minneapolis meeting. That chronicle includes
charges of heresy against Cole and Taussig, formally filed by a United
Methodist clergy but denied, prior to trial, by a UMC bishop.

Wisdom's Feast was first published in 1986 under the title of *Sophia:
The Future of Feminist Spirituality.* Based on the success of that first
trial balloon, *Feast* was reissued two years later under its current title
and was instrumental in formalizing the kind of re-imagining exercised
in Minneapolis.

Not only, then, do Cole, Ronan, and Taussig speak with the authority
of intimate experience, but they also bring to this new edition a keen
sense of the practical. Their summary of what happened in the decade
between 1986 and 1996 in Sophia studies and politics is an invaluable, if

partisan, one. The bibliography, incorporated into the body of the text, of recent scholarship is exhaustive of the significant sources. And the second half of the edition is given over, here as previously, to orders of service and suggested liturgies, allowing every reader to see for him- or herself the actual words and forms around which the controversy continues to swirl.

17. Many of the participants left Minneapolis exhilarated. Some, like Mary Ann Lundy, a staff member of the Presbyterian Church USA who had been instrumental in getting denominational funding for the event, lost their jobs. But nobody among the participants and no body among the represented denominations escaped without some considerable conversation (see Nicastro, "Re-Imagining the Church," 14, 15).

For example, months later the General Assembly of the Presbyterian Church USA, the governing body of the denomination, convened in Wichita, Kansas. The meeting, where normally attention is focused upon the election of the church's moderator or leader and on administrative business, was given over so completely to trying to figure out what had happened in Minnesota and why that little else of import seemed to transpire. In fact, when *Christianity Today,* the leading journal of American Protestantism, covered the assembly, correspondent Timothy C. Morgan devoted all but a paragraph and a half of his full-page report to the impact of Re-Imagining upon the assembly's agenda.

From the point of view of our present discussion, perhaps an equally pertinent part of this is what Morgan uncovered as causative or particularly aberrant doctrinally to many of the delegates to the assembly. In reporting on those aspects of the Re-Imagining Conference that had caused the greatest agitation in Wichita, Morgan identified gender-feminist theology as the chief culprit and summarized its tenets. In a precis of the four major principles in Morgan's gender-feminist theology, the third was "Individual experience of God is an essential component in shaping one's belief" ("Re-Imagining Labeled 'Reckless,' " *Christianity Today,* July 18, 1994, 49.)

Two months later, *Christianity Today* followed Morgan's coverage with an article, "Testing the Spiritualities" by James R. Edwards, professor of religion and chair of the Department of Religion and Philosophy at Jamestown College, who references the Re-Imagining Conference as his proof text. Edwards finds that "many Christians, however, are confused about the resurgence of the spirituality that rushes to fill the vacuum in America," and then asks, "Is spirituality per se Christian? Is it neutral? Or are all non-Christian spiritualities anti-Christian?" He concludes that not all are good and that "spirituality, then, is not something about which Christians should be undiscerning" (*Christianity Today,* September 12, 1994, 25).

18. Once more, there is no attempt to exclude Islam here, but only a recognition that the rumblings within that faith have not yet reached quite the same proportions of volume as in the other two. So far as I know, the idea of a female iman has not yet come up for serious consideration, and Islam, as we have noted elsewhere, is chary of any manipulation of the Koran, including any translations out of the Arabic and any additions or emendations. While traditional and progressive Muslims alike seem eager to argue that Islam has never suppressed women in its recognition of differences in gender roles and obligations to the faith, there are evidences, nonetheless, of increased interest lately in a fuller incorporation of women in Islam and Islamic religious history. An annotated bibliography of some current studies of Islam and of this issue of gender within it may be found in "This Was the Year for Books on Islamic Faith, Culture and Politics" by Henry Carrigan (*Publishers Weekly's Religion Bookline,* August 15, 1996, 10).

19. I mean to suggest here not only the obvious cults — the Jonestowners and the Branch Davidians — but less socially and politically volatile phenomena like the Elvis movement, which has increasingly taken on the terminology and symbols of Christianity as it has moved from fan-club to cult status and on toward who yet knows where. Those inclined to pooh-pooh or disparage such activities as silly or inconsequential emotionalism may want to review newspaper coverage of the twentieth anniversary of Elvis's death (week of August 12–19, 1996) or, as a particularly crisp summary, Robert Campbell's review of *Graceland: Going Home with Elvis* (Karal Ann Marling, Harvard University Press, 1996) entitled "The King in His Castle" (*New York Times Book Review,* August 25, 1996, 9). The coup de grâce, however, is *In Search of Elvis: Music, Race, Art, Religion* (Westview Press, 1997) — it also triggered its own *New York Times Magazine* cover story — by Vernon Chadwick, the University of Mississippi English professor who has become the most influential interpreter of this aspect of the Elvis phenomenon.

20. Many contemporary Christians, particularly feminist ones, embrace Sophia not only as divine Wisdom, but also as the Bride of Christ. Interested readers will find *Jesus: Miriam's Child, Sophia's Prophet* by

prominent theologian Elisabeth Schüssler Fiorenza (Continuum, 1994) to be particularly informative. (The book won the $10,000 Continuum Book Award in its year of publication.) Two other recent volumes, both from Lindisfarne, that may be of interest are *Sophia: The Wisdom of God* by Sergei Bulgakov and *Theosophia: Hidden Dimensions of Christianity* by Arthur Versluis.

21. Whether Gnosticism is a religion or a religio/philosophic attitude lies outside the range of our present discussion. For that reason, so too do the tenets that characterize it. But it still seems prudent to at least note the fact that Gnosticism involves far more than just the "knowing" of my main essay. The dualism of Gnosticism's perspective, for instance, is a huge part of its/Sophia's claim to fame as representative of the most primal tensions in Judaism, Christianity, and, to some extent, even Islam. In this latter regard, Sufism is frequently referred to as a gnostic religion and is, not coincidentally, the fastest-growing division of Islam in this country. Etc., etc.

22. Richard Scheinin, "Wondering about the Gnostics," *Publishers Weekly*, August 15, 1994, 45. More to the point, however, for a popular but brilliant and truly informing overview of contemporary religious experience as seen through the historical lens of Gnosticism, the reader should see Harold Bloom's *Omens of Millennium* (Riverhead Books, 1996).

23. Brent Walters, professor at San Jose State and an authority on early church history, has become, by extension, one of the country's foremost experts on Gnosticism as well. Walters articulates the gnostic experience clearly and in pretty dramatic terms. "It's like a light bulb that's been turned on inside: 'You *did* not know, and now you *do* know.' It is a redemptive process" (as quoted in Scheinin, "Wondering about the Gnostics," 45.)

24. This is very close to the problem Paul addresses in his now-famous letter to the early church at Corinth: "And if I should have prophecy and should know all mysteries and all knowledge, and if I should have all faith so that I could remove mountains, and have not love, I am nothing" (1 Cor. 13:2).

25. Redfield's *The Celestine Prophecy* reveals rather didactically but in fictive form the nine insights that lead to spiritual health. The book was first published privately, but became an underground bestseller within a year. Warner Books then bought it up for commercial publi-

cation in 1994 and, at the time of this writing over two years later, it has been on the national bestseller lists without interruption since.

Prophecy is generally regarded and reviewed as a gnostic novel, as is its sequel, *The Tenth Insight* (Warner, 1996). It is also regarded by some religionists as approaching the status of scripture or authoritative text for New Age religion, having already spawned commentaries and innumerable small-group reading bodies across the country.

There are few more irrefutable testaments to the power of contemporary popular religious fervor than the publishing histories of the "insight" or gnostic books like *Prophecy* or Betty Eadie's now-famous near-death chronicle, *Embraced by the Light.* It too was rejected by mainline publishers and then, after being privately published, became such an underground seller as to command commercial attention. At the time, in June 1993, that Bantam bought *Embraced*'s paperback rights, their six million dollar advance was thought to be the largest ever given for reprint rights in American publishing history. In the same vein is Neale Donald Walsch's *Conversations with God* (Putnam, 1996), which has followed the same track from small-press publication to underground success to commercial publishing with a big advance and bestsellerdom.

26. This is particularly true of books like *The Five Gospels: The Search for the Authentic Words of Jesus* by the scholars of the Jesus Seminar, which, when it was published by Macmillan in December 1993, not only went on bestseller lists across the country (the volume remained on *Publishers Weekly*'s religion list for nine months, for example), but also triggered public burnings and demonstrations. A discussion of other recent editions of extracanonical texts along with bibliographic information about them may be found in Scheinin ("Wondering about the Gnostics," 49).

27. Prominent Jesus scholar Marcus Borg, in listing the theological themes to which "particular attention" is paid in his masterful *Meeting Jesus Again for the First Time* (HarperSanFrancisco, 1993), cites first "the emergence of both 'Son of God' and 'Wisdom/Sophia' christologies in early Christianity" ("Meet the Author," GTU Bookstore on Ecunet, January 19, 1996.)

28. In addition to Borg, the most frequently quoted and photoed are scholars like John Dominic Crossan (*The Historical Jesus: The Life of a Mediterranean Jewish Peasant* [HarperSanFrancisco, 1991]; *Jesus: A Revolutionary Biography* [HarperSanFrancisco, 1994]; etc.);

Robert Funk (*Honest to Jesus: Jesus for a New Millennium* [Harper-SanFrancisco, 1996]; etc.); Luke Timothy Johnson (*The Real Jesus* [HarperSanFrancisco, 1995]; etc.); Burton Mack (*Who Really Wrote the New Testament?* [HarperSanFrancisco, 1995]; etc.); John Meier (*A Marginal Jew: Rethinking the Historical Jesus — Mentor, Message, and Miracle* [Doubleday, 1994], etc.); and Bishop John Spong (*This Hebrew Lord* [HarperSanFrancisco, 1993]; *Liberating the Gospels: Reading the Bible with Jewish Eyes* [HarperSanFrancisco, 1996]).

29. While most of the more populist writers within the field of Jesus Studies believe earnestly in the devoutness of their cause and can articulate with winning sincerity their positions, the most complete and best argued *apologia* I have seen is Dom Crossan's "Why Christians Must Search for the Historical Jesus," *Bible Review,* April 1996, 35–45.

30. Like most trends and shifts, the Genesis "boom" was not so much a boom as the slow building of a wave that was not visible from a distance until it was almost cresting. For booksellers, librarians, and publishers, however, there had been indications for at least two years of a gathering interest, evidenced in an increasing number of books on Abraham (as opposed to the more usually celebrated Moses) and Noah as a prophet (as opposed to his animals and the Flood) and Jacob (as opposed to the more colorful Joseph), etc., etc. That is to say, not only was the number of books with content origins in Genesis increasing, but also the emphases in those books had begun to shift from cultural to theological ones.

31. For a succinct, but annotated, overview of these titles, see Rahel Musleah's "A Reader's Guide to Genesis Books," *Publishers Weekly's Religion Bookline* (October 1, 1996, 6, 7).

32. As the months since the initial Moyers showing have progressed, they have provided perhaps the ultimate confirmation of this; for it is in how and what we write about life and faith for our children that we confirm or deny in the most irrefutable of ways the validity of what we say. While Bible story books have been with us from time immemorial, the winter of 1996 produced two or three examples of what looked very much like a new kind of children's Bible book, one that plays to the mystery and invites the imagination.

Faith has always required narrative imagination. The ability to envision precedes the ability to move above a fight-or-flight instinctual level. Yet historically we have been unwilling to instruct a child's imagination through Bible story. Indoctrination and enculturation, not the skills of adoration, were the genre's raison d'être; but perhaps no longer. When I look at books like Rabbi Susan Sasso's story of Naamah, Noah's wife, and of how she was told by God to collect and save aboard the Ark all the seeds of the earth (*A Prayer for the Earth,* Jewish Lights) or Sheryl Prenzlau's *The Jewish Children's Bible: Genesis* (Pitspopany Press) I see books that for the first time in my lifetime as a working religion book professional invite our children to pass with us through Genesis into that which informs it.

33. This is not my pun, but is borrowed from any number of newspaper religion writers from around the country who dubbed the winter of 1996 as "the winter of the second flood" in honor of the Genesis inundation.

34. For a detailed study of these ideas and metaphors see Diarmuid O'Murchu, M.S.C., *Quantum Theology* (Crossroad, 1997).

Chapter Nine: For the Love of Theology

1. Lest this appear to be just a gratuitous slam on my part, let me ameliorate it by two additional statements. First, my concern for the consequences of this attitude and my agitation over its ubiquity are so keen that I would do anything, including gratuitous slams, to try to call attention to the problem. Second, in conversation — and it is almost entirely conversational data that I am responding to here — I rarely if ever encounter this attitude of scornful nonengagement among our more pastoral and respected theologs.

My favorite, newest case in point is a lunch I shared with Martin Marty in Chicago just after the Democratic National Convention had been there in September 1996. While the conversation around the table ranged fairly widely, the recurring *leitmotif* of many of Marty's comments was his ongoing concern with this very issue. He expressed, in fact, a poignantly pastoral grief over the popular American confusion (which he attributed directly to homogenizing, abundantly accessible media) between generic faith and actual religion. It was not the first time I had wished for a tape recorder instead of a fork when in Marty's company.

2. It is imperative here, in the name of intellectual honesty if nothing else, to acknowledge two things. First, in the case of *Touched by an Angel,* television show and sermon do *not* differ in one very important

way. While she may be an angel by cathode light, in the cold light of day Della Reese is herself a preacher complete with her own pulpit and her own congregation. Second, we must acknowledge the fact that image is always more powerful than word; and any discussion that puts the two of them in the same sentence needs to recognize that fact immediately.

Just as an aside, it is worth noting as well that this dominance-of-image principle has led to some other interesting media applications beyond the predictable ones. For instance, Visual International is a South Africa-based company now moving actively in the American market, and its cause and product is the word-for-word translation of the entire Christian Bible out of print format and into video by means of an adroit combination of acting with unobtrusive, on-screen verse citations. While the whole is a fifteen-year project, Visual now has three of the sixty-six books — Matthew, Acts, and Esther — on the market. The results are spectacular. They also are very persuasive confirmation not only of the principle in question, but also of Visual's own preproject research that found that, even among the interested, 20 percent of us are more likely to look than read.

3. Nor do I mean to suggest that all of established or formal religion is pleased to ignore or discredit the importance of these media expressions of faith. Probably my favorite "official" — authorized, if you prefer — religion magazine for laity is *St. Anthony Messenger*, a Roman Catholic family publication that I find myself reading every month, not as a professional reviewer, but just as a pleasured reader. One of the column that attracts me to such faithfulness, I must confess, is James Arnold's "Movies/TV" in which *St. Anthony* goes so far as to review theologically television's commercials as well as its programming — which is the kind of clear-eyed, hard-headed religious realism that always deserves kudos in my opinion.

4. Once more, I find myself not wanting to belabor a point, while at the same time being concerned lest we manage to underestimate its importance as a result of some false economy.

It would be impossible, I suspect, to exaggerate the role that referencing plays in any group's ability to speak cohesively to one another over a sustained period of time. I know it would be impossible to exaggerate the shock to every cultural system when the citations and fixed terms of referencing undergo abrupt change, which is exactly what happened in this country in the decades of our mid-century and which has bombarded our god-talk and social policy with equal ferocity ever since. Nor is this abrupt interruption in conversational referencing as it appertains to god-talk just a matter of new clichés from films, e.g., "Build it and they will come," etc. The theology implied in referencing a Yellow Submarine instead of the Land of Nod just east of Eden is as different as it is informing.

In many ways, the cultural literacy that E. D. Hirsch captured and then championed so persuasively in his 1987 book by the same name — *Cultural Literacy: What Every American Needs to Know* (Houghton Mifflin) — was, alas, already moribund when Hirsch paused to celebrate it. The younger the body of speakers, the more apparent that truth is today, not just on the streets, but also in homes and businesses and even many schools and colleges. It certainly is apparent in god-talk.

I was confirmed in this — and with considerable amusement, I might add — when I read the headline blazoned across page 46 of the *New York Times Magazine* for June 4, 1995. It read, and I quote in entirety: "In its own, sly, serious way, *Pulp Fiction* is engaged in a sustained theological inquiry into good and evil. The intervention of the Big Kahuna challenges the relativistic framework of the *Godfather* movies." I understood the headline, but believe me, I was referencing like crazy out of a culture that wasn't even around in 1987.

5. For a sense of just the Judeo-Christian side of this phenomenon, interested readers may want to look at "Evergreen Audio Favorites" by Terri Castillo (*Publishers Weekly's Religion Bookline,* July 1, 1996, 3).

6. At the time of this writing, the original *Chicken Soup for the Soul* (Health Communications) by Jack Canfield and Victor Hansen has sold 5,450,729 copies to be exact. Multiply that figure by the number of readers per individual unit for this type of book (probably five to seven). Add to that figure the fact that there have been nine additional Canfield and Hansen spin-offs, the most recent being *Chicken Soup for the Woman's Soul* with Jennifer Hawthorne and Marci Shimoff and *Chicken Soup for the Soul at Work* with Martin Rutte, Maida Rogerson, and Tim Clauss in late 1996. The result should give even the most dubious pause to consider.

7. Knopf, 1995.

8. So great is the perceived impact of the small-group movement and particularly of the small-group movement in relation to Moyers's Genesis work, that *Library Journal,* the professional journal of the library industry, published a major preairing article, "Something to Talk About," by Barbara Hoffert et al. featuring Moyers's work and review-

ing other similarly appropriate titles (September 1, 1996, 140–43). One of the more delicious subnotes in this whole thing, of course, is that Moyers got the idea for his Genesis when he himself stumbled upon a small-group discussion of Genesis at Jewish Theological Seminary in New York several years ago.

9. *Emerging Trends*, September 1996, 3.

Chapter Ten: In the Palaces of Cyberspace

1. For a very fine introduction to every person's place upon the theological ladder and to the overall hierarchy of modern theology, see Stanley J. Grenz and Roger E. Olson, *Who Needs Theology? An Invitation to the Study of God* (InterVarsity Press, 1996).

2. Dale Lature, an expert on the relationship between god-talk and the Internet, spoke to this point by saying: "I think that in the case of cyberspace communications, we are seeing a much larger attempt by people with theological concerns to participate in the new media. That is, a higher percentage of participation than there was in the communication revolution that was happening during, or probably resulting in, the Reformation. I think the reason why is that the new media today as represented by Computer Mediated Communications are more widely accessible than was the printing process in Reformation times" (<dlature@iac.net>! http://www.iac.net:80/ dlature/ united/webtheo.html) for May 29, 1995.

3. Mark Kellner is an expert on computing, having written on the subject since 1983 for the *Washington Times*, contributed to many other periodicals, and served as editorial director of both *Portable Computing* and *Mobile Office*. His expertise, however, has become even more narrowly defined over the last few years, during which he has emerged as perhaps our leading authority on religion and computing.

When IDG Books (http://www.idgbooks.com), the firm that publishes all the "For Dummies" computing titles, perceived in 1995 the size of the theology/religion revolution going on in computing and cyberspace, it was Kellner to whom they turned. In May 1996 IDG published Kellner's *God on the Internet*, a 336-page, nineteen-chapter introduction to the myriad Internet religion sites — commercial, restricted, and homepage — that were operative at that time (their number having expanded even while *God* was in production.) The volume has become a kind of

starting point — an instant *sine qua non,* in fact — for anyone wanting to understand and/or enter the geography of electronic theology and
religion.

No dewy-eyed romantic, Kellner is very aware of the dangers (i.e.,
integrity of information, etc.) as well as the benefits of cyberspace and
of the fact that both are markedly exaggerated when they have to do
with faith — with its morbidity and mortality principle, that is. Kellner
deals openly, for example, with such events as the near destruction of
the World-Wide Church of God when it dropped in the three-month period of January to March 1996 from a membership of ninety thousand
to one of fifty thousand as a direct result of Internet communication
among members unmediated by ecclesiastical leadership, or with events
like the institution of renegade "virtual parishes" by dissident priests like
Jacques Gaillot that threaten the established order by providing a means
of circumventing it entirely.

While one assumes, based on human history, that increased communication will in the end prove to be of inestimable benefit, wisdom decrees,
as does Kellner, a judicious rather than a precipitous movement into this
brave new world.

4. One of the charges most often leveled at experiential churches
and at the seeker-oriented segments of megachurches is that they simply
cannot — or dare not, many of their critics say — provide theological
instruction. Whether this is a fair charge or not, it is an omission for
whatever reason and a legitimate concern that at least the megachurches
are not impervious to. The question is how to both be doctrinally
specific and seeker attractive.

5. In August 1996 at the annual meeting of the Religion Newswriters
Association in Chicago, Mark Kellner (see above) spoke on this very
matter of change within the status quo. He told the nation's religion
writers that "computers and computing are going to change the way
hierarchial religious organizations work because you have people talking
across levels, not up and down."

6. My proof-positive *du jour* of this fluid equality as an enacted fact
rather than a narrative one came when Indiana University Press promoted as its lead "title" for the Fall/Winter 1996 catalog and publishing
season, not a book but a CD-ROM. *Investigating Olduvai: Archaeology of Human Origins,* created by Jeanne Sept in collaboration with the
Teaching and Learning Technologies Lab at Indiana and released in February 1997, was tested for several years at the university in instructing

graduate students and even some undergraduate majors and nonmajors in archaeology. It introduces Mary Leaky's Olduvai Gorge and permits the user not only to learn but also simulate the methods of archaeology in virtual field work. Having been refined in the university's classes, the CD-ROM moved out of its beta phase in 1995 and is now being used as a standard "text" in Indiana's curriculum. *But....*

...But the university also saw *Investigating* as a product having significant general-trade potential because of archaeology's appeal for armchair scholars and, given the implications of early human origins study, particularly for those with theological and religious interests as well. "Many sailors, one ocean" takes on a whole new significance in such circumstances.

7. Poor Gutenberg, like René Descartes, is showing up in more than his fair share of disadvantageous word-play lately. Here's a recent one that I like as much for its sentiment as for its pun: Through his "Editor's Space" column in Bethlehem's *Diocesan Life,* Bill Lewell, communication minister for the Episcopal Diocese of Bethlehem, Pennsylvania, encourages his readers to participate ever more actively in cyberspace communication with one another and with their diocesan officials. He closed out his March 1996 column by observing: "Some say Gutenberg spawned the Protestant Reformation. A new electronic revolution will eventually have an even greater impact on our church. It's a virtual reality."

8. The push toward seeing that every child in this country is computer-literate and every adult has reasonable access at public expense to a computer and the Internet is a political reality as well as a moral necessity. Championed since 1992 by Al Gore and both political parties, funding that will eventuate in "reasonable access" is already being put in place. Lawrence Grossman, former head of PBS and former president of NBC News, has produced a magisterial overview of this process — its whys and wherefores, its pros and cons — in *The Electronic Republic* (Viking, 1995)

In reviewing Grossman's book for the *New York Times* (August 18, 1995), Michiko Kakutani concludes by saying: "His [Grossman's] book not only illustrates Marshall McLuhan's belief that 'as the speed of information increases' politics tends to move toward the 'immediate involvement of the entire community in the central acts of decision,' but also de Tocqueville's prescient observation that American democracy 'is constantly in the process of democratizing itself further.' " As in politics, so in religion.

9. This kind of statement always smacks of hyperbole. Or perhaps it is just that we use so much hyperbole these days that even honesty smacks of it. The unadorned truth, however, is exactly as stated. Almost every standard religion work imaginable, from the *Guru Granth Sahib* of the Sikh tradition to the *Commentary of St. Jerome,* is available on CD-ROM as of this writing. More to the point, however, are things like "Project Gutenberg" that post in cyberspace the less frequently called for texts of our faith traditions in order that the interested may download directly into their own hard drives. (Albeit with major questions like "integrity of information" and "publisher liability" still unresolved, a circumstance that presently suffuses Internet publishing of any sort with inestimable potential mayhem.)

10. The facts here are pretty astounding. A survey funded jointly by *Publishers Weekly* and Zondervan Publishing in 1996 showed that 42 percent of all those shopping in general commercial bookstores that year had purchased a Bible or a book dealing with Christian themes within the past twelve month period. Of that number, well over a third had done so within the month in which the survey was conducted.

Once again, however, observers in positions like mine all too frequently respond to and report upon the areas of heaviest gross movement, rather upon those of proportionally heavier movement in analyzing market activity. We tend, in other words, to look at statistics like the sales — five million and counting — of the new *Catechism of the Catholic Church,* which by anybody's definition is Christian and doctrinal, and say,"Wow! Look at that!" In reality, were the activities of exploding access viewed in proportion to total size of population, they would be far greater and more consistent in Judaism than in Christianity.

"English translations and commentaries on classic texts have burgeoned so rapidly that they now represent the largest collection of Jewish primary texts in a language other than Hebrew, says Seymour Rossel, the publisher of the Union of American Hebrew Congregations Press. 'No other community in the history of the Jewish people has placed so much emphasis on translating and interpreting texts,' he notes" (Rahel Musleah, "Jewish Sacred Texts," *Publishers Weekly,* October 14, 1996, 42).

11. The most blatant example of this within Christendom at the moment is probably the work of Fr. Jacques Gaillot. Fired by pope John

Paul II in 1995 from his position as bishop of Evereaux in Normandy because of his controversial stand on gay marriages, condom distribution, and noncelibate clergy, Gaillot suffered reassignment by the Vatican to Partenia, an ancient city in the Sahara that has been nothing more than sand and more sand for centuries. Undeterred in his isolation, Fr. Gaillot used the World Wide Web to create the first "virtual diocese"; and from Partenia's Internet site, he continues, at the time of this writing, to pastor his flock in both French and English while continuing as well to promulgate his views on social justice.

Far less splashy but just as portentous of opportunities ahead is Worldwide Faith News on the Internet (http://www.wfn.org), a project of the National Council of Churches of Christ in the USA. Officially launched August 31, 1996, WFN stores almost instantaneously news releases, policy statements, and other similar and/or related documents for national and global denominations as well as ecumenical agencies and other faith organizations. The result is a constantly changing, situation-responsive collection that is available for journalists, professional religionists, organization members, and the just plain interested or curious. Never before in the history of religion has such a resource for instant communication and authoritative, exhaustive sourcing been available to anybody, much less to all comers.

12. One of the raciest and most thorough short overviews of this phenomenon is "The Power of Babble" by Richard Ostling (*Time*, September 9, 1996, 58–59).

13. Edward Mendelson, professor of English at Columbia and a contributing editor to *PC Magazine*, published an absolutely charming as well as informative essay, "The Word and the Web," in the *New York Times Book Review* (June 2, 1996) in which he connects the whole business of hyperlink capability directly to the medieval scriptoria and the monks who so painstakingly illuminated their manuscripts and annotated them with cross-referencing. Computophobes with a religion bent or theological itch should regard Mendelson's essay as required reading, as well as therapeutic of their condition.

14. It's important to remember here that the release itself could not have happened had the computer not opened up the Scrolls in the first place. It was the computer's ability to take infinitely small pieces of the Scrolls and arrange and rearrange them electronically — a little like solving a jigsaw puzzle by computer — without the potentially ruinous

damage of physically handling that allowed scholars to reassemble and reconstruct them in the first place.

15. Evangelical Protestant Christianity seems more acutely aware of this potential market and of the ways to exploit it than any other branch of organized religion at the moment. Almost every major Evangelical house has been aggressively developing doctrinally specific, highly sophisticated interactive electronic teaching products for the young adult and juvenile markets since early 1996. The catalogs of firms like Tyndale House, Questar Publishing, Baker Books, WORD Kids!, Tommy Nelson, etc. reveal the richness of ever-increasing possibilities being explored by this branch of Christianity. It will be ten to twenty years before the success of their efforts can be confidently measured, but meanwhile every preliminary indication points in their favor.

16. In an unsigned 1994 Associated Press story (October 2), David Burke, director of translations for the American Bible Society, gave historical perspective to this shift, interpreting it "as part of a progression from oral traditions to reading and back to oral traditions." While Burke is hardly the only observer to routinely make this connection now, he was certainly one of the first.

17. For a superb and zesty as well as deeply informed study of this fact, see *The Soul of Cyberspace* by my colleague Jeff Zalesky (HarperEdge, 1997).

18. Another notable "first" for me in understanding the orality of electronic communication was the publication in mid-1996 of *Holy War On-Line: A Debate in Cyberspace* (MMI Publishing) that was transcribed, not exactly written, by David Zolt. As the title suggests, the book is a hard-copy, print-format presentation of a sustained, AOL message-board conversation about theology. The telling thing, though, was the fact that MMI positioned the volume in its marketing literature as having "more in common with *oral history transcripts and private diaries* than ordinary books" (emphases mine).

19. Taken from "The Daily Brief," Intelligent Network Concepts, Inc., Wednesday, August 14, 1996 (http://www.tiac.net/users/incinc/).

20. The increase in theological interest was marked enough for Steve Case, president of AOL, the country's largest commercial on-line server, to use his New Year's Greetings letter to AOL's membership on January 1, 1996, to announce the opening of an entire new area on "Religion and Beliefs."

21. As reported by columnist Terry Mattingly on Scripps-Howard News Service, June 19, 1996.

22. "Sorting through the Flood of Religious Information on the Internet," *Emerging Trends,* 1, 2.

23. This data was first relayed to me in a personal conversation in July 1996 by George Barna himself. Not only using the adjective "shocking," Barna also reached over and signed the notepaper on which I had recorded his findings. BRG has since released the same findings in television forums, though so far as I know at the time of this writing, the data has not yet appeared in print.

24. A goodly portion of this paradigmatic shift is to orality, of course. Probably the classic text on these issues and their interrelatedness is still Walter J. Ong's *Orality and Literacy: The Technologizing of the World* (Routledge, Chapman and Hall, 1982).

25. Lewis C. Henry, compiler, *5000 Quotations for all Occasions* (New Home Library, 1944).

26. In a rollicking piece of front-page reportage, "Not Just Sunday-Go-to-Meetin' — Religion Buffs, Clergy Surfing the 'Net Build Church in Cyberspace," (January 9, 1995), Ray Waddle, religion news editor for the *Tennessean,* interviewed a number of prominent religionists and clergy on the subject of religion and the Internet. Almost all of them made reference to the anonymity factor. Morris Chapman, then head of the Southern Baptist Convention, the nation's largest Protestant denomination, told Waddle, "People are more forthright [i.e., on the Internet] — it seems to be the nature of the medium."

Waddle himself summarized the Internet's interrelation with religion in this way: With the click of a computer button, users can request prayers, find companionship, and rage against theological enemies with relative anonymity. Shut-ins have a new voice. So do dissenters and malcontents. It's faster than print, more candid than Sunday school, more democratic than a deacons' meeting."

27. See n. 2 above.

28. Dale_Lature.parti@ecunet.org on May 29, 1995.

29. Dale_Lature.parti@ecunet.org on August 3, 1995.

30. *Silicon Snake Oil: Second Thoughts on the Information Highway* (Doubleday, 1995; issued in paperback by Image Books in 1996). An interesting collection of the thoughts of nineteen thinkers on this same subject is Sven Birkerts, ed., *Tolstoy's Dictaphone: Technology and the Muse* (Graywolf, 1996).

31. Dale_Lature.parti@ecunet.org on September 7, 1995.

32. http://www.logos.com.

33. While Logos has led the field in innovations and in sales to date, there are other serious competitors for customer loyalty. Parsons Technology is becoming a household word in Bible software, as is Kirkbride. Biblesoft, White Harvest, and Jones Digital Century have interesting new products. So too do religion book publishers like Zondervan, Abingdon, and Oxford University Press, to name but a few.

34. IDG, 1996.

35. And the conversation has indeed been global. One of the most articulate early responses came from London and was penned (predictably) by Karen Armstrong. Entitling her piece for the *New York Times* on the Rhem affair as "Whose Heaven Is It?" Armstrong speaks compassionately about Christians for whom talk of "the salvation of unbelievers" is uncomfortable and rejoices with those like Rhem for whom it is inevitable (August 31, 1996). Readers may also wish to see "RCA Rebukes Pastor, Church," *Christianity Today,* October 7, 1996, 86, for a summary of the situation as of that date.

36. So far as I know, the first seminary to try this bold new integration of levels was the Church Divinity School of the Pacific, a member institution of the Graduate Theological Union in Berkeley. CDSP's experience was so remarkably fulfilling to all concerned that it has now become a regular part of the seminary's curriculum as well as a model for the rest of the country.

37. Dale_Lature.parti@ecunet.org for August 3, 1995.

38. Taken from comments made by Kellner in addressing the Religion Newswriters Association convention on August 31, 1996, in Chicago.

39. In an interview granted to Diane Winston of Religion News Service and published by RNS on October 11, 1994.

40. At one time I did my own fair share of this talking, so there is no finger-pointing involved when I say that everybody from William Bennett on has drawn this analogy in this way between present and past times. There are even concerted efforts like Michael Horton's CURE — Christians United for Reformation, which publishes a journal called *Modern Reformation*—that are dedicated to effecting reformation with the "r" capitalized.

41. Taken from a keynote address delivered in Washington in January 1994 by Dykstra at a gala given by the Alban Institute to honor Loren B. Mead, its retiring founder.

Chapter Eleven: With Constantly Changing Tools

1. The paradigm of "spiritual coalitions" belongs to Martin Marty. It, along with many of the other ideas I have summarized in the preceding paragraphs of my argument, is beautifully presented by Marty in a 1993 interview with Daniel J. Boorstin, former Librarian of Congress and author in his own right. Those wishing to gain a sharp but succinct overview of the present roles of religion, theology, and spirituality in postmodern culture could do no better than to read Marty's dazzling responses to Boorstin's insightful questions and commentary ("Post Modernism: Of Science, Religion and Secular Liberal Society," *New Perspectives Quarterly*, June 22, 1993, 55ff.).

2. A collection of papers on this very subject and its implications, *Christianity and Civil Society* (Orbis Books, 1995), was edited by Rodney L. Petersen in 1995 and contains work by such leading theologians as Robert Bellah (*Habits of the Heart* and *The Good Society*, most notably) and Max L. Stackhouse, Stephen Colwell Professor of Christian Ethics at Princeton Theological Seminary.

Whether the reader decides to push further into the intricacies of the whole matter later or not, it is essential here to recognize that theology is greater than religion at least in so far as it justifies a religion to its constituency while remaining less institutionalized and thereby more dynamic. This facility is of particular importance in postmodern society. Petersen, in the opening paper of *Civil Society*, summarizes the points I have been making quite clearly. "Religion," he writes (18), "may hold a society together, but, to paraphrase Stackhouse, in an emerging global social order that is not rooted in the memory of common experience, more is required," namely, theology (18). He also notes that "clarity about what theology has to contribute to a civil society in distinction from religion and social science is a theme running through the following papers," and concludes that the thoughtful reader and observer might even wonder whether all religion should not indeed be "subjected to theological evaluation" (15).

3. In this absorption we must include agnostics and atheists, many of whom seem as intent as do the god-driven upon establishing for themselves the definitions of their own spiritual theory of everything.

4. In the interest of keeping things simple, I do not want to become simplistic, especially not in so sophisticated a spot as this one. Historically, Christianity has certainly recognized a distinction between the

body of belief and the institutionalized exercise of belief (that is, to use the correct terms, between *kerygma,* or the salvific good news of Jesus, and *didache,* or teachings of the church about how the good news is to be interpreted, applied, and housed). The point I wish to make, however, is that what once was seen as the two faces of one head, albeit held there in tension, has now come to be seen as an either-or dichotomy.

5. Robert Fulghum in his bestseller *From Beginning to End: The Rituals of Our Lives* (Villard, 1995) in many ways wrote the descriptive as well as prescriptive bible on this. Arguing throughout his book that the sacred flows from the individual into ritual and then into religion, Fulghum says, "Reformation did not cease with Martin Luther. Re-form-ation is on-going, led by the need of live people — and followed, however reluctantly, by organized religion. The rituals change when the forms of celebration no longer fit our yearnings to celebrate the realities of present circumstances.... What does not change is the yearning.... It is neither right nor wrong — it is the way it is" (137).

6. While inelegant, my sow metaphor was deliberately chosen, for it best evokes, I think, the rather gluttonous or lusty surge currently in theological interest, especially among the young. For instance, there has been a 36 percent increase in enrollment of undergraduate majors in religion in 1990–1995; and 44,000 entering freshmen at 427 American colleges declared a religion or theology major in the 1994–95 academic year, according to Religion News Service (*Publishers Weekly's Religion Bookline,* July 1, 1996, 1).

7. The discomfort is so real that it needs, not a print citation for validation, but a street-level one. If I had the proverbial nickle for every time I had heard a conversation opened with, "Well, of course, I'm not religious, but I am spiritual and pretty damned moral as well," I would indeed be a wealthy woman. The sustained necessity for such an apologetic opening gambit has more than compensated for any lost fiscal rewards, however, by serving as proof-positive of my point.

8. Even this position represents concepts that are relative newcomers in human history. Robert Bellah in his paper "The Church in an Individualistic Society" (*Christianity and Civil Society,* Orbis Books, 1995) argues, for instance, that "since Judaism and Christianity are themselves 'historic' religions, they exist somewhat uncomfortably in modern society," and that "Protestant Christianity, with its strongly individualistic tendencies, has gone farthest in accepting the place to which modern culture assigns religion" (3).

9. Stanley Hoover, director of the Center for Mass Media Research in Boulder, Colorado, is an expert on religion and the media. He is among those who believe strongly that only public religion as we know and presently understand that term will be operative in the future. "In this commodified religious culture," he told the Religion Newswriters Association's annual convention in Colorado Springs in July 1995, "religion doesn't exist unless it exists in public."

10. One of the most dramatic examples of this perception for me came on September 9, 1996, when *U.S. News and World Report* ran as their cover story "The Faith Factor — Can Churches Cure America's Social Ills?" by Joseph P. Shapiro with Andrea Wright and entitled the piece itself "Can Churches Save America?" (46–53). The whole article dealt unremittingly with exactly what its titles would anticipate: the social utility of institutionalized religion and its benefits to psychological and cultural life. So much for any connection with more ethereal matters.

11. Or maybe there is a connection with divinity, at least for the cynical. In "Straying from the Way," author Kennedy Fraser offered an extended critical essay based loosely on David Hare's play *Racing Demon* (*The New Yorker*, December 4, 1995, 48–63). Arguing that many hallowed British institutions including the Church of England had collapsed over the last few decades because of "radical 'conservative' government, on the one hand; the crumbling of the hidebound old class hierarchies, on the other," Fraser concludes that "it would scarcely be surprising if a religion shaped for a very English God showed signs of strain now that England has nothing outside itself to rule or conquer." We might conclude, in other words, that different gods ordain different ecclesial strokes, which does not make the result any the less ordained, I suppose, just different.

12. This is true across the board. Rabbi Eric Yoffie, new president of the Union of American Hebrew Congregations, is quoted as having said in his inaugural address on June 8, 1996, that one of the prime challenges reform Judaism's leaders must teach their youth immediately is that "fervent prayer in a Reform synagogue should not be seen as eccentric or embarrassing" (as reported by Terry Mattingly, Scripps-Howard News Service, June 21, 1996).

13. The most exhaustive demographic study available today of just exactly what religion means spiritually and privately is, to my way of thinking, George Barna's *The Index of Leading Spiritual Indicators*

(Word, 1996). Barna writes that "What is not lost in this spiritual upheaval is the new perception of religion: a personalized, customized form
of faith views which meet personal needs, minimize rules and absolutes, and which bear little resemblance to the 'pure' form of any of
the world's major religions" (132).

14. The most all-incorporating demographic description of the con-
duct of religion in each of these contemporary guises is, in my opinion,
George Gallup's *Religion in America: The 1996 Report of the Princeton
Religion Research Center.*

15. This is especially true today, as in the days of King Arthur, among
our younger citizens. In a sidebar about Generation X captioned "The
First Thing to Understand," the editors of *Next* (April 1996) wrote that
Gen X is "the first generation that grew up without absolute truths,
believing that the highest virtue is tolerance of the views of others" (1).

Chapter Twelve: From One to Many and Back Again

1. The fierceness here is most present in younger Boomers and the
older, just-now-being-enfranchised Busters. In many ways, it is also a
product of cumulative literacy, but of a slightly different kind from any
which we have discussed; it is the product of enormous, painful literacy
about the actual world and about the lives being lived in it. Poverty, danger, disorder, and illness foreshorten tomorrow into right now and breed
their own strong but primitive generosity. In current Christian thought,
this phenomenon is causing more and more observers to predict that the
church of the twenty-first century will be much nearer in disposition to
that of the first century than to that of the twentieth.

2. One of the most lucid and authoritative presentations of the characterizing role of these values is in a paper written by Glenn T. Miller,
academic dean at Bangor Theological Seminary. Entitled "Theological
Table Talk — Dreaming" (*Theology Today*, July 1995), the exposition
first came to my attention (as has so much else of worth in my professional life) by way of Martin Marty, who reviewed a portion of Miller's
conclusions in *Context* (October 15, 1995, 2, 3).

3. One of the most complete — almost disconcertingly complete, in
fact — summations before-the-fact of what the changes were going to be
and why ran in the July–August 1986 issue of, predictably enough, *The
Futurist* (20–23). Interested readers will want to reread "The Future of

Religion in America — Toward a Public Church?" by Hugh Myers just for the pleasure of seeing how completely yesterday's predictions are on their way to becoming today's story.

4. While the names are familiar, the sheer scope of the movement they comprise is almost beyond comprehension. This was conveyed to me most graphically in the summer of 1995 when I was in Colorado Springs on business and discovered, almost incidentally, that there were at that time over one hundred national and international parachurch organizations headquartered in Colorado Springs alone.

5. Just here one needs to stop for a "Yes, but...." The "yes, but" in this case has to do not with the megachurches (which are indeed ahistoric), but with the presence of another response or accommodation. Concomitant with the growth of para- and megachurches has been an increase in liturgical practice. Many individual congregations and many denominations that have had no history of using traditional liturgy have begun to incorporate it into worship. Additionally, there has been for some time a kind of "liturgical mobility" among Christians; that is, there has been a movement from less liturgical to more liturgical denominations as a compensatory response to perceived needs and changes. In a way, this shift is "ahistoric," of course. The irony is that its ahistoricity should involve a moving back into history. One of the best recent summations of this is Peter Steinfels's column, "Beliefs — Two Divergent Roads to the Christian Life: Megachurches vs. the Liturgical Legacy," *New York Times* (May 20, 1995).

6. Charles Trueheart published an exhaustive essay on what he calls the Next Church as the cover story for the *Atlantic Monthly* in August 1996. "Welcome to the Next Church," which covers far more than we can here, should be compulsory reading, in my opinion, for anyone who wants to participate seriously in Christian, and perhaps just in American, religious ecclesiology during the next decade.

7. Part — a large part, actually — of this flexibility and ease within new affiliations is due to a lack of personal religious history or religious knowledge among younger Boomers and older Busters. I lurked for months in late 1995 and much of 1996 in an Ecunet chat room titled "Ministering to Gen X" where many of the participants were clearly not only clergy but X-ers themselves. One conversant who won my affection for his poignant, wistful sincerity opened his postings every day with the header: "We are the first generation born without God." Enough said.

8. Again for demographic reasons, this is most visible, among America's less populous traditions, in Judaism. I laughed out loud when I read the opening paragraphs of Walter Ruby's "Who's Winning?" (*Moment,* April 1996, 30–39): "Jerome Epstein's business card reads 'CEO,' and he sounds like one. 'We took a careful look at what we were selling and came up with a program of product development.'...Hardly unusual language for a businessman, but Epstein's card also reads 'Rabbi' and his business is selling religion." Ahh, well...

ALSO BY

Phyllis A. Tickle

Re-Discovering the Sacred
Spirituality in America

"After 20 years in the religion-book publishing industry, and 15 in academia, Tickle has literally written the book on religious books. An important read for anyone interested in the nation's religious mind."
— *The Syracuse Herald Journal*

0-8245-1460-2; $19.95

At your bookstore or, to order directly from the publisher, please send check or money order (including $3.00 shipping for the first book and $1.00 for each additional book) to:

The Crossroad Publishing Company
370 Lexington Avenue, New York, NY 10017

We hope you enjoyed God-Talk in America. *Thank you for reading it.*

crossroad